New Directions in Mentoring

This book is in memory
of Amelia Allen
whose artistic spirit
fills these pages
just as it lives within
the teachers and administrators,
parents and students,
at The Florida State University School.

New Directions in Mentoring:
Creating a Culture of Synergy

Edited by

Carol A. Mullen
and Dale W. Lick

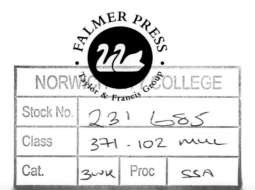

First published 1999 by Falmer Press
11 New Fetter Lane, London EC4P 4EE

Simultaneously published in the USA and Canada
by Falmer Press
Routledge Inc., 29 West 35th Street, New York, NY 10001

Falmer Press is an imprint of the Taylor & Francis Group

© 1999, C. A. Mullen and D. W. Lick

Cover design by Caroline Archer

Typeset in Times by Graphicraft Limited, Hong Kong
Printed and bound in Great Britain by Biddles Ltd, Guildford and King's Lynn

British Library Cataloguing in Publication Data
A catalogue record for this book is available from the British Library

Library of Congress Cataloging in Publication Data
A catalogue record for this book has been requested

ISBN 0 7507 1011 X (pbk)
    0 7507 1010 1 (hbk)

Contents

List of Figures and Tables   vii
Acknowledgments   ix
Credits   x
Foreword from the Field   *Marilyn J. Haring*   xi
Foreword from the Leadership   *Jack W. Miller*   xiii

Preface: Navigating a New Mentoring Pathway: The Search Begins   1
                    Carol A. Mullen

Part I   **Mentoring a New Culture**   9

Chapter 1   Introducing *New Directions for Mentoring*   10
                    Carol A. Mullen

Chapter 2   Adventures in Mentoring: Moving from Individual
                    Sojourners to Traveling Companions   18
                    Carol A. Mullen, Frances K. Kochan, and Fanchon F. Funk

Chapter 3   Proactive Comentoring Relationships: Enhancing
                    Effectiveness through Synergy   34
                    Dale W. Lick

Part II   **Mentoring Partnerships**   47

Chapter 4   Birth of a Book: A Narrative Study of a Synergistic
                    Comentoring Process   48
                    Carol A. Mullen

Chapter 5   Creating Synergy in a Mentoring Relationship with a
                    University Student Volunteer   71
                    David S. Greenberg

Chapter 6   The League of Mentors: A Strategy Beyond the
                    Faculty Handbook   79
                    Freddie L. Groomes

Chapter 7   Profiles in Mentoring: Perspectives from Female School
                    and University Voyagers   87
                    Fanchon F. Funk and Frances K. Kochan

Contents

Chapter 8   Becoming Seamless: Dynamic Shifts in a Mentoring
               Commitment   104
               Lori L. Franklin

Chapter 9   The Principal as Mentor: From Divergence to Convergence   116
               Eileen L. McDaniel

Chapter 10   Spiritual Mentoring: A Synergistic School Therapy   125
               Sandy R. Lee

Chapter 11   Coloring Outside the Lines: Portrait of a Mentor-Teacher   133
               Debi P. Barrett-Hayes

Chapter 12   Discovering Mentoring Relationships: A Secondary
               Teacher's Reflections   142
               Margaret L. Ronald

Chapter 13   Mentoring Preservice Teachers: The Positive Impact of
               Professional Development Schools   157
               Diane Sopko and Susan Hilgemeier

Chapter 14   A Mentoring School Leader: Successes and Trials of the
               Voyage   172
               *Edward M. Vertuno with Carol A. Mullen and
               Fanchon F. Funk*

Chapter 15   Lifelong Mentoring: The Creation of Learning Relationships   187
               Carol A. Mullen and William A. Kealy

Part III   **Mentoring Leadership**   201

Chapter 16   Multiple-Level Comentoring: Moving Toward a Learning
               Organization   202
               Dale W. Lick

Chapter 17   From School to Family: A Voyage of the Soul   213
               Frances K. Kochan

Chapter 18   A School Director's Vision: Lighthouse, Beacons, and
               Foggy Crossings   227
               Glenn Thomas with Carol A. Mullen and Dale W. Lick

Epilogue: A New Mentoring Pathway has been Navigated:
               The Search Continues   242
               Carol A. Mullen

Notes on Contributors   248
References   253
Index   265

List of Figures and Tables

Figures

1.1	Being rebirthed as comentors N. Kennedy (1998)	10
2.1	A synergistic foray along an unknown pathway A. Allen (1996)	18
3.1	Comentoring under a rainbow of synergy J. Johnson (1998)	34
4.1	Nuts 'n bolts of book-making D. P. Barrett-Hayes (1998)	48
4.2	Please let me I N C. A. Mullen (1997)	64
5.1	Reaching in for a new life to mentor J. Johnson (1998)	71
6.1	Introductory handshake at program orientation B. Langston (1992)	79
7.1	Dancing bolts connecting C. Delissio (1998)	87
8.1	Dual keyboarding partners J. Foxwell (1998)	104
9.1	Creating synergistic relationships K. Kittendorf (1998)	116
10.1	Spiritual tree of life J. J. Fenno (1998)	125
11.1	Coloring outside the lines A. Allen (1996)	133
12.1	A culture wheel mentoring tool M. L. Ronald (1998)	151
13.1	Hand that provides support to hands that aspire J. Johnson (1998)	157
14.1	A sign of the times: A school's dual identity W. A. Kealy (1998)	172
15.1	A holistic mentoring model of abilities, needs, and resources W. A. Kealy (1998)	193

16.1   Multilevel synergistic comentoring   202
       R. Bitar (1998)

17.1   A school community called family   213
       J. Johnson (1998)

17.2   Impact of a "school as family" program on faculty involvement   225

18.1   The lighthouse beacons/beckons   227
       C. Andrews (1998)

19.1A Factors facilitating group process   244
       Partnership Support Group (1998)

19.1B Factors hindering group process   244
       Partnership Support Group (1998)

Tables

3.1   Synergy audit items analysis of the PSG Project   44
4.1   Group-based situational definitions of mentoring   66
4.2   Strategies for developing comentoring support groups   67
15.1 A manifesto of seven mentoring postulates   196
      W. A. Kealy (1998)
17.1 Impact of participation in "school as family" program   220

Acknowledgments

The professional mentoring narratives on which this book is based were supported by the school and university governing ethical research committees of The Florida State University School (FSUS) and The Florida State University (FSU), Tallahassee, FL. We gratefully acknowledge the progressive vision embodied in this endorsement. We especially wish to thank those school and university faculty who invested their time, energy, and faith in the Partnership Support Group (PSG). Together, the senior editor/project leader, coeditor, and a total of 28 contributors functioned as a close comentoring team to develop this project. It was brought to completion within the 1997–98 academic year. We extend a very special thanks to the art students who patiently worked with us, rendering our themes in intriguing, aesthetic forms.

We wish to thank by name those who helped to mobilize, sustain, and complete this collaborative project.

First, Eileen L. McDaniel, Elementary School Principal at FSUS, affirmed the value of this comentoring action research project. She joined the PSG herself and continually encouraged the teachers and administrators in her laboratory school to commit to its agenda and vision.

Next, Debi P. Barrett-Hayes, art teacher, generously orchestrated the design production of the original artworks for this book. She communicated with Carol A. Mullen throughout the phases of the project, regularly working with her in the art classroom. Together, Debi and Carol shaped each other's vision of the artworks in coordination with the students. The students responded to Debi's mentorship with deep appreciation. Rami Bitar, one of Debi's art students, kindly assisted by preparing the camera-ready artworks on his own time. Among other activities, he scanned the students' slides and performed the necessary digital manipulations.

Further, William A. Kealy, Associate Professor at FSU, provided technical support on the production of the additional figures and graphics in the book. He generously redesigned all of the authors' concept maps to improve them in terms of legibility and aesthetics. Dr. Kealy also solved our computer problems and ensured communication among our different processing systems.

Finally, Anna Clarkson, Senior Acquisitions Editor at Falmer Press, took on this demanding project with grace and professionalism. While meeting with Carol Mullen at the 1998 Annual Meeting of the American Educational Association in San Diego to discuss her book prospectus, Ms Clarkson responded with enthusiasm. From there, Ms. Clarkson expeditiously moved this book through the review and production phases. The Partnership Support Group is delighted to have our project and vision sponsored by Falmer Press, a long-standing member of the Taylor and Francis Group.

Credits

We, the editors, are grateful to The Florida State University School art students and their parents for official consent to "exhibit" their artworks in the book. We also appreciate the permission granted by those school professionals, identified in Chapter 8, to include their actual names.

This book project was orchestrated by Carol A. Mullen, principal investigator, and it was officially endorsed by the human subjects committees of The Florida State University and The Florida State University School in May 1997. Accordingly, this edited volume complies with the 1997–98 school and university's research and development guidelines. As recognized, anonymity of research participants is not relevant in this project as they are, at one and the same time, the contributing authors and artists as well as the subjects of this book. Anonymity has been respected where the writers resourced their own participant populations through interviews and other action-based research strategies.

Editor's note: The artworks appearing in this book were produced as original designs by student artists who were guided by Carol A. Mullen's interpretation of each writer's salient images and themes. All artworks were selected and captioned by the senior editor in consultation with the authors.

Foreword from the Field

Marilyn J. Haring, Dean, School of Education,
Purdue University

It is an exciting development that a book on *new directions* for mentoring has been written inasmuch as many, including myself, have concluded that the traditional model of mentoring has exhausted its potential to foster innovative practice, especially on a large scale. That traditional model, called grooming mentoring, is severely constrained by its hierarchical, power-laden, and dyadic nature. Thus, grooming mentoring does little to foster the collaborations that are characteristic of the 1990s and, presumably, beyond. Instead, grooming mentoring – by facilitating the development of beginning researchers who fit the image of established ones – has contributed to practice that has maintained the status quo.

Happily, new people have been empowered to shape agendas in educational research and practice. They are practitioners and students in the K–12 and higher education arenas, as well as those who are more readily identified as university researchers, and their approaches and results often are markedly different from those of educational research in the past that issued from the grooming mentoring model.

Thus, there is a pressing need for mentoring models that depart radically from the assumptions of the traditional model. Comentoring is such a departure. It embraces reciprocal and synergistic relationships. It is characterized by practice that is dynamic and has no agenda to preserve hierarchies, power imbalances, or institutions as we know them. In fact, the agenda for a comentoring model as the basis of research and practice is to connect people of varying levels of power and privilege who join together to pursue mutual interest and benefit. As such, comentoring is an instrument of innovation through partnerships, and it is an ideal basis for the practice of action research.

Readers of *New Directions for Mentoring: Creating a Culture of Synergy* are treated to an exploration of collaboration among empowered participants in the Partnership Support Group (PSG) at The Florida State University and The Florida State University School. Although action research long has been expected as a natural outgrowth of university-laboratory school collaborations across the country, the success of the PSG is both unique and multifaceted. Most school-university relationships have failed to meet even modest expectations for action research, and the PSG has met those expectations admirably, as publication of this book attests. In addition, the PSG clearly is focused on egalitarian mentoring supported by the comentoring model. I know of no other such collaborations that have utilized comentoring, either as a vehicle for action research or as a focus for the learning and growth of its participants.

New Directions for Mentoring: Creating a Culture of Synergy is a spectacular contribution to mentoring practice. It artfully explores the conceptual dimensions of a mentoring process that will be new to many readers, even as it demonstrates far greater possibilities for mentoring than many have imagined. And for those who already have been engaged in the scholarship and practice of egalitarian mentoring, this book will provide inspiration to press forward.

Foreword from the Leadership

Jack W. Miller, Dean, College of Education,
Florida State University

This book is filled with terms that recognize a new pedagogy for professional growth. Included are concepts of comentoring, professional peer networking, partnership support groups, and communities of teacher/researchers. A "new age" of learning spirited by emerging technological methods of transmitting and warehousing information, a new metaphor for cooperative learning, and the active construction of knowledge by learners and teachers are all presented.

At the outset a question occurs, is all mentoring that is valuable, equal? Or, does comentoring imply equality of contribution to teaching and learning? Surely, valuable is not synonymous with equal. While unquestionably the mentor and mentee both have things to learn from each other, the notion of total equality belies the reality that in most relationships what is to be shared is not equally distributed across the partners. Background of experiences are not equal. Prior thought on a subject is often not equally shared, nor is the opportunity for growth. This is not to say that one point of view is of value and the other is of no value. Rather, it is likely that in any given situation the total "value" to be contributed to meaningful learning will be different between "teacher" and "learner."

Perhaps a marriage is a good framework from which to consider a comentoring relationship. While many believe in marriage as an "equal" partnership in its totality, certainly what each member has to contribute to the other is not equal, situation by situation. In some instances one partner has far more knowledge and background and can contribute greatly to the advancement of the other, while in other instances those roles will be reversed. This takes both individuals who are willing to teach to learn and a recognition that these roles can change, based on the type of learning to occur.

In a marriage equality is often preserved by both members feeling that they must contribute more than "their half" of all the effort to the relationship. The fact that it is not mathematically possible to contribute over 100 per cent is unimportant. What is important is that both partners feel it incumbent upon them to put the majority of the effort into making the relationship succeed.

This analogy carries back to learning environments involving professors, college students, classroom teachers, and K–12 students. For example, few university professors have the recent relevant experience in the classroom that teachers who daily instruct young people have. Conversely, very few classroom teachers have the opportunity to spend as much time reading and reviewing current literature and searching out useful information as do their colleagues in the university. When people from these two groups work as partners in a comentoring relationship, recognizing that each partner has something to contribute and to gain, and further recognizing that in some instances *Partner A* will contribute more, and in other instances *Partner B* will be the biggest contributor, powerful change can occur. Under these circumstances the value of the comentoring relationship and the professional peer network is seen. Amos Bronson Alcott (1968) in *Orphic Sayings*, when discussing the teacher, noted, "The true teacher defends his pupils against his own personal influence. He inspires self-trust. He guides their eyes from himself to the spirit that quickens him. He will have no disciple" (p. 590). Over a century ago Alcott described the spirit of comentoring in the true teacher. We see similar models today. Joyce, Bennett, and Rolheiser-Bennett (1990) explain the empowerment of teachers through cooperative research as they discuss how to change school cultures through staff development. They note that:

> Proposals both for the 'empowerment' of teachers and for an increase in the use of knowledge base in education depend upon the realization of a radically revised workplace with very different relationships . . . and much greater attention to the application of professional knowledge. (pp. 33–4)

This reconceptualized role and comentoring between those charged with the development of new knowledge and the preparation of teachers, and those charged with the responsibilities of carrying out the role of teacher, is vital to not only effective practice but to the creation of new knowledge, thus shaping future practice.

Given the recognition that comentoring is potentially powerful and that it does not require exactly equal contributions to be a shared endeavor, then a second question arises: Do problems of equal *effort* occur in such learning environments?

Slavin (1995) discussed cooperative learning in general and noted concerns: "There is one important pitfall that must be avoided if cooperative learning is to be instructionally effective. If not properly constructed, cooperative learning methods can allow for the 'free-rider effect' " (p. 19). An individual may take advantage of a comentoring relationship by allowing peers to assume the majority of the work and by not making a full contribution. While one would hope that this is not typically the case, it unquestionably occurs. To return to the marriage analogy, it is possible for one of the partners to work on being effective in the relationship while the other makes little or no effort, creating a codependent, rather than a coequal relationship. The same imbalance can occur in the professional development relationship.

While such problems in a shared relationship often exist, they can be outweighed by the power and heuristic value of the sum of the individual efforts being much greater than the additive parts. In some cases a comentoring relationship may provide a free ride on the "cooperative learning train," but in far more instances a strong synergy develops. In describing the philosophy of the Mars Pathfinder project team, Pritchett and Muirhead (1998) note, "Some people are more creative than others, but anyone you encounter might possibly be the person to spark a breakthrough idea. Innovation feeds on multiple points of view" (pp. 32–3).

The chapters in this book describe varying and effective comentoring relationships. Equal, not because each partner brings exactly the same qualities to the table, but largely equal in terms of effort, and mutual respect and valuing. In each of the case studies you will see very different kinds of comentoring relationships. A "road map" is defined for a powerful kind of culture in which synergy is built by the work of partners, with each contributing.

Preface: Navigating a New Mentoring Pathway: The Search Begins

Carol A. Mullen

This book is about paving walkways that matter. It is about bringing together those life forms that already exist in our schools and universities to create new partnerships. Our schools and universities are filled with the potential for promising collaboration at higher levels of integrity, creativity, and synergy. What is needed, then, are constructive ways to think about partnership and to link different professionals and their educational contexts. This book proposes that new forms of mentorship are needed in order for a partnership culture to develop in our lives.

This book is, more specifically, about a recent innovation in mentoring theory and practice that was spearheaded at a school-university research site in Florida. It highlights the work of the Partnership Support Group (PSG) that was formed to tackle issues of mentoring, action research, writing, and publication across diverse faculty groups. This collaborative project brought together teachers, professors, administrators, and graduate students to study their own issues about and processes of mentoring. Participants conducted action research that resulted in this book on new directions for mentoring that support the creation of cultures of synergy.

This book shows that guided learning and shared investigation promote the kind of scholarship that honors equality, voice, learning, representation, and fairness. We offer strategies for focusing on educator development (rather than teacher development) within professionally diverse collegial networks that support the new scholarship. Our professional story concludes with recommendations for conducting collaborative research within partnership contexts.

Over the last 20 years research about teaching has been directed at teacher (rather than educator) development. Carter (1993), Clandinin and Connelly (1992), Elbaz (1983), and other teacher research proponents have led the way in promoting this new paradigm. Sleeter (1998) asks: Whose voice is heard in collaborative project settings designed to facilitate teacher thinking? This question implies that teachers' voices may not be as fully developed or represented as they could be in the educational literature. Researchers may need to function as navigators to ensure that teachers' voices are heard, at least in their own projects.

This book asks: What practices invite and enable school practitioners to conduct collaborative research with university faculty and to benefit? More directly put, how might university researchers ensure that growth and benefits are realized by participants beyond the learning that is often a byproduct of research? Researchers

1

can find ways to include participants in the very publishing opportunities and visibility channels they/we so earnestly seek.

The authors of this book have attempted to take a step forward. We struggled as developing educators and leaders from our various places of contact and work. With this book we hope to raise consciousness about the need for synergistic and beneficial mentoring practices among different professionals. We also hope to offer some guidance for establishing partnership groups that value comentoring, or mutually supportive, research processes and goals.

The "Foreword from the Field" launches a perspective on our book as one that advances new forms of mentoring relationships and research in school-university environments. In her own research, Dean Marilyn Haring has studied the role of mentoring, together with networking, reflection, and socialization, in the development of female administrators and academics (e.g. Haring-Hidore, Freeman, Phelps, Spann and Wooten, 1990). This emphasis fits with the need that we believe exists for guided leadership in the lives of all school and higher education professionals, especially women, persons of color, students, and novice researchers and writers.

Dean Jack Miller's "Foreword from the Leadership" is a view of mentorship as a kind of marriage between different but equal partners in the collaborative arrangement. This metaphor of mentoring nicely sets the tone for our vision and support group mosaic, one that brings together those who are culturally different to proactively learn from one another. My own Preface offers a complementary view, one that prepares the reader for encountering an applied study of reciprocal mentoring in the lives of diverse educators.

Teacher educator narrative

My commitment to initiate the Partnership Support Group and to complete an edited book as an outcome of comentoring for faculty renewal originated in three sources. The first was my assumption as a newcomer to Florida in 1996 that the school-university faculty would be involved in joint research projects, and that I could join their efforts. Instead, I found a need for a collaborative faculty project that would provide guidance for school and university faculty about researching and writing for publication. This book reports on the collaborative project that I established at The Florida State University School–The Florida State University (FSUS–FSU). Collins (1997) recommends that academies need to "highlight model collaborative projects being conducted by higher education faculty and teachers in the public schools" (p. 52).

The second source stemmed from my awareness that interinstitutional arrangements are plagued with social problems that result from how universities work *on* rather than *with* schools. Goodlad (1988) insists that there is a distinction between satisfying mutual self-interests and creating symbiotic, equal partnerships, one that he carries over to schools and universities. In the context of the PSG project, symbiotic teamwork underscored the need for meaningful research, relations, and publication as goals. The school practitioners' contributions were viewed as valid and necessary for shaping projects equally.

The third source was rooted in my insights into a previous mentoring study in Texas that resulted in a book (Mullen, Cox, Boettcher and Adoue, 1997). However constructive our work in redefining traditional forms of mentoring, this group of educators did not include the membership of school practitioners. I came to believe that a new partnership group would require that school faculty be integrated as comentoring researchers and change agents.

New directions for mentoring

We, the navigators of a joint institutional culture, came together as designated "captains" and "crew members" at first. But then we moved beyond our titles once the value and practice of a synergistic comentoring approach was established. And with this new practice came the need to re-examine those stories about mentoring that informed who we were as professionals.

We decided that the old story about mentoring needs to be pulled apart, reconfigured, and drastically altered. It would have us believe in a Hollywood story wherein the protégé is cared for throughout the torrents of life by a selfless, enduring elder. This is, for the most part, a fantasy, especially in a culture as transient as education. The new story of mentorship is in an early phase of development. However, in the Partnership Support Group we worked to make the new story come to us.

In the support group I used field-based research strategies to help develop a new professional story. As a framework, *planning* and research coordination between the university and school proved an essential first step. Biweekly meetings, regular follow-up, and interpersonal contact proved vital to sustaining the *process and productivity* of the group. *Assessment* took many forms. An early collection of participant profile data helped steer the direction of the project. Mentoring context or discussion data (gathered through transcribed conversations and pattern analysis of themes) provided insight into the development of not only our project work but also our group identity. Boyle and Boice's (1998) model of systematic mentoring identifies three similar phases, but with emphasis on program development.

New trends in higher and further education

Current trends on collaboratively oriented studies indicate that university faculty are continuing to publish research almost exclusively. It does not follow that professors who conduct reform initiatives with school practitioners provide space for participants to represent *and* author their own work. Pounder's (1998) book on teacher teams and restructuring schools for collaboration is the result of university faculty research and authorship. The PSG book, in contrast, results from the individual and combined efforts of professors, teachers, and administrators. It also provides a context of consolidated group support that integrates novice action researchers as authors.

Another trend in teacher education that contrasts with current models is embodied by Ann Lieberman's challenge. She has attempted to awaken the academic community to include the voices of school practitioners and their knowledge in an agenda for future research (in Glaser, Lieberman and Anderson, 1997). Such visionary thinking inspired my development of the PSG, but only in a general sense. Field-based research, which is growing in popularity, includes practitioners' perspectives only as data sources and case study exemplars. In my view, this does not go far enough to support participants in becoming published authors.

As I see it, another trend in teacher education perpetuates a view of the mentoring relationship as somehow self-evident, when in fact its forms, contexts, and consequences vary. While the PSG faculty support group took shape within the paradoxical spaces of a school-university culture that unifies *and* separates contact; that reveals *and* conceals opportunities for cross-cultural mentoring; and that inspires *and* discourages learning and new identity construction. The PSG project survived because it somehow managed to inhabit these contradictory walkways.

The support group functioned as a proactive "mentoring mosaic" (Head, Reiman and Thies-Sprinthall, 1992) wherein the strengths and qualities of multiple partners were tapped, transformed, and transcended to promote new learning. This interactive process is indispensable for cultivating peer mentors; for compensating for traditional mentoring relations and dissatisfactions; and for facilitating larger, team-oriented projects (Kealy and Mullen, 1999). Traditional relations can exclude vital aspects of the mentee's development as well as synergistic relations leading to such benefits as comentorship and coauthorship. Within mentoring mosaics, individuals interchange roles as mentors and protégés, optimizing the sharing of cultural knowledge, learning of new skills, and conditions for identity transformation. Networks that guide learning require a facilitator (which can be a dual or rotating responsibility) who keeps the project, process, and individuals on track within a guided, flexible structure. This particular set-up offers definite advantages to busy but interested professionals.

Our approach to interinstitutional research

Promising enough on theoretical grounds, what does a mentoring mosaic look like in practice? And, how can such a network prove beneficial to creating reform within school-university partnerships and other learning organizations? The content and structure of our book illustrate aspects of various comentoring networks which include collegial relations, action research, mentoring and leadership, learning organization, higher education, practical and transforming synergy, collaborative structure (comentorship and coauthorship), research story and metaphor, and artwork/aesthetic forms of inquiry.

The authors bring to this book our pieces and ways of telling a promising research story about mentoring. The storytelling strategy proved indispensable as a research tool because we all exchanged stories that helped us to make "gut level" sense of our studies of educational issues. We needed our stories and each other's to help us to embark on, and describe, our voyages. We had no predetermined map for guiding us. Bends, forks, and contours, often unforeseen, kept us in conversation about what we were trying to do and become. I was often reminded in our travels of Darwin's (1839/1989) effort to examine new land but in the form of raw materials that had been transformed into a diversified landscape. In many ways, this describes for me the "country" of our stories, this book.

Organization of this book

This book is organized into three parts. The first part, "Mentoring a New Culture," explores perspectives that support the role of mentorship in helping to create a new community culture; the second, "Mentoring Partnerships," provides many examples of mentoring experiences, programs, projects, processes, and activities of school-university partnership professionals; and the third, "Mentoring Leadership," offers creative visions of mentorship for educational relationships and systems. The examples in Part 2 are our professional research stories; these demonstrate an informed, experiential awareness of mentoring themes and issues. In some chapters, this awareness is played out self-referentially as a developmental story of learning about mentoring issues. Other chapters are grounded in mentoring constructs and patterns of learning based on documentation, analysis, assessment, and research sources. We have included artworks in our research stories, an outgrowth of our synergistic relations with the art teacher and students at FSUS, the campus laboratory site of our project.

In Chapter 1, I introduce the book project using overarching concepts to discuss its themes of professional renewal, comentorship and coauthorship, action research, and shared cultural development across institutional/interpersonal spaces. I define key terms and map out the purposes and scope of the book as well as the value of this project; its relationship to the educational literature; its audiences and applications; and work with student populations.

In Chapter 2, I, along with coauthors Frances Kochan and Fancy Funk, provide a metaphoric view of this book as a journey from individual sojourner to traveling companion. The topics covered include the book expedition itself; a group membership profile; a map of the "old world" (university laboratory schools) and a current map (of one such school); the unique role and function of our joint faculty research initiative; the publication culture of a school-university setting; the mentoring language adopted by our network; and the power of what one group can imagine and do.

In Chapter 3, Dale Lick presents a new practical approach (coming from the change management field) for enhancing comentoring processes by applying the concept of synergy. He includes prerequisites for synergy and steps to develop highly viable relationships. Further, a synergy audit tool is offered for assessing the effectiveness of comentoring processes.

In Chapter 4, I provide a contextual account of the development of the Partnership Support Group (PSG), an innovative network which supported the making of this book through an intensive collegial process. Relevant sociopolitical issues are advanced to provide insight into how our "training" in higher education affects perceptions and practices of research as well as authorial outcomes. Implications for educational cultures as places that need to redefine power structures and relationships to promote justice and equality, or synergistic comentoring relationships, are addressed. New directions for ethical development in research are advocated.

In Chapter 5, David Greenberg focuses on a mentoring relationship with a university volunteer, and asks, "How can synergy be created and what obstacles exist to this synergy?" His professional mentoring story pursues this question through the mentor–mentee relationship of a French instructor and Haitian university student.

Next, in Chapter 6, Freddie Groomes reflects on The League of Mentors, a supportive university-based program developed to improve the success rate of untenured professors of color. This long-term initiative involved the participation of established faculty as mentors to aspiring faculty or mentees. It resulted in an increased number of faculty achieving promotion and tenure. A significant feature of the program was the willingness of the participating mentors to advise.

Coauthors Fanchon Funk and Frances Kochan, in Chapter 7, describe the role of mentoring in the career and personal development of female administrators and professors in K–12 and higher education. This study compares and contrasts their narrative experiences with other female mentors who have made similar "voyages."

Lori Franklin, in Chapter 8, describes some metamorphic qualities of a professional mentoring relationship shared between a library assistant and supervisor. Their daily work and learning is an inspiring story about the value of collegial bonding and heightened synergy.

In Chapter 9, Eileen McDaniel discusses the role of the principal in a K–12 setting as a rich mentoring opportunity. With the addition of functioning in close collaboration with the university community, the experience of teaching–learning is multilayered. This narrative focuses on mentoring relationships that, while unique to university laboratory schools, could be transferred and applied to other educational settings.

Sandy Lee, in Chapter 10, provides a personal and professional account of how her interest in mentoring was built through a spiritual foundation in her life. She provides links to her work as a therapist at FSUS and offers a view of the mentoring relationship as not only academic but also spiritual and therapeutic.

Debi Barrett-Hayes tells the story, in Chapter 11, of her mentoring efforts aimed at the artistic and professional development of her students. She provides a close-up of a special relationship shared with a gifted female student and their highly synergistic development. Debi's portrait of the mentor-teacher is seen as an enriched professional responsibility of a teacher's commitment to students, the school, and the community.

In Chapter 12, Margaret Ronald investigates her teaching experiences at FSUS using a reflective, action-based framework. She asks: "How can a language teacher use the concept of mentoring as a vehicle to better understand students, to improve classroom effectiveness, and to progressively evolve as a professional?" New classroom learning approaches are introduced.

Diane Sopko and Susan Hilgemeier, in Chapter 13, ask: "What is it about the Professional Development School (PDS) experience that helps to prepare preservice teachers for their first year of teaching?" The authors explore the experiences of preservice teachers who constructed personal understanding about teaching within PDS partnership settings. This account is based on inquiry into the lives of preservice teachers, mentor teachers, and university faculty at three different Professional Development Schools in collaboration with Texas A&M University.

Edward Vertuno in Chapter 14, tells the story of his experience as a former, long-term director of FSUS. He discusses changes in the school as a result of a number of different events, such as redefinition of its mission. This story, rich in history, was told to myself and Fanchon Funk, and we in turn reconstructed it for this account.

In Chapter 15, I (with William Kealy) explore *lifelong mentoring* as a newly emerging concept for rethinking educational relationships and partnership systems. We describe how lifelong mentoring offers a vision of ongoing learning throughout the human life cycle, inseparable from personal and social development. We provide a discussion of needs, abilities, and resources that play a role in mentoring relationships. An original mentoring model and description are illustrated to raise questions about how mentoring networks generally work.

In Chapter 16, Dale Lick narrates a new approach to comentoring in schools called the "whole-faculty study group process." The intention behind this model of school reform is to significantly increase faculty partnership; enhance student learning and school effectiveness; and recreate schools as learning organizations. The author provides the practical knowledge required to understand and successfully implement the study group process.

In Chapter 17, Frances Kochan relates the story of the impact of a university school's internal restructuring effort which "touched her very soul." Using a case study approach, the chapter describes how faculty and staff changed as a result of being involved in the transformation from a school organization to a "family."

Chapter 18, Glenn Thomas' story (with Dale Lick and me) focuses on the creation of a new university school and the importance of fostering an organization of lead-mentors that models vision and its effective translation. A metaphor of the lighthouse and its beacons is used to project light onto the role of leadership in creating a new collaborative culture.

The Epilogue provides an overview of the comentoring group process and a collective assessment. "Facilitation" and "hindrance" are used as key concepts for addressing benefits and shortcomings in our joint professional project. This discussion provides two original concept maps. I end by providing recommendations for guiding collaborative action research studies.

We, the authors, offer an exploration in partnership creation that is grounded in place. During these times of keen interest in global awareness, localized places are being overlooked. The stretch of the horizon has become favored, almost at the expense of worlds hidden within the grassy clumps that populate our own river's edge. While the PSG has studied the "horizon" of mentoring frameworks and systems, our stories give special attention to the grassy clumps in our own world – those intricacies in our own overlapping stories as developing mentors.

Many "lighthouses" or significant others offered us powerful signals during our new travels, but these were inevitably incomplete. We had no choice but to search by the light of our own beacons, however faint and cloudy these might be. We became voyagers whose finished works contain the raw materials of our new learning. Our chapters remain awash with jottings from our mentoring logs. We offer our book, this diversified landscape, to you in the hope that it will offer something of value in your own journey.

Part I

Mentoring a New Culture

1   Introducing *New Directions for Mentoring*

Carol A. Mullen

Figure 1.1:   Being rebirthed as comentors (Nathan Kennedy, 1998)

We, the authors of this book, ask: How can synergistic patterns and pathways of comentoring among differently situated professionals be created? And, how can these connections be aimed at purposeful collaboration, productivity, and publication? We provide examples of mentoring relationships and networks that embody the value of collaborative learning, despite conflict and tension, and that result in democratic practices resulting in professional authorship.

For an intensive year (1997–98), the Partnership Support Group (PSG) dialogued and experimented with original material written and produced for this book. The PSG is a name that I gave the comentoring support group to underscore the effort of a school-university collaborative, a research university and university laboratory school working together to promote deeper professional links. By so doing, we, a group of teachers, professors, administrators, and other practicing professionals, as well as art students at The Florida State University (FSU) and The Florida State University School (FSUS), pursued an agenda of mutual interest and benefit.

The lead title of this book, *New Directions for Mentoring*, underscores the focus of this book. Our cross-institutional support group process, professional research story development, and making of this book all gave explicit attention to mentoring in its varied forms and meanings. The variation we produced demonstrates approaches to mentoring from traditional to more progressive forms and meanings. Regardless, the PSG upheld a concept of mentoring as reciprocal and highly supportive throughout the group, research, and book developmental phases. As we worked together, we wanted to capture the synergy we experienced and the community of researchers we built through the PSG. We also wanted to highlight the community that we had extended and even, in some cases, created through our individual and joint action research.

The second part of the title of this book, the metaphor of *Creating a Culture of Synergy*, means that the generation of synergy, or inspiration, empowerment, and energy, enables conditions for greater innovation, productivity, quality, and equality. In our case, synergy was produced in new areas of mentoring, community, and educational change. Because we had all experienced heightened forms of synergy through our research, relationship, and community efforts for this project, we decided that it needed special attention. Our synergistic comentoring bonding, then, provided a catalyst for our pursuit of new directions for mentoring and research. We value human forms of coengagement, relearning, and narrative and voice representation. Our projects, now chapters, illustrate the creation of symbiotic relationships and comentoring activity settings; redirected learning within, and transformation of, learning organizations; and new vitality of teachers' and professors' voices, identities, and lives.

We set our sails to deliberately learn from one another and to develop as a synergistic comentoring team. This comentoring practice of actively learning from others has supported the development of our specific topics of mentoring as well as our practices of collegiality and authorship. The general problem we recognized was how to support a comentoring approach to applied research within a power-based educational culture. The practice we therefore attempted was nonauthoritarian yet guided among different professionals within a school-university setting that, like most other partnered environments, has not traditionally enabled such endeavors.

Comentoring, to me, is a complex learning process that deserves study, careful practice, and mindful negotiation. It is a way of being that energizes people to develop appreciatively and critically while creating and sustaining synergistic development in concert with others. Through an active exchange that supports opportunity, dialogue, enthusiasm, and change, professionals can develop as they awaken to new ways of thinking, feeling, and acting in their immediate environments (see Figure 1.1). In contrast, the self functions without energy and inspiration to teach devoid of learning; to see only organizational and interpersonal barriers to change; and to avoid uncomfortable forms of "newness," involvement, accountability, and assessment.

Comentoring for professional renewal

Throughout this book, we, the Partnership Support Group (PSG), focus on these two fundamental themes:

1 comentoring promotes the development of different approaches to action research among professionals/learners interested in understanding mentoring relationships and systems, as well as research and practice, and

2 when those within a shared culture use comentoring perspectives and strategies to represent and reflect on experience, synergy can be produced; professional renewal can be advanced; and relationships at all institutional levels can be enhanced.

This book is primarily about the use of comentorship as a framework for generating new directions in mentoring; forms of teaching/learning and relationships; and research and publication, within a school-university culture. The authors each advance their own study of mentoring that focuses, in some cases, on mostly the school or university culture, and, in other instances, on tensions within the educational culture as a whole. Individual and joint mentoring projects are accompanied, in each chapter, by our research and professional stories, action-based inquiries, and graphic illustrations.

By "research story" I mean the study of narrative as more than story, that is, as a form of inquiry into cultural reform issues (Mullen, 1994). Our studies have been designed to focus on site-based learning in a range of contexts that blend the professional with the personal. We believe that Goodlad's (1988) call for symbiotic arrangements between public schools and colleges of education is vital and that it can be created through the development of a synergistic comentoring program. Strategies that support such comentoring activity include various forms of proactive communication, skills development, documentation, and shared processes and products.

We also wish to contribute our story of new initiative and reform to the canon of large-scale consortium work undertaken by the Holmes Group since 1987. This new structuring of institutions – involving 90-plus nationwide Professional Development Schools (PDSs) – was created to establish working partnerships among professors, teachers, and administrators to improve and reform practice. The principles of partnership used to guide a PDS consist of reciprocity, experimentation, systematic inquiry, and student diversity (the Holmes Group, 1995). To this list I, along with the Partnership Support Group of a school-university culture external to the jurisdiction of the Holmes Group, add *comentorship*, *synergy*, and *coauthorship*. These terms express a shared commitment to the development of an active research agenda that supports practicing professionals in representing their own voices, perspectives, and contributions in the educational literature (Mullen, in press a; Mullen, in press b). Even current scholarship paradoxically represents university professors' lenses and interpretations of practicing professionals, not those of teachers and administrators it seeks to represent.

With this new perspective on shared research, author representation, and egalitarianism in mind, we wish to add this aspect of inquiry to the school-university bridge between research and practice. We also hope to contribute to the work of PDSs or research laboratory schools established nationwide through the effort of the Holmes Group to produce serious educational change (Weber, 1996). We recommend that university faculty can assist in a leadership role within public school faculties by creating or assisting focus/study groups of coresearchers that clearly benefit everyone involved.

As mentors who are also mentees and comentors, we do not presume to provide insights into all of the critical issues pertaining to educational forms of mentorship within school-university cultures. Rather, we invite new and critical perspectives on our own conversations and reports. We see mentorship as a taken-for-granted phenomenon in life and within educational institutions and domains, community life, and family systems. Mentoring activities can provide powerful ways of furthering the reflection and development of mentors and the mentored. The research stories and professional accounts we offer provide a structural device or aesthetic through which readers can form their own impressions. Our distinctive, interpretive patterns were made available to us through inquiry into humanistic studies of mentoring perspectives and practices. This permits the deeper examination of educational lives, development, and dilemmas, rendering these accessible to others. Our chapters therefore have educational and human value beyond the merely private or confessional.

In this edited volume, we reconceptualize traditional forms of mentoring by focusing on researchers' actual engagement in and expression of learning contexts. We see development in terms of learning to negotiate and clarify expectations, roles, and directions leading to the transformation of relationships through strategies which can enhance school-university collaboration and faculty renewal. Teachers and researchers can use this book to entertain new ways of engaging in and representing their mentoring relationships with others, including students, administrators, and each other.

The term *mentoring* is used in this book to suggest a process of expanding and deepening liberatory practices and habits with, and alongside others, in the academy, schools, and other settings. We emphasize the primacy of personal experience; negotiation of understanding; practical knowing informed by theory; and applied theory shaped by human values. Our mentoring stories have implications for curriculum, and partnership and leadership, development. We uphold that enriched understanding can evolve from life-affirming and self-conscious perspectives on mentoring stances and activities. Traditional mentorship in teacher education, teaching, and academic research can be characterized as a relationship in which professors guide, facilitate, and transfer experiences and knowledge to apprentices, students, and junior-level professors. The traditional approach to mentoring suggests a relationship based on higher authority or expert knowledge. While conventional approaches to guiding professionals and students provide needed support in some instances, there are many times when a multidimensional view of mentorship reflecting a flexible, interactive process is more appropriate and even desirable (Mullen et al., 1997).

The definition of mentoring is expanded, in our book, to mean an empowering interaction among individuals who learn/research together for the purpose of personal and institutional change. Support for comentoring dynamics among professionals creates an environment where individuals share processes and purposes, ambiguities and uncertainties, writings and new research.

Our stories converge to show that progressive forms of mentoring teach mentors and neophytes about their strengths and abilities through supportive interaction, reflection, and collaborative self-study. A supportive context, such as that reported as needed within a school-university setting, will allow educators and students to develop their professional skills, research knowledge, and capacity for human connection. Those involved in a comentoring network, like the one we advocate, will constantly be learning from each other; building on what is heard; seeking comentoring opportunities; and sharing with wider and newly emerging communities.

Throughout these chapters, examples of mentoring studies, programs, processes, activities, projects, and systems are shared that we have actually conceptualized, implemented, and analyzed. In some chapters, formal assessments are also provided. We seek to provide more explicit awareness of human interaction and activity through an applied understanding of our mentoring-based research stories. Readers are engaged in each chapter in a search for effective and inspiring mentoring approaches in their own settings and roles as teacher–researchers and other professionals. The sociocultural context of this search, and the political underpinnings of work for justice and equality, is an impulse that runs throughout much of this book.

Purposes and scope

Mentoring as a form of faculty and professional development and change at interpersonal and institutional levels is, even with this book, at an early phase of development. No one perspective can be provided to manage all of the textured nuances. In qualitative forms of inquiry, the aim is to represent and understand experience as nearly as possible as its participants live it. This requires that teacher–researchers depict and consider their relationships with their participants and themselves. This we have attempted to do in relation to others. We provide a collection of teaching and research narratives and tools that promote reflection, helping mentors and protégés to reimagine their roles. The actualities of each case are embodied in our lived experiences and reflections. We take readers to the scenes we depict with developmental impact. Our distinctive ways of telling and weaving together our individual and shared stories of teaching and research include self-narratives, dialogues, transcriptions of live conversation, artworks, tables and charts, figures and poems, and various other forms of cultural identity representation.

New Directions for Mentoring has six specific purposes:

1   to argue for and to provide examples of mentoring in relationships, programs, schools, universities, school-university collaboratives, and focus support groups that foster personal and professional development;
2   to express teacher–researcher synergy using reflective research stories and professional accounts that highlight significant mentoring moments and patterns;

3 to draw attention to the taken-for-granted but genuine capacity for human beings to mentor and to be mentored in return;
4 to promote transformation of perspective, and reform of traditional mentoring structures, that have yet to facilitate ways of eliminating inequality and injustice across professional ranks;
5 to show that personal and professional life has greater meaning when infused with critical and appreciative mentoring dimensions, and support group functions; and
6 to underscore the importance and value of teachers, professors, administrators, and students working together to create a new mentoring community inclusive of sustained conversation, empathetic connection, coauthoring opportunities, and promising results.

Unique aspects and distinctive features

The promotion and transformation of educator perspectives as well as the reform of ineffectual mentoring situations/systems provide the overarching framework of this book. The articulation of effective mentoring roles, relationships, and systems is accompanied with a combined narrative and critical pedagogical approach. For example, the same page within our book can present argument and story as well as personal commentary, analysis, critique, exemplar, research, and artwork. As facilitator, I encouraged and guided the development of visual composites, featuring the synthesis of cognitive, emotional, and aesthetic aspects of new learning. Although we express a unifying perspective on the pressing need for comentoring as professionals, each author has explored the new learning while blending it with the preferred style and voice that each chapter demonstrates.

Accordingly, this edited collection has these five distinctive features:

1 argues for and provides examples of mentoring relationships, programs, systems, and activities that are developmental. The book contains aesthetic features, such as artworks;
2 emphasizes that, if researchers, teachers, and other professionals are to develop, they need to work together to highlight partnership forms of new learning and reciprocity;
3 is grounded in the belief that the experiences and perspectives of mentors and the mentored offer crucially important insights for better understanding of professional work and values;
4 draws on a wide range of classroom contexts and stakeholders invested in inquiry, including teachers, teacher educator–researchers, curriculum designers, and artists; and
5 offers a comprehensive array of applications of action-based forms of synergistic comentoring or successful partnership within and across schools and universities.

Relationship to the educational literature

This book is related to a number of other scholarly texts concerned with the practical. It is concerned primarily with perspectives on, and approaches to, mentorship. We, the authors, explore the role of mentorship as directed collaborative practice in the lives of teachers, professors, administrators, and students. Our Partnership Support Group (PSG) was extended, through our chapters, to include high school students and university and school faculty. This comentoring group is shaped by, and concerned with, school-university partnership issues.

This book is different from yet similar to my edited publication, *Breaking the Circle of One* (Mullen et al., 1997). The 1997 book attempts to show that research circles, such as those consisting of professors and graduate students, have the potential to be "broken" to dissolve hierarchy and isolation and to bring new awareness to comentoring development. Like the former book, this new one results from this value orientation. It is also an outgrowth of professionals' conversations and writings within a self-study collaborative support group context. However, the purpose, local context, group process, specific methods and organic models of learning, populations, and writings are all unique.

For *Breaking the Circle of One*, a relatively small focus group in higher education produced accounts related to mentoring in our personal and professional lives. With *New Directions for Mentoring*, the support group consists of a more diverse population of educators, including teachers and administrators, whose work is shaped within a school-university environment and active program in action research. In *New Directions for Mentoring* the comentoring process was, in contrast to the 1997 book, deliberate, programmatic, and carefully documented through my own case study reflection and analysis. (Chapter 4 offers a discussion of the new support group process, and the Epilogue provides an assessment of this work.)

Practical guides to mentorship for teachers, principals, and other leaders in schools constitute the majority of texts available in the area of mentorship. Our book offers a different perspective, one that embraces site-based learning and applications but with analysis of theory and practice.

Finally, books on collaboration within school-university contexts differ substantively from our own. This new book is the result of the combined writing and research efforts of professors, teachers, and administrators. Books, like Pounder's (1998a) on collaboration in schools, result from the research efforts of university professors. In contrast, the premise of *New Directions for Mentoring* is that promising educational change needs to involve school professionals directly in designing synergistic, collaborative or comentoring practices. A norm of equality and shared power requires that teachers function not just as "organizational interfaces" but also as integrated team players who have voice.

Audiences and applications

Our book addresses gaps in the available literature on school-university collaboration and Professional Development Schools, mentorship and leadership, synergistic comentorship, teacher–researcher inquiry, theory and practice, and professional development and socialization. Although our edited collection has a unifying framework, it exemplifies a range of approaches to research on mentoring development. It provides a focus for work with multiple audiences. We seek to help readers to pursue their own mentorship work using the study group process.

Our book has several innovative applications at the undergraduate level. First, it is applicable to foundation courses on developing a personal philosophy of teaching. It is relevant to curriculum and instruction courses in elementary and secondary education; leadership and cooperative learning; and multiculturalism and diversity. In such courses, accounts of the classroom experiences of others are invaluable for providing material for prospective teachers to reframe. The book provides stories, reflections, research, visuals, metaphors, graphic displays of text, and poems on professional experience that can be used vicariously. It has several substantive applications at the graduate level. First, it could serve courses on leadership as well as qualitative and quantitative educational research, teacher development, and educational philosophy.

Inservice teachers and administrators participating in graduate degree and thesis work could gain from the learning and assessment illustrated. Our book could also serve more broadly across audiences, however, as a foundational text for ideas on, and strategies for, doing research with groups of professionals engaged in comentoring, research development, and action- and site-based inquiry. Our book's case study approach to "real" educational experiences, dilemmas, paradoxes, and issues could appeal to graduate student–professionals.

This book could prove worthwhile to heads of subject departments, staff development officers, and superintendents who plan professional development programs for schools and school boards. It is a useful guide for teachers who wish to design, execute, and assess collaborative development processes and programs. This text could help supervising administrators to use humanistic mentoring approaches when implementing inquiry plans. It could also assist in dealing with loss of morale, stress, and burnout. These problems can accompany traditional approaches to teacher development, involving transfer, redundancy, mandated change, top-down decision making, and the delivery of packaged courses.

Building synergy with student populations

Throughout the book, we included original artworks made by art students, our extended team players at The Florida State University School. While some of the artworks were reconstructed to fit the mentoring themes of the book, most were created especially for it. The abstract, nonrealist set of images presented here evolved out of a new collaboration between art teacher, Debi Barrett-Hayes and me. I worked in direct consultation with the art students and the authors to translate vision and create image. Examples of artworks that were developed to capture our central themes include images of rebirth, synergy, growth, creativity, and community. It is important to our practice of partnership development and synergistic comentoring in education that the students be included directly in the making of this book.

2 Adventures in Mentoring: Moving from Individual Sojourners to Traveling Companions

Carol A. Mullen, Frances K. Kochan, and Fanchon F. Funk

Figure 2.1:   A synergistic foray along an unknown pathway (Amelia Allen, 1996)

The journey begins

We are a teacher–researcher group of explorers who have embarked upon a journey down unknown paths. Our goal is to delve within ourselves, our work communities, and our relationships to discover our potential to recreate and renew them all.

Our journey formally began when Carol Mullen, a former adjunct professor and consultant at The Florida State University (FSU), invited university faculty to engage in a joint research project with The Florida State University School (FSUS), a university laboratory school on the FSU campus. The initial focus of the research endeavor was to share stories of mentorship as a means of understanding the structured learning process in an in-depth manner. No single way of defining mentorship was offered to the university and teaching faculty. The intention was to avoid limiting participation and the potential for different expressions of, and approaches to, mentorship. All faculty members who had an interest in mentoring, and possibly a related story to tell about their own work and lives, could join this focus support group.

The project on mentoring took its own course as various ideas about what mentoring might mean were forwarded by potential members struggling to understand whether their ideas were "legitimate." Those who joined the group became more and more open, empowering themselves to decide what "counted" as a worthwhile perspective to share about mentoring theory and practice. We became navigators who supported each other in exploring meaningful ideas and practices of mentoring within a range of relationships, programs, and activities.

On another level, this research story is about the need to support collaborative efforts to think, do, and publish research among teachers, professors, administrators, and others. We came together, as the Partnership Support Group (PSG), seeking new relationships for pursuing alternative research avenues as well as better organizational structures within which to learn. As the members of this group, we comentored our way to this book with an eye towards developing new directions in community building and team learning. These new directions support the continuing challenge that faces our school and university to find ways to jointly build a world-class educational program at all levels.

The design of the PSG was aimed at the creation of a group of writers who would commit to using a participatory, dialogic framework within which to engage counterpoints of interest. We not only attempted to understand the content of our mentoring studies, but also the process we engaged in while meeting biweekly during 1997–98. Although anyone could join who valued storytelling, no "one" story would matter more than any other, and no one person would be more highly valued than the others. This conceptualization of teachers respects them as educational storytellers whose knowledge is practical, experiential, and purposeful (Clandinin, 1986; Elbaz, 1983). When viewed as full partners in generating knowledge, teachers can benefit from curriculum innovation (Connelly and Clandinin, 1988) and reform.

The group process would be one of reciprocal learning and nonhierarchical teaching despite differences in status, popularity, and knowledge. Each member intentionally served as a comentor to other faculty from both the university and the school. For example, beginning teachers did not just listen attentively to experienced professors' stories and suggestions, but actively shaped the entire process. And their own stories were similarly "heard" by professors who expressed a keen interest. We blended together as a single organism, shedding the many layers of clothing that artificially separate teachers and professors, guides and travelers. We used our individual and cultural differences to further our project ends and to become informed when gaps in knowledge about each other's worlds became evident. For this reason, this context-sensitive chapter could only have been written jointly by PSG members who collectively directed and redirected one another's attention and new learning. Among other efforts, we, the authors, expanded each other's perspectives about the university and school's different cultural practices. We also shared local documents and recorded events to provide context and clarity.

The book expedition

This book is based on our dialogue, yet it also reflects a development and refinement of it. We talked our way through the project, defining and redefining our shared intentions for the group process. For the purpose of this book, the term *mentoring* is understood in its traditional sense as the teaching of specialized knowledge and skills as well as intervention strategies in career development and learning (Merriam, 1983). But, in addition to this "top-down" view of mentorship, which is discussed in some of the chapters, all contributions incorporate a contemporary idea of mentoring. We view mentoring, regardless of context, as a relationship of shared roles and responsibilities. In some chapters, this concept of mentoring is taken more broadly. In such cases, mentoring is presented as a collaborative enterprise in which distinctions between teacher and learner, expert and novice, become entangled or even indistinguishable. At such times people become engaged or engulfed in a comentoring situation wherein their mutual learning becomes vital. Formal distinctions between mentor and protégé can altogether dissolve. This process favors reciprocal learning (Maynard and Furlong, 1995) and synergistic interchanges that, in themselves, reflect new directions for mentoring. The Partnership Support Group demonstrated this range of mentoring possibilities in the research stories we shared, as is evident in the diversity of topics in our chapters and our approach to them.

Although we originally intended to share mentoring stories that dealt with the shaping influence of a school-university community, our group expanded the parameters of our sharing. Some of our stories about mentoring practice deal more or less exclusively with the university or school context, depending on where the author is physically, psychologically, and biographically situated. Other stories include existence outside of this particular educational community that impacts on our work and sense of self. As might be expected, even these personal and professional stories have had a profound influence on our experience within the support group and hence the school-university and university school culture. We sought to understand the varied contours of mentorship embodied within our relationships and cultures and the healthy change which we were trying to foster within them. This publication is essentially a book of narrative research accounts that pulls together our mentoring stories shared through dialogue and writing. As Figure 2.1 conveys, this book has resulted from our synergistic forays into a new expedition along partially discovered, but mostly unknown, pathways that have paradoxically connected/separated FSU and FSUS, two learning organizations.

The traveling companions

As a group of comentoring sojourners, our membership shifted for several months, but then became fully launched with a diverse group of 17 people. We represent beginning and experienced teachers and professors as well as administrators, librarians, dissertation candidates, family school therapists, consultants, and school directors. In a number of cases, individuals played two or more of these professional roles, crossing over between the school and university as part of their daily lives and professional dreams. The members of this group each knew various people within it and had had opportunities to share connections across cultures.

The teaching experience within our PSG ranged from first year to 40 years among the teachers, the most experienced teacher also being the latest arrival at the school. Among the professors, teaching experience included, in its various configurations, public school, technical community college, prison, and university, ranging from one decade to four decades. One member had been president of three universities. Our support group also included two former directors and the current director of The Florida State University School. While the core group met regularly, a few members joined as part of our electronic-based network. Still others contributed to the project towards the end, everyone producing chapters with Carol Mullen's guidance and feedback; library sources and materials; and extensive editorial revisions and writing modifications to which Dale Lick made contributions.

We were diverse as well as a group of men and women, mostly Euroamerican (white) although also bicultural, African American, and Pacific Islander. We were monolingual and bilingual, ranging in age from our late 20s to mid-60s. The teachers were practitioner focused and the professors were research oriented, but everyone also demonstrated, to varying degrees, interest in theory and practice. Along with the professors, one teacher and several administrators held doctoral degrees (and, in a few cases, were ABD meaning "All But the Dissertation"). Areas of research and teaching specialization included educational leadership and principalship, curriculum and teacher development, inservice and preservice teacher education, elementary childhood education, peer coaching, special education, organizational change, affirmative action, pluralism and diversity, counseling therapy, family school therapy, modern language development, library science, mass communications, educational technology, and prison education. Some of these areas, such as educational leadership and principalship, and curriculum and teacher development, provided the theoretical and biographical framework for authors' action-based studies on mentoring and synergy.

Our PSG includes members who are published researchers, ranging from beginning to experienced. For example, the professors have published their own single-authored and coauthored books. One teacher and an administrator joined with the explicit intent of seeking guidance for writing a book. Most of us, but not all, have written one or more articles. We therefore have had varying degrees of publishing experience with academic journals in such areas as mentoring, collaborative inquiry, action-based research, faculty development, organizational change, and institutional reform. It is important to emphasize that our inclusive comentoring practice and value-orientation embraced those who desired to publish regardless of past experience.

Finally, and also notably, we represented a balance in the number of individuals (nearly equal) from the school and university setting. Carol Mullen had wanted to create a comfortable environment and an egalitarian set of dynamics where status distinctions among faculty would only be made where necessary to our stories, or helpful to our ends. The entire school faculty was invited to join the group to fulfill dreams of professional development and to lend support to those "teachers [who] are reluctant to view themselves as investigators and [who] resist notions of 'experimentation in their classrooms'" (McDaniel, 1988–89, p. 5). (See Chapter 4 for details of the invitation.) University faculty who had a reputation for promoting caring relationships with teachers and students, with an interest in mentoring, were invited to join on an individual basis. Those university faculty who committed gave legitimacy to our comentoring functions and values. Those who did not join sometimes expressed views of inservice teacher populations as nonscholarly and of university laboratory schools as mismanaged research sites – perceptions, whether founded to some degree or otherwise, that reinforce serious barriers to organizational change.

As professionals, our voices communicated diversity across subject areas and specializations, throughout various levels of education, and within our own lives. Differences were evident in our institutional status, range of experience, cultural and racial identity, orientation in education, scholastic inclination, gender, age, style of interaction, life circumstances – and even by our degree of commitment to the group and writing process. Yet, each member demonstrated the need for synergistic (or highly reciprocal) relationships. This commitment in turn served as a structure that sustained our group within an organizational culture which vied for our attention and energy. We, the comentoring support group, were intrigued, and at times overwhelmed, by the challenge of writing together for publication. We moved ahead like the caboose of a train, envisioning the end, but without a specific plan as to how to traverse our course until we had gathered, talked, and negotiated.

No ready-made maps exist for us, the faculty, to develop partnerships beyond those adjoining walkways that traverse our university laboratory school and college of education. Familiarity and even prior connections do not necessarily foster comentoring among professionals whose cultures are different. Carol Mullen's research focus, which the PSG carried out in action-based mentoring projects, became formed around the question: How can synergistic patterns and pathways of comentoring be meaningfully created among university and school faculty to purposefully develop collaboration, productivity, and publication?

One vital pattern was to establish visibility and regularity as process characteristics. We held all of our regular biweekly meetings in the Knowledge Center, the school's new media resource unit, developed to serve as a joint-use facility with the college of education and other units throughout the university. Such patterns supported a re(new)ed and intentional community with a strong desire for mutual discovery as well as interpersonal and institutional change.

A past pathway

University laboratory schools (or laboratory or university schools), such as FSUS, have their roots in the belief that theory and practice should be interconnected through the creation of school-university partnerships. The use of laboratory schools was intended to facilitate this experiential and organizational development, but without notable progress. Laboratory schools, which have been a part of the system of teacher preparation since the 1820s, have focused almost exclusively on providing practice teaching sites (Weber, 1996). Many states had included them as part of the "normal" school movement in which campuses established for preparing teachers included a laboratory school (Kramer, 1991). As the normal schools closed and teacher preparation became part of colleges of education, many universities included such campus laboratory schools. In 1926, the American Association of Teachers Colleges adopted a standard suggesting that all teacher colleges maintain a training school under its own control. This standard also allowed the college to work with a school district if they could have sufficient control over the clinical teaching site(s) (American Association of Teachers Colleges, 1926).

In the early 1900s the role of laboratory schools expanded when John Dewey (1900/1990; 1929) established a school at the University of Chicago, and a few others like it. He believed that this school should be not just a center for clinical education but a place where teachers would seek answers to the question of how an environment can be created in which all students can succeed. There are currently over 100 laboratory schools in the United States serving elementary and secondary schools, and slightly fewer serving preschool settings (Kramer, 1991).

University schools seem to be perfect settings for originating theories of education and discovery in research, especially action- and field-based. They also seem ideal for establishing the credibility of teachers and professors as research partners in the educational enterprise. However, what should have been a "perfect match" has in fact been marked with serious problems. Throughout their history, laboratory schools have had a variety of missions – as places for systemic research (Dewey, 1900/1990; 1965); settings to develop curriculum reforms, provide inservice education, and disseminate information about promising practices (Bonar, 1992); and as major sites for teacher training (Page and Page, 1981; Weber, 1996). This confusion in clarity of purpose has been noted as a possible reason for their elimination from many campuses. It is also clear that interinstitutional partnership via laboratory schools has proven difficult to accomplish.

The concept of a partnership between professors and teachers was intended to extract the best from the worlds of theory and practice (Tanner, 1997). Yet, the century-long practice of linking universities and schools in a working relationship for promoting school reform has an unrealized history riddled with conflict and even collapse (Clark, 1988). The differences in cultures between schools and universities (Darling-Hammond, 1994) is one of the primary reasons for the difficulties which have plagued these schools. The goals, values, cultures, and governance styles of these institutions are very different (Colburn, 1993; Restine, 1996; Sarason, 1993). Schools tend to have an action orientation while universities are typically reflective and research driven. Teachers' central focus is on teaching and students as well on the school culture. Comparatively, university faculty focus on teaching but publication of research also must have a primary place in their world. From the perspective of the university faculty, school teaching is insufficiently guided by evidence from research while, from the perspective of school teachers, educational research bears little resemblance to the "real world" of the classroom.

While university schools in theory were developed to blend these worlds and foci, the differences have indeed remained. These differences have hindered the ability of the sites to fulfill their initial promise as settings for jointly developed and implemented research that would assure success for all faculty and students. The scenario has traditionally been that campus laboratory schools support the development, implementation, and dissemination of university-based research. Professors and graduate students conduct empirical and action studies in these nearby K–12 classrooms, publishing "their" research. University researchers have been accused of acting intellectually superior; often they work *on* schools rather than *with* them to achieve mutual goals (Hargreaves and Fullan, 1992; Sarason, 1993). Researchers' work at all levels of engagement must incorporate ethical considerations, including the question of who is credited for authorship of published works.

There are other reasons why collaboration between university and school faculty is not the norm. Collaboration on research and writing projects in the social sciences (more so than the sciences) in universities is rare. Institutions of higher education tend to be places of isolation and autonomy where individualism rather than joint work is rewarded (Massey, Wiley and Colbeck, 1994; Mullen and Dalton, 1996). Hafernik, Messerschmitt, and Vandrick (1997) assert that "many faculty have been told by deans that single-authored papers are required for tenure and promotion [and to distinguish] oneself in order to stand above others" (p. 32). Given the pressure on university faculty to publish single-authored articles and the suspicion of administrators of works produced collaboratively, it is no wonder that the school-university culture is at odds with itself.

The Partnership Support Group comentoring project was motivated by, and framed with, these ethical-cultural considerations. The project supported joint inquiry, productivity, and publication; it discouraged systemic barriers to collaboration and goodwill. The participants helped generate a richer conception of inclusive forms of action research practice and leadership development. The larger intent in the formation of this group was to draw attention to the need for a new ethos of school-university partnership that promotes egalitarian practice in research and publication (Mullen, in press a; Mullen, in press b).

A local pathway

Historically, The Florida State University School laboratory facility was intended to function as an embodiment of John Dewey's philosophy for improved instruction/quality of schooling for students. It was to serve as a place for university professors to carry out research in a controlled and "guaranteed" environment. Additionally, it was a place for student teachers to receive a thorough practicum, assisting the university with the best teachers possible for preparing the public schools of Florida. The College of Education would have the advantage of being associated with highly educated and experienced teachers. There has been incentive, then, for this school-university collaborative to regulate organized learning situations so that theory could be translated into practice, and practice into theory (*Florida State College for Women Catalogue*, 1951).

Throughout its days, the name of the school has changed to signify its evolving mission and purpose. Its original title as The Training School was soon changed to The Demonstration School, the practice-teaching arm of the FSU School of Education. As the "Dem" School, it had the local name of Florida High which continues today. But even this name was officially changed because of the misleading image it created of the K–12 school as a secondary school only (*Florida State College for Women Catalogue*, 1920–1931).

In the 1969–71 era, the mission of the university school was redefined and hence subjected to the condition that it could stay open only if it adapted to a specified research purpose. This "pressure" was in keeping with the switch in priority other laboratory schools were making from teacher preparation to research during the 1970s and '80s (Weber, 1996). In order to facilitate this vision on a local level, most of the student teaching activities were, for a period of time, eliminated. Moreover, the student admissions' policy was changed to a four-factor criteria of race, gender, IQ, and socioeconomic status. One goal was to remove the influence of elitism on the school (with FSU faculty predominately enrolling their own children). Another goal was to match the population distribution from its six surrounding counties, giving researchers access to a controlled student population for their studies.

The student population at FSUS has been regulated now for several decades to (a) promote student equality and access to high quality schooling; (b) increase the probability that innovative curricular projects tried at this school will have generalizability and credibility, and (c) ensure a multiculturally, ethnically, and economically diverse population within which students could learn tolerance and good citizenship. Currently, approximately 1,041 students comprise this school population along with 62 teachers, an elementary and a secondary principal, and a director – all represented, with contributions from each population, in this book.

Before 1974, the laboratory school had "moved away from involvement of teacher education activities. We have been charged by the Board of Regents with becoming a research and development center. We expect to become developed in these terms" (Ed Vertuno, a former Director of FSUS in Rand, 1974, p. 3). In keeping with this research and development mission for the school, Florida State University students and faculty who have needed a student population to conduct research have used this facility. Projects are monitored by the human subjects committee at FSU as well as FSUS's Research Coordinator (a PSG member) who evaluates them for feasibility; for ethical considerations of "human subjects"; and for their fit with FSUS's mission statements. If endorsed at the school and university committee level, a research project schedule is negotiated and established. This is the entry process underlying how Carol Mullen's study, upon which this book is based, was supported within this educational milieu.

The school experienced another name change from Developmental Research School to Florida State University School in 1990 when the legislature passed a bill in which all university schools were to be identified as Developmental Research Schools. According to Glenn Thomas, current Director of FSUS, 60 research projects were carried out in 1997 and each student was used in research on an average of at least three times (Knowledge Center dedication ceremony, January 1998). This number is fairly typical given the total research projects that have been conducted annually at the school over the last five years.

A research pathway

School-university joint research initiatives, involving faculty across institutions, appear to be of value in fulfilling the mission of the school. However, oral narratives, interviews, documents, and pertinent publications indicate that the majority of these research initiatives have been conducted by individuals immersed in their own research. Research can instead be used to build a dynamic school-university community of coinquirers needed not only in university and school settings but also as part of teacher education reform in North America.

It would be an overstatement, if not falsehood, to claim that joint research activities have been altogether overlooked at the school. Numerous examples show that such efforts have and continue to be conducted. These endeavors have sometimes functioned as part of a research initiative, such as the revision of the elementary language arts program that was established by a former college dean during the late 1980s. Other projects have involved a single university professor forming a partnership, with one or more FSUS faculty, or with the school administration, to work with the school in developing and evaluating a curricular change. Other efforts have involved FSU departments in revising undergraduate education programs as well as the K–12 curriculum, such as those developed in mathematics and science education as well as in the physical education program. These departmental projects usually included school and university faculty as well as graduate assistants. FSUS teachers have even served as adjunct instructors who teach courses at the university.

The FSUS faculty and staff have also created research projects in which university faculty were invited to participate. One of the most comprehensive of these was the Family/School/Community Partnership Program (see Chapter 17). This project focused upon restructuring the university school – and the relationships experienced among school personnel, university faculty, students, parents, and the community – in order to create an environment more supportive of the needs of families and students. This program entailed a joint research effort of FSUS, the State Department of Education, and the Center for Policy Studies (CPS) in the College of Education at FSU. University professors got involved in the planning, implementation, and evaluation of the initiative which lasted for three years. In addition, new relationships were formed with the Schools and Colleges of Social Work, Psychology, and Nursing. Many of the synergistic relationships that developed, and which provided services to students, remain operational today, four years after the project was officially concluded. Although some of the structural and relational changes initiated through the restructuring effort continue, the research relationships formed with individual faculty and the CPS ended when the formal funding ceased.

During the early 1990s, another project, specifically focused on developing and publishing joint research projects, was initiated. This involved teams of teachers, faculty, and undergraduates engaged in action research projects. Topics were originated by school faculty. Data were collected and analyzed by undergraduates with assistance from university faculty, reviewed by school faculty, and developed into written documents. A special journal issue of a Florida state-level publication guest-edited by Catherine Emihovich (1992b), the university coordinator of the project, was contributed to by six faculty, three professors from FSU and three teachers from FSUS (as well as an undergraduate student). Although this was a successful endeavor, the project and publication were relatively small-scale compared to *New Directions for Mentoring*. The earlier project was discontinued when the two principal coordinators, the university professor and the school director, left.

Although many of the projects and research activities conducted at the school have added to the research base and even been significant in their impact, most have similarly ended when those who had a special stake moved onto other interests. Most of the projects, initiated by university personnel, focused primarily on a curricular or content area. Those few action-based school projects, attracting teachers and professors at various times, were sporadic and different in their emphases. The project reported in our book is unique in its focus upon mentoring and the potential for partnership – the capacity of faculty to learn from, and teach each other while changing the operational scope of institutional roles and the very way in which research is conducted, reported, and shared. Likewise, this is the first time that a jointly written publication, with a national audience involving a significant number of faculty from both institutions, has resulted from a group's research efforts at FSU/FSUS. Like dolphins aspiring to swim through rainbows, we have delighted in this comentoring opportunity to develop alongside our academic "cousins" in the school and university community.

Pathways through cultures

The work of mentorship and collaborative inquiry has yet to be successfully developed and sustained, on a large scale, throughout this school-university culture. This is not surprising. The Florida Board of Regents Policy along with the Florida Statutes and University Policies have established criteria for promotion and tenure for faculty at The Florida State University (FSU) and The Florida State University School (FSUS), respectively. These seem, on the surface, to be similar for the university and school cultures but actually differ rather significantly. Although both cultures emphasize faculty activity in the three areas of teaching, research, and service, FSUS evaluates candidates on the basis of effectiveness in the context of the mission of the school and the teaching profession. FSU, in comparison, evaluates candidates on the basis of recognized standing in the discipline and profession accomplished, in large part, through effective instruction and scholarship (e.g. the production of new knowledge, publication, and dissemination) (Faculty Handbook, 1991; Miller, 1997).

The faculty within the laboratory school are highly qualified, experienced teachers hired with a bachelor's degree and five years teaching experience, or a master's degree and three years teaching experience. Those with doctorates among the school faculty are in the minority. While it may at first seem confusing that these teachers are also professors affiliated with the College of Education who are ranked (i.e. University School Assistant, University School Associate, and University School Professor), they are also evaluated in accordance with the school's advisory board policy. Further, the school culture is not completely self-determining. Recommendations for tenure and promotion are made not only by the director of the FSUS but also by the Dean of the College and the President of the University. Historically,

> the promotion policies affecting the school were exactly the same as for the university in terms of publication, and they all went through the College. In 1976, a special tenure and promotion track was initiated by me on behalf of the FSUS faculty. We got in general the process that they're doing now which still goes through the College, but the criteria are different. They match [more closely] what the teachers are doing and what their expectations are. (Ed Vertuno, former Director of FSUS, interview, 24 February 1998)

While there is some pressure to publish at the laboratory school since faculty must go through a tenure, review, and promotion process somewhat similar to that of FSU, the publication requirement is not as stringent as for university faculty. As evidence, a total of three articles were published as part of the research/presentation activity of the school faculty in 1996–97, yet the support provided to the R&D efforts of university faculty is impressive. With this new comentoring reform initiative, the FSUS administration was pleased to be able to report multiple chapter publications in the context of a new, unprecedented highlight – "FSUS and the College of Education faculty collaborated on a book to be published by Falmer Press about professional mentoring of school colleagues" (Florida State University School–Florida High, 1998, p. 3).

The emphasis at this university school is more on teaching; on applied research focused on designing and facilitating context-sensitive school programs; and on proffering classroom sites for others' studies. Research and development activity is not only an established practice at FSUS but also a primary function upon which it is evaluated. This emphasis on the service function of the school (i.e. assisting university researchers versus leading or coleading research) helps to explain the impoverished state of comentoring that exists at intensive levels, including joint research and publication. The teachers themselves are less preoccupied with research and publication, and more concerned with responsibilities related to citizenry at immediate and holistic levels. This difference is evident by virtue of the school's full-service programs in such areas as dropout prevention, family-school-community partnership, and parent volunteer programs.

Even though an argument can be made to "leave well enough alone," we think a fundamental flaw is apparent in a system that nonetheless requires some publication and dissemination by its school faculty who are simultaneously the conduit for the university's research. Mullen and Dalton (1996) have developed a shark metaphor to expose and examine the "underbelly" of this symbiotic phenomenon:

> Teacher educator-researchers rely on human resources and practical settings to trial and test their developing theories of teaching, learning, and researching. Socialized to act as sharks, university faculty exist in a 'symbiotic relationship' with schools. . . . Chumming, although a cooperative effort, can be an unfriendly proposition within research, dissertation writing, and publication enterprises. . . . Pilot fish and remora survive as shark's 'companions' because they serve clean-up functions. (pp. 59–60)

Clearly, teacher educators could benefit by becoming more aware of how they are perceived in their roles as researchers and, at the same time, more self-critical of their research agendas. In this PSG project, we often confronted preconceptions held by us as university and school faculty. Changing school-university cultures into genuinely collaborative research communities will require a fundamental shift in how teachers and professors relate to, and learn from, one another. Such a shift in perception and relationship has the potential for significantly enhancing, and perhaps transforming, school and university effectiveness and, moreover, well-being.

Teachers are not, generally speaking, considered the professional equals of professors, even within a culture where they are systemic counterparts. In part, this inequity is reflected in the teacher development literature that targets teachers for reform, regarding neither their knowledge nor the professional growth required of researchers to properly engage in school studies. An alternative approach to teacher development proposed by Thiessen (1992), and empathetically embraced by the PSG, is that "teachers should develop themselves" through action research strategies (e.g. the comentoring faculty–student support group practice as described by Mullen et al., 1997). However, self-initiated action research is not often attempted at our partner school and, according to Goodlad and his proponents, this typifies most collaboratives and schooling places.

Teachers require conceptual and emotional support as well as skills-based assistance to undertake action research at the levels of leadership and scholarly development. Without these various forms of support, teachers will not gain the learning, rewards, privileges, and reputation that the world of publication can afford. There is a strong possibility that teachers, and other school practitioners, who research their own practice make more effectual mentors and community-builders. The movement toward teacher empowerment underscores the need for educational reform in both schools and universities. This need is compounded in school-university systems whose research and development mission requires participatory cooperation by school and university faculty. Emihovich (1992a) conducted an action research project in our partnership context in Florida only to conclude that "Despite the positive effects of collaborative efforts, vexing problems in differential status and power between faculty in public schools and universities still need to be resolved" (p. 12). Faculty partnership obviously involves "more than working together to achieve the university faculty's research goals or to provide staff development for the school on its assigned topic. . . . [there] is a [strong] need for equal responsibility by and benefits for each partner" (Peel, Wheatley and Brent, 1997, p. 3).

Ethical considerations need to overlay researchers' work at all levels of engagement. This includes authorship or the public representation of participant contribution. We have only begun to develop an ethic of research responsibility in higher education. Dialogue that upholds this direction will help generate more expansive treatments of all forms of research, especially participatory studies aimed at teacher development and thinking.

Languaging our journey

According to Corcoran (1995), the professional development of teachers is typically top-down. Such "training" fails to make much of a difference because it is too far removed from day-to-day practice. By contrast, this book uses a collaborative action research framework. We have created our own version of what this might involve by deliberately using both comentoring and synergy as reform approaches to interpersonal and institutional life. We explore the developmental professional experiences of teachers who are, at one and the same time, the subjects of study and the researchers themselves. Our action research accounts are dedicated to story forms of narrative inquiry (Clandinin and Connelly, 1992; Connelly and Clandinin, 1988); shared knowledge creation and stimulating communication (Freire, 1994); coauthored forms of writing that promote comentoring or collaborative learning (Diamond and Mullen, 1997); and activism for personal and social change (McIntyre, 1997; Mullen, 1997; Mullen and Dalton, 1996).

Comentoring can be viewed as an expression of personal and social change. It involves an authentic collaboration of persons in which everyone's story is valued and encouraged, and through which the organizational culture itself is reworked. The mainstream academic definition of mentoring is being expanded here to include interaction among coinquirers invested in researching their own practices. We borrowed from other groups in education who have also developed their own language of mentoring. Notably, a women's studies class described its own development as a process of comentoring which "gives a name to supportive assistance provided by several connected individuals. Placing the prefix 'co' before 'mentoring' reconstructs the relationship as nonhierarchical; 'co' makes mentoring reciprocal and mutual" (Bona, Rinehart and Volbrecht, 1995, p. 119). Comentoring further gives a name to a process that is "social, active, and appreciative of differences among individuals in terms of their backgrounds, talents, and learning styles" (Bona et al., p. 119). In other words, comentoring also values diversity in such areas as ethnicity, gender, status, age, ability, skill, learning style, and subject-matter discipline.

Descriptions of mentoring by Krupp (1992) and Wunsch (1993), with theorizing by Noddings (1995), focus on trust, reciprocity, and mutuality which partly characterize the synergy of our support group. Other characteristics of our group fit with those described as essential by Denton and Metcalf (in Peel et al., 1997) – "risk taking, commitment, tolerance for ambiguity, energy, and compassion, [all of which] contribute to the success of collaborative activities across institutions" (p. 3). Participants had in common the desire to seek support for specific forms of guidance not readily available in our settings. Our comentoring enterprise was elusive in the context of this search for systematic guidance and strategic learning in our professional domains.

Within the Partnership Support Group, university and school faculty and administrators intentionally cooperated to exchange research ideas and to promote synergy through storytelling. Synergy can be viewed as a sibling concept of comentoring, an energy which enables the experience of comentoring to occur at increasingly effective levels (see Chapters 2 and 4 for an elaboration). Where there exists *synergy* among people, the result exceeds the efforts of all individual players who energize and inspire each other as the basis for new approaches to learning (Murphy and Lick, 1998). Comentoring and synergy can function as sister concepts in action-based studies of professional development involving leadership and mentorship activity. It is possible that where comentoring creates and sustains synergy, conditions can be met for developing teamwork and, moreover, creative expertise which, in turn, can provide opportunities for new learning.

Bereiter and Scardamalia (1993) define creative expertise as "the process of expertise directed toward creative goals" made possible through "opportunities for learning and experimentation, suitable levels of challenge, a secure and supportive environment that encourages the progressive tackling of higher-level problems, and a good match between talents and demands" (p. 147). These conditions for developing aspects of creative expertise were of concern in the PSG where we facilitated learning, challenge, and security – all within a demanding framework and timeline made feasible with the positive effects of comentoring and synergy. The promise of our work is the opportunity it offers for "tackling higher-level problems" across faculty domains aimed at promoting learning relationships that result in shared research agendas, writing, and publication.

Navigating new pathways

Despite the reputation of university faculty as reflective practitioners (Goodlad, 1988), professors have had little to say about the mentoring that occurs within their own academic context. Further, the mentoring literature itself falls short in revealing the processes by which students and faculty are actually mentored within universities (Sands, Parson and Duane, 1991) and schools (Little, 1990), and even, as we suspect, partner schools. Occurrences of mentoring are, in fact, often difficult to detect for two reasons. First, mentorship has many functional components (e.g. befriending, advising, encouraging, promoting) and goes by many names, such as collaborating, peer coaching, assisting, instructing, and colearning (Little, 1990).

Second, mentoring may be particularly hard to identify in an educational setting (as opposed to a corporate one) because boundaries that distinguish it from teaching are not clear-cut. Faculty who mentor, or who are mentored, do not necessarily have a language or defined process for what they do.

Researchers have developed many conceptual frameworks and programs to mobilize the efforts of school-university partnerships (e.g. Lieberman, 1988; Oakes, Hare and Sirotnik, 1986). Some programs, called "teacher networks," "enriched professional roles," "collegial work" (Darling-Hammond, 1996), and "peer coaching" (Showers and Joyce, 1996), have even included mentoring components. By and large, however, these efforts have not generated collaborative forms of mentoring in significant ways. On the contrary, commitment to school research has typically resulted in scholarly opportunities and advancement for university researchers only.

What, then, does it mean to develop new patterns and pathways that transform the top-down view of schools as service facilities and universities as rightful owners? As Frances Kochan (1992), former Director of FSUS, has reflected:

> The relationship between researchers, typically from universities, and classroom teachers in schools has taken on a hierarchical relationship, with the university researcher viewed as superior to the practitioner. The result has been that the impact of research upon practice has been diluted and there has been little integration of research and practice. (pp. 28–9)

And, as Carol Mullen (1997c), higher education faculty, has proposed, the metaphors we use expose those culturally pervasive dynamics and mindsets in need of institutional change. For example, the metaphor of "post-sharkdom" draws attention to a "sharkdom" world that can be imagined differently:

> Within the world of post-sharkdom, the individualism, power, and status that shape traditional academic relationships are confronted. Communities of comentors, intent on breaking the circle of one through reeducation, might share leadership and tasks as well as dreams, fears, and truths. Self-study, collaborative projects can be taken on by those who value joint human effort and the revitalization of life in academe. Such projects are ideally forged among selves without a human cost, despite institutional rules and games of sharkdom. (p. 151)

Within the taken-for-granted world of "sharkdom," teachers are targeted for development, a euphemism for change, and professors supported as the sole (or main) researchers and beneficiaries of scholarly productivity. Given this widely accepted premise underlying theory and practice, it is challenging to locate examples in which teachers and professors function as explorers of the same project, reaping rewards commensurate with contribution and ability, not status or power.

Creating new pathways

This book provides perspectives on, and views of, mentoring by those who belong to a focus group within a school-university culture. Isolated no more, we have become engaged, intertwined in our own practices and each other's settings and lives. Our professional mentoring stories respond to Schwab's (1978) criticism of research that either fails to be grounded in "the practical" or that does not reflect an understanding of context involving actual persons and real settings. In the course of our study, guiding principles were identified that support site-based initiatives, self-directed professional inquiry, and mutually rewarding practitioner–researcher relationships. Chiefly, however, this project is concerned with the mentoring life of an educational culture that has the potential to become a major center for collaborative inquiry among school-university faculty. We take seriously the potential value of our work for other professionals whose partnership arrangements or plans could benefit from an influx of new ideas.

Educational domains need a guide for putting into action the "symbiosis" called for by Goodlad to ensure the viability of "interinstitutional collaboratives (Goodlad, 1988)." Joint research activity may provide just such a guide because although teachers and professors do not collaborate together nearly enough, for reasons including mistrust and misunderstanding, there is, for some faculty, a shared desire to do so. There clearly exists a need to redefine traditional mentoring structures and relationships that isolate teachers and researchers as well as those that promote such structures on an ideological but not a practical level, thereby also limiting organizational success. This book yields a collaborative model – partly deliberate, partly organic – for nurturing a research community and partner relations among individuals across institutions, and even time and space.

As a strategy for strengthening the partner school-university culture, intentional forms of mentoring across faculty and organizational lines have yet to become an important element in the educational picture. Needed, then, is a realistic but hopeful school portrait that can serve as the basis for stronger collaborative cultures; more effective forms of collegiality; and inclusive strategies that promote equality at all levels of professional service. *New Directions for Mentoring* supports this vision for educational reform that incorporates the elements of comentoring, synergy, team learning, writing and research, action-based inquiry, partner support group development, and collegiality in purpose, process, and ongoing practice.

We, the PSG, realize that we constitute one group of collegial partners within several school-university landscapes. Yet, we have learned, in the words of Wallace Stevens (1972), the power of "What one star can carve" (from "Six Significant Landscapes" v. 5, 1. 46, p. 17).

We invite our reader to consider these questions as you participate in our journey: How might you include others in your circle or sphere?; How might you join others in their circles or spheres?; What are some strategies that can be drawn from a single microcosm or community to stimulate desirable change? We encourage the use of this book of our professional research stories, ideas, tools, and experiences to help chart your own mentoring agendas, pathways, and cascading changes.

3   Proactive Comentoring Relationships: Enhancing Effectiveness through Synergy

Dale W. Lick

Figure 3.1:   Comentoring under a rainbow of
synergy (Julie Johnson, 1998)

Mentoring and comentoring, when successful, are powerful approaches to the human dynamics and learning accomplishments of groups of two or more people. Unfortunately, such approaches are often uneven in success and effectiveness. In this chapter, I unfold a new intentional and proactive approach for the significant enhancement of the effectiveness of comentoring processes. The fundamentals of this approach come from the field of change management and involve the application of the concept of synergy and the creation of synergistic relationships.

I will discuss and illustrate this new approach to comentoring processes, including the four prerequisites for synergy as well as four key steps in the development of synergistic relationships. Further, a synergy audit procedure is presented that assesses the effectiveness of the comentoring process.

About mentors and comentoring

Mentors and mentoring have been situated and defined in the literature in many ways. Most of these descriptions have suggested that a *mentor* is "a person who acts as sponsor, advocate, guide – or who teaches, advises, trusts, critiques, and supports another to express, pursue, and finalize goals" (Vanzant, 1980). Typically, good characteristics for mentors include being interested, supportive, competent, sharing, unexploitive, positive, and involved (Cronan-Hillix, Gensheimer, Cronan-Hillix, William and Davidson, 1986).

Comentoring has many of the same desirable characteristics as mentoring, but this process is one whereby members of a group also provide supportive assistance to one another (Bona, Rinehart and Volbreht, 1995). In a book written by university faculty and graduate-researchers, a community of comentors is described as a "self-study group that [united in order] to celebrate our comentoring webbings within and outside the group and to share these on deeper and more sustained levels" (Mullen, 1997c, p. 153). Ideally, in a comentoring situation, each member offers encouragement to everyone else; this expands understanding and improves the group's effectiveness and productivity (see Figure 3.1). A comentoring group might be a teacher study committee that explores a common interest and that assists members to increase their capacity for understanding (Murphy and Lick, 1998). The Partnership Support Group (PSG) provides just such an example.

Powerful comentoring is fundamental in the business world. The foundation for it comes from relationships among people such as "Treat them as adults. Treat them as partners; treat them with dignity; treat them with respect" (Peters and Waterman, 1982, p. 238). One of the leading practitioners of this approach is Jack Welch, Chief Executive Officer, General Electric who says, "The idea flow from the human spirit is absolutely unlimited. It's creativity. It's a belief that every person counts" (Byrne, 1998, p. 98). Welch is a master coach whose leadership approach is an outstanding example of comentoring; he teaches while being taught in turn.

Another fascinating example of comentoring comes out of telementoring, an area that describes online exchanges among various people collaborating on a project (Education Development Center, 1996). Communication among the comentors can draw on a large pool of people. Telementoring allows senders and receivers to choose when and how to communicate.

The essence of comentoring that I hope to capture goes beyond that expected in most school, university, or corporate committees or "typical" groups. I am interested in how comentoring within groups helps individuals, and the group, to rise above the potential of any individual in his or her wisdom, expertise, and effectiveness. My own interest in this direction has been established by the members of the partnership group, which is the basis of this book. As I move from a discussion of mentoring to comentoring in groups, I aim to broaden the mentoring process by adding reciprocal learning among members.

Team building

Effective comentoring groups are capable teams. A comentoring group will not live up to its capacity if it does not have genuine teamwork. Often teams exhibit self-destructive or self-defeating tendencies, making it harder for them to accomplish their full potential. Senge (1990) on "learning organizations" in America relates what he calls the "myth of teamwork": "Most teams operate below the level of the lowest IQ in the group. The result is 'skilled incompetence,' in which people in groups grow incredibly efficient at keeping themselves from learning" (p. 9).

Teamwork can be defined as the willingness and ability of members of a group to work together in a genuinely cooperative (i.e. interdependent) manner toward a common goal or vision (Murphy and Lick, 1998). According to Conner (1993), "Teamwork requires insight and ideas, open discussion, and respect for the values and input of others" (p. 190). Teamwork is the vehicle that allows common comentoring groups to attain uncommon results.

A good example of teamwork is California's giant trees. The sequoias, with their roots barely secure, grow in groves. When strong wings blow, the intertwining/interdependent roots of the sequoia trees help hold up each other. Another notable illustration of teamwork was evident by the US hockey team in the 1980 Winter Olympic Games. Rather than just picking the top players, the coach selected individuals who could function under pressure as a team. In a field of eight teams, the US team was ranked 7th. Maybe they didn't have the best players on the ice, but they did have the best team as they brought home the gold medal! In my estimation, they exhibited a synergistic team, collectively striving for a common vision.

Synergy defined

Authentic team processes experienced within, and exhibited by, a group is called *synergy*. This occurs when the functioning of a group allows it to get the maximum results from available experiences and resources. Effective comentoring teams are synergistic and self-directed. *Synergy* commonly refers to how the whole is greater than the sum of its parts. In *synergistic relationships*, individuals work together to produce a total effect that is greater than the sum (effect or outcome) of their separate efforts (Murphy and Lick, 1998).

The concept of synergy is discussed widely for groups in the community, in business and education, as an approach for enhancing processes effectively. For example, Covey (1990) describes synergy as one of the seven key habits. Senge (1990) discusses team learning as one of the key disciplines of successful groups; synergy is noted as the critical part of team learning.

In those areas of life where synergy has been successfully generated, it has proven to be a powerful tool that increases effectiveness. This is applicable to comentoring groups. Consequently, it is my intention here to bring synergy to a new level of consciousness, especially as it applies to comentoring groups. My question is: What is the process for using synergy effectively to enhance the efforts of comentoring groups in schools and elsewhere?

Much of the literature that discusses synergy does not provide an adequate basis for its use with comentoring groups. On the other hand, some sources from the change management field (e.g. Conner, 1993; Murphy and Lick, 1998), provide a new foundation for identifying and effectively applying the fundamentals of synergy. I share the essentials here.

Synergistic relationships

If a group is only as productive as the sum of what the members could produce individually, the group has a *self-destructive* or *static relationship*. Levels of group dysfunction unfortunately come about because of such dynamics as poor communication, inefficient management, lack of trust, defensiveness, self-centeredness, lack of commitment, and competition. No doubt we have all experienced groups composed of bright, capable individuals that may have also been equipped with financial and other resources that, despite these advantages, proved inefficient.

A third type of relationship, the desired one, is the *synergistic relationship*. The synergy of a mentoring group is the combined cooperative action of persons who generate additional energy beyond that consumed by them, producing a total outcome beyond individual attainment. In a genuinely synergistic mentoring group, members energize and inspire each other. The diversity of ideas and openness available to them provide the basis for new creative ideas and problem-solving approaches. Covey's (1990) idea of synergy is that "You begin with the belief that the parties involved will gain insight, and that the excitement of the mutual learning and insight will create a momentum toward more growth" (p. 264).

A good real-world analogy of synergy is found in a healthy marriage. In such a marriage, the spouses develop a caring support system in which they genuinely and openly cooperate to provide sharing, assistance, and encouragement toward commonly held goals (see Miller's Foreword).

The power of synergy, or synergistic relationships, is illustrated by an eight-foot wood 2 by 4 that is placed on blocks at its ends. The board will hold 100 pounds of weight before it breaks. If, however, one takes two eight-foot 2 by 4s and glues them together, the pair will hold a staggering 800 pounds! Why? The glue bonds the two boards together, so that when the fibers of one board run in a different direction, one gives strength where the other is weak. The bonding significantly increases the total strength capacity not by two-fold, but by eight-fold.

Synergy prerequisites

When considering the *capacity* of a comentoring group, I consider the group's *willingness* and its *ability* (Conner, 1993). If either of these factors is missing, the group will have a lesser capacity. The same applies to the potential capacity for synergy development. That is, for a comentoring group to be synergistic, it must be willing to do what is required to bring about synergy *and* it must have the ability to do so. Most groups fail to be synergistic because they are not willing to work at becoming effectual, or they lack the ability or circumstances.

Conner (1993) found that the core dynamics for the development of synergy in a group were *willingness* – arising from the sharing of common goals and interdependence – and *ability*, growing from group empowerment and participative involvement. As seen from my examples, synergistic relationships are both powerful and productive. Unfortunately, most comentoring groups do not function synergistically. They either fail to understand these prerequisites for synergy or they do not apply them very well. Why might this be? Because developing and maintaining synergy in a comentoring group, though vitally important, is not an easy task.

Willingness: common goals and interdependence

The first step in creating a synergistic comentoring group is the development of common goal(s) or shared purpose(s) that can help keep everyone on track. Many comentoring groups do not make the required effort to clarify what they are trying to accomplish, or how to accomplish their plan. An example of common goals for a comentoring group of teachers might be to understand a new learning process and how to successfully implement it in their school. An example of common goals established by the authors of this book was to function as an effective comentoring team in developing research approaches to mentoring and in applying synergy themes where relevant.

Willingness to seek, create, and continue to focus on common goals for a comentoring group is key to its maximum success. The same can be said for the comentoring group's willingness to function interdependently, that is, in a genuinely cooperative and mutually dependent manner. Members of a comentoring group do not have to agree on everything to have a synergistically functioning team. In fact, having different ideas and producing tension by bringing forward diverse information, opinions, and approaches are some of the building blocks for developing constructive, synergistic relationships. However, to be synergistic and effective, comentoring groups must function interdependently like two soldiers in a foxhole during a battle.

Ability: empowerment and participative involvement

Common goals and interdependence inspire cooperation; they are necessary for people to work together synergistically, but more is required for groups to be fully synergistic. For comentoring groups to operate effectively, members must feel empowered and they must participate in the work of the group. That is, *empowerment* and *participative involvement* are key *abilities* that members must have to function synergistically (Conner, 1993). People *are empowered* when they believe that they have something valuable to contribute to a situation, and to its outcome or effect.

With comentoring group members feeling empowered, each individual is more willing to share his or her perspective, increasing its potential for new ideas and expanded creativity. In such a context, if members feel comfortable saying what they feel or think, then they can contribute importantly to its goals and processes. However, the process of empowering comentoring group members is not always a straightforward or transparent task.

The ability of comentoring groups to operate synergistically requires both member empowerment and participative involvement. This approach offers potential for substantially increasing the effectiveness of the group. In such an environment members function as an entity that learns and reflects together, inspires and empowers members, enhances creativity, plans initiatives, makes decisions, solves problems, and evaluates results. The approach relies on a team learning where the "search" is itself an expression of synergy – the search to know, understand, apply, and create and develop professionally.

Synergy process

Prerequisites for a synergistic comentoring group include the willingness to establish common goals and develop a genuine interdependence among its members as well as the ability to create circumstances that provide empowerment and offer participative involvement so that members interact openly in their work. Given these fundamental prerequisites for synergistic comentoring groups, the question now becomes: What is the process for creating these synergistic prerequisites within comentoring groups? To respond, I turn to Conner (1993) who tells us that an effective *four-step process for building synergy* in comentoring groups is: interaction, appreciative understanding, integration, and implementation.

Interaction

Webster's New World Dictionary defines *interaction* as "action on one another or reciprocal action or effect" (Guralnik, 1986). The first step in the process indicates that if comentoring groups are to be synergistic, they must be interacting; that is, they must have members acting on one another or reciprocating. To encourage interaction, all members must share and also express themselves. What is desired is a balanced interaction by the members of the comentoring group. Interaction can be especially effective when the sharing adds constructively to knowledge, as when someone in our partnership group would suggest meaningful ideas for another author's chapter. On the other hand, those who interact too much or inappropriately diminish a comentoring group's effectiveness.

The *three elements of interaction* that reduce comentoring group problems, such as misunderstanding, alienation, and confusion, and that enhance group potential, are *effective communication, active listening,* and *creating trust. Effective communication* means direct communication that reflects a nondistorted sense of what the communicator believes.

A word of caution: In many groups the typical approach is the competitive one where each person is an advocate for certain ideas, making a particular case at each opportunity and even countering contrary ideas. Instead, the merits in other members' ideas need to be appreciated in order to avoid destructiveness.

Trust is fundamental to the development of synergy in a comentoring group. As the sessions of the partnership group continued, each author became more open, sharing not only information and ideas, but also concerns about writing and areas of desired assistance. I remember an instance when a group member was struggling with the concept of synergy and where it was being manifested in his story. When he shared his concerns, the group immediately responded, dramatically expanding his understanding which included how synergy might apply to his chapter. When this level of trust occurs, the comentoring group has an opportunity for effectively resourcing the values and diversity of perspectives that each member offers.

Appreciative understanding

One of the keys to help comentoring group members deal with their "tender" sensitivities is the operational concept of appreciative understanding. According to Conner (1993), *appreciative understanding* is the capacity to value and use diversity. To assist group participants toward the experience of appreciative understanding, each member must understand why others see differently, and why it is necessary to appreciate differences.

Four steps for building appreciative understanding (i.e. win/win means and relationships) are to create an open climate, delay negative judgment, empathize with other members, and value diversity (Conner, 1993). The effective communication, active listening, and trust generated by genuine interaction by comentors lay a foundation for appreciative understanding to develop. In particular, even with the inevitable differences of opinions and perspectives, conflicts, and possible misunderstandings, members realize that all of this is fundamental to surfacing important issues; understanding different frames of reference; seeing from a different angle; and generating building blocks for new and potentially better solutions.

An *open climate* is one in which comentors encourage productive tensions and constructive discussions to take place; foster win/win relationships; and help members understand relevant issues and gain new insights. By creating an open climate, members learn to appreciate conflict and differences, utilizing them to broaden their basis of understanding toward the development of potentially more valuable responses and re/solutions.

We have probably all been in a group discussion where someone offers a thought that seems ridiculous, and yet from that source comes a cascade of ideas leading to new insight, and even better problem solving strategies. Most new and creative ideas come from sensitive members who are extremely vulnerable to attacks by others. At the same time, such ideas often have the highest potential for leading to innovative solutions and productive synergy. Consequently, comentoring groups function best, and have greatest potential for synergy, when members exhibit the discipline and sensitivity to delay forming negative judgments.

Empathy is defined as the "projection of one's own personality into the personality of another in order to understand him [or her] better," or as the "ability to share in another's emotions or feelings" (Guralnik, 1986). When we empathize with other comentoring group members, we allow ourselves the opportunity of knowing what they are experiencing and feeling. When individuals empathize with others, they create conditions for increasing the group's chances of generating team synergy and solution building.

Most of us are sensitive about our cherished values and ideas; as a result, we tend to slowly share as we "test the water" to see how others will respond. Yet, these perspectives in a comentoring group represent the very diversity that gives the group its unique potential. By genuinely *valuing diversity* in a comentoring group, members are showing their respect for each other's person, values, ideas, and creativity.

Integration

Synergistic interaction and appreciative understanding provide a strong foundation for effective comentoring groups. With these effective relationships and mechanisms in place, a comentoring group assumes a strong position to take on the difficult task of integration. *Integration* is the process of considering all of the input from the group, evaluating its value and usability, and creatively pulling together the appropriate and/or relevant information and perspectives to generate the best available solution or outcome. Experience has shown that the effectiveness of the integration process is often enhanced by tolerating ambiguity and being persistent, flexible, creative, and selective (Conner, 1993).

Many of the problems facing comentoring groups may be extremely complex, yet groups have a tendency to seek quick, easy solutions. Frequently, this approach proves to be nonproductive, leading us down a path to a less valuable result. Consequently, in order to function in a comentoring capacity, groups must shift from the more typical "quick-fix" or "how-to" approach to problem solving to become more persistent with ambiguity.

Implementation

The first three steps in the process to generate synergy – interaction, appreciative understanding, and integration – provide a comentoring group with a foundation for moving in the direction of a desired effort or outcome. Thus, the remaining step in the synergy process is to effectively implement the various parts of the desired outcome. Key elements of successful *implementation* are to strategize, monitor and reinforce, remain team focused, and update (Conner, 1993).

To increase the likelihood that the comentoring group outcomes will be implemented effectively, the group must strategize, creating a plan for the implementation process that sets its direction, manages its resources, determines its priorities, and ensures that the various implementation steps are compatible. Once a strategy and plan have been developed and the implementation process begun, it is critical that the process be monitored to assure that the plan is followed and progress sustained.

In the implementation process, there will be the potential for some members to move ahead more rapidly. Uneven movements increase the risk for people being out-of-step with each other, reducing the synergy of the total effort. Consequently, it is important to remain team focused, respecting the group's common goals and interdependence.

During the implementation process, circumstances and environments may change. When this happens, there should be an updating according to the comentoring group's implementation or action plan.

A synergy audit

As my reader attempts to apply the concepts discussed to create synergistic comentoring groups, it will be beneficial to monitor your efforts. My synergy checklist could prove helpful during this reflective process. I provide question sets for identifying and assessing the synergistic effectiveness of comentoring groups.

1 *Common goals*: Has your comentoring group agreed upon and written a clearly and precisely stated goal(s) for its work?
2 *Interdependence*: Has the interaction of your comentoring group been interdependent (i.e. mutually dependent and genuinely cooperative)?
3 *Empowerment*: Does each member feel that what he or she has to offer is important to the group and valuable to the final outcome?
4 *Participative involvement*: Do the members feel that they openly participate in the discussions of the group?
5 *Interaction*: Do the members interact effectively? Do they actively listen? Have trust and credibility been created?
6 *Appreciative understanding*: Do the members exhibit appreciative understanding of other's ideas? Does the group exhibit an open climate? Does it value diversity? Do members delay judgment and empathize with others?
7 *Integration*: Do members tolerate ambiguity and exhibit persistence in their deliberations? Are they flexible, creative, and selective in their issues and anticipated results?
8 *Implementation*: Is the group successfully able to manage the implementation process?

In Table 3.1, I apply my synergy audit to efforts of the Partnership Support Group, the faculty-administrative comentoring group that gave rise to this book, our action-based project.

The conditional items in the audit suggest places for improvement, the major concern being that some members unevenly attended work sessions, especially toward the end. As a result, their energy and diversity were not fully added to the group decision-making process. Consequently, they themselves did not receive the increasingly positive impact of its helpful mentoring benefits. However, the leader–facilitator of the partnership group, Carol Mullen, proactively maintained a high level of communications with those both attending and unable to do so. This high level of synergy assisted members in being focused, motivated, and informed.

Synergy development

Creating strong, effective comentoring groups means taking necessary steps to build synergistic teams that are proactive and intentional in their commitment and effort. The cost for not operating in this manner is high and even wasteful of human energy. Here I offer several procedures for the creation of synergistic relationships:

1 At an initial meeting, introduce the concept of synergy and discuss how it can help the group to become an effective comentoring team.
2 If the group is amenable to comentoring and synergy, take time to learn about synergy and its application. An early understanding can pay handsome dividends later.
3 Once understanding of synergy has been established, develop an agreement to the effect that the group will strive to function as a learning team and in fulfilling the synergy guidelines.
4 If someone exhibits nonsynergistic behavior, this should be diplomatically dealt with.
5 Periodically, members of the group should apply the synergy audit to themselves.

Traditional mentoring and synergy

Even though mentoring and comentoring are, in some ways, different processes, they nonetheless have much in common. In terms of their differences, the typical mentor acts as a sponsor, advocate or guide for the mentee, while, in the latter, those in groups serve as both mentor and mentee to one another. On the other hand, these teaching/learning processes are similar in that they both deal with people and relationships involving common goals, interdependence, empowerment, participation, and trust.

This chapter attempted to show how synergy plays a crucial role in increasing the support of comentoring relationships by providing an open-ended set of

Table 3.1: Synergy audit items analysis of the PSG Project

Common goals:	
Discussed goals?	Yes, at the onset of the project, and included related readings, individual writing, team support, and publication.
Agreed upon goals?	Yes, this was outlined in detail in the project plan, submitted to FSUS and FSU for formal institutional review, and then reviewed and approved by the partnership group.
Clear, precise goals?	Yes, goals were precisely written and understood.
Written goals?	Yes, right from the beginning.
Interdependence:	
Interaction and sharing?	Yes, these have been unusually good.
Mutually dependent?	Yes, especially good for those in attendance, but otherwise partially limited.
Genuinely cooperative?	Yes, particularly good for those attending, uneven otherwise.
Empowerment:	
Feeling input important?	Yes, positive, receptive feelings for those in the work sessions; mixed otherwise.
Feeling input valuable to outcome?	Yes, feeling of respect and value for those attending, more limited for others.
Participative involvement:	
Members can openly participate?	Yes, feeling of openness and "friendly waters" in work sessions.
Do members openly participate?	Yes, almost everyone present was willing to be vulnerable and share in the work sessions
Interaction:	
Members interact effectively?	Yes, high level of constructive exchanges for those attending and participating.
Members communicate effectively?	Yes, members expressed themselves well.
Members actively listened?	Yes, individuals were attentive and wanted to learn. They utilized what they heard in their subsequent materials and discussions.
Trust and credibility in the group?	Yes, high level of sincerity and trust, even for those missing sessions.
Appreciative understanding:	
Appreciative understanding exhibited?	Yes, high level of appreciative understanding exhibited with only an occasional slip.
Open climate?	Yes, positive leadership set the right tone.
Value diversity?	Yes, almost always in the work sessions.
Delay judgment?	Yes, people respected one another and were open to new perspectives.
Empathize with others?	Yes, this was a group that genuinely felt for each other.
Integration:	
Exhibit persistence?	Yes, reasonably so, especially due to faith in the group leader–facilitator.
Tolerate ambiguity?	Yes, handled it well and with hope.
Flexible?	Yes, most were open to others as they tried to enhance their personal understanding and writing.
Creative?	Yes, a widely creative but focused group.
Selective?	Yes, particularly so relative to the group's input into each chapter's creation.
Implementation:	
Written implementation plan?	Yes, developed early and refined over time.
Ensures steps, progress, priorities?	Yes, priorities, steps, and benchmarks clearly defined and monitored.
Process remains team focused?	Yes, followed an agreed upon process that helped to maintain team focus throughout.
Plan continuously updated?	Yes, good initial plan with ongoing refinements.

guidelines. Since mentoring also encompasses the same fundamental elements of people and relationships, a similar potential exists for the application of synergy in different forms of mentoring relationships. In particular, two people can also become an effective team by developing a shared synergistic relationship. This goal can be accomplished by the mentor and mentee arriving at an understanding of the concept of synergy and then applying its elements.

I end by comparing synergy to the image of a rainbow. A rainbow is an arc containing the fundamental colors of the spectrum in consecutive bands. The glass-constructed artwork of the rainbow in the opening image visually compares the beauty of a rainbow to the overarching synergy in successful comentoring. A comentoring group functions as a full spectrum, representing the diversity of its members.

Carol Mullen next provides a contextual treatment of the comentoring framework.

Part II

Mentoring Partnerships

4   Birth of a Book: A Narrative Study of a Synergistic Comentoring Process

Carol A. Mullen

Figure 4.1: Nuts 'n bolts of book-making (Debi P. Barrett-Hayes, 1998)

Crafting books with wings

The Winged Victory is a statue of a Greek goddess. She might also be the "soul" of books that grow wings. When authors make books, they are preoccupied with daily concerns and tasks. They are not aware of crafting or even growing wings themselves. Instead, ideas get generated and materials produced, all with a final product in view. The "hardware" of a book suggests this physicality – pages, fastened together. Bounded within a cover. Print and graphics suggest "hardware images." Even these "parts" are fitted together to create a sense of the whole.

The technical process of making books is not straightforward. Technical issues overlap with the production of meaning. The support group that gave rise to this book negotiated most technical issues, a process that kept returning us to conceptual, emotional, and spiritual ideas. For example, during our work on the table of contents, we strove to manage the hardware of our book's "soul." We wanted an organizer. So, we tried to formulate a sequence that would be helpful. Each chapter was therefore situated to fit our understanding of the whole. However, we would falter. We had become entangled in questions of interpretation, which continually forced a fluid, creative, and challenging understanding of the process.

Each time we met we would again tackle our need to create the table of contents. By doing so, we would talk about what is meant by mentoring in the literature and in our own lives, and how mentoring itself relates to concepts of synergy, learning, collaboration, and community. As we physically designed the "nuts and bolts" of our project, something new would emerge in our thinking. Like the book, we were in a state of becoming. On the surface, it would seem as though our ability to manage the book was less than seamless. Regarding technical and structural considerations, we were simply unable to constrict our talk during those times that we desired order and certainty. Emergence, uncertainty, and possibility would demand attention at the table while the "nuts and bolts" of our project were being formulated and negotiated. This book was, for me, an experience in working with hands committed to "making" our metaphysical world (see Figure 4.1). Finished books, although fastened with hardware and hardware images, are not in a state of rest. Like authors, they are paradoxically "grounded with wings."

Growing wings as partners in research

New Directions for Mentoring is a book about what can happen when people seek to grow wings, or new ways of becoming researchers, mentors, learners, collaborators – and authors. Our Partnership Support Group (PSG) provided an opportunity for establishing an interactive, flexible structure to communicate across faculty lines. A group of faculty from The Florida State University (FSU) and The Florida State University School (FSUS) were, for the first time, brought together to create a partnership of action researchers and authors. Our writing is about discovery of new forms of mentoring, learning, research, identity, community, writing, and expression. It is also about breaking inherited circles of limited choice. We no longer wish to live and work as cultural isolates. We want to grow wings as partners in research.

Current progressive thinking in the teacher education literature promotes a view of teachers as capable storytellers, researchers, and curriculum and policy makers. However, a more radical position is that teachers need to literally become authors and researchers of their own professional practices and work. Otherwise, their lives will continue to be understood on terms other than their own. To empower practices of teacher authorship is to undertake new directions in mentoring and to question the ways in which order and power have been privileged within the academy.

As storytellers and writers, we, the group members, challenged ourselves to find a new way to become more fully human and alive. Together, we shared protected insider knowledge, our vulnerability, and our commitment to the hard work and honesty demanded of growth. Revealing comments made by group members include:

- "I would think that you'd want to build trust [with your mentee] particularly involving this issue of race, because later on he may say, 'You used me,' or 'Why didn't you share this with me, I don't like hidden stuff.' You reduce the likelihood of that if you're up front about what you're doing."

- "I understand from what you're saying that my mentoring log is kind of dry when I'm reading it and more animated and better described when I look up and speak to you face-to-face, and look away from my notes, right?"
- "The difference is in the storytelling – in the reading of your log you're giving your experience in the abstract, which is fine and correct, but when you relate it as a story it touches us much more than in the abstract mode."
- "Cultures are so rigid in the schools and universities that in fact a small study group is unlikely to have a very large impact on what's going on within that organization. We aren't very good learning organizations with respect to the learning of the organization itself."

We came to see ourselves not just as a community of learners but of coinquirers. As the Principal Investigator of this book project, I shared with my sojourners the enthusiasm that

> It is possible, and can even be intellectually invigorating, to navigate between these galaxies [of university and school]. Indeed, such travel can sensitize us to the differences in values, languages, mythologies, and convictions between subcultures, including those of the academic and the layperson. (Barone, 1992, p. 22)

Barone, a university professor, is concerned with promoting cross-cultural navigation in education. He wants us to "enhance our own status as professors, thus becoming *more* of who *we* can be" (p. 22). As a PSG navigator, my travel within the school-university culture has drawn attention to areas of mainstream academic canons that require rethinking. For example, I have learned that teachers each have their own special way of framing and illustrating collaborative action research and learning teams. It would be very difficult for a university researcher to anticipate the richness of this diversity and to capture it alone. I am arguing for a completely equal exchange in school-university collaboration in which academics have as much to learn as teachers and in which each professional group shapes the pedagogy, purpose, and practices of the other. Each side enters the world of the other and provides support to create something new. From this viewpoint, mainstream academic canons need to become critiqued as systems of research built upon authority, privilege, status, and reward.

An alternative canon would force researchers to set goals of collaboration, one of which would be to provide guided research practice and opportunities for joint publication. As this new practice implies, researchers would be held responsible for explaining why participants, when excluded from projects and publishing plans, have not been included. When professors intentionally comentor with teachers, the learning and status of school faculty will be enhanced. Practitioners can then become *more* of who *they* can be.

Without the development of their own distinctive voice and actual signature on published scholarship, the contributions of teachers and school administrators in collaborative research serve to support the project aspirations of university faculty.

On a larger scale, the potential for school-university collaboratives to function as cultures of synergy, or places where mutual human growth is supported, is weakened. I write not as a public school teacher, but as a teacher educator-researcher. I realize that not every study, setting, and collection of persons is conducive to comentoring, especially at the level of joint publication. On the other hand, I also believe that we in academia need to redefine our own sense of purpose and power in order to navigate the outer edges of these walkways to include all who wish to use them. We also need to reconsider our sensibilities about teacher development and the reward structure if we are to occupy a new intellectual-ethical sphere. Guided and shared publication is a new sociocultural practice that can transform those worlds we seek to understand better in significant ways. University faculty face serious socializing pressures. Nonetheless, we need to rethink mainstream research canons. These have a serious impact on shaping teacher educator identity as well as that of other professionals, including our participants.

In this chapter, I consider ways in which the Partnership Support Group revealed metaphoric qualities and how it supported comentoring relations. But first I look to the larger issues in higher education and teacher development that informed my need to create this project.

Collaboration as energizing walkways

"Walkways" is my literal expression for the concrete pathways that connect colleges of education and university laboratory schools. These walkways are frequently used by professors to do research in these schools and by student teachers to become certified teachers. The walkway as a symbol of joint life is consequently less inclusive than it could otherwise be.

The work of the PSG led its members to understand that the adjoining walkways needed to become two-ways paths not only for researchers, but for administrators and teachers who were engaged in collaborative research projects. When we make teachers visible we find that they have cultural and local knowledge about schooling processes, social relationships, and community needs. Some new educational reform initiatives benefit from teacher input yet still require joint efforts to conceptualize and implement research. The walkways that connect institutions could be substantially strengthened if they were also used to facilitate collaborative projects aimed at the teacher development of school faculty *and* teacher educators. These walkways, representing interpersonal, intellectual, and cultural connections, are therefore also boundaries. The metaphor of the walkway suggests that school-university relations need to become energized to support symbiotic, equal partnerships.

In recent years, educators have begun to further an evolutionary process in mentoring. Little (1990) identifies the "mentor phenomenon" as a "model of human relationship that is difficult to achieve within the confines of bureaucratic arrangements" (p. 299). By *mentorship*, I mean the traditional teaching relationship in which professors guide, facilitate, and transfer knowledge to teachers, students, and junior faculty. Traditional mentoring falls short of satisfying the deeper, multiple demands required for professional partnership development. Opportunities for authoring research as equal partners in professional development are not accommodated in the traditional mentoring model.

Comentoring offers a viable alternative to traditional mentoring wherein status and power shape relationships and contexts as well as research development, outcomes, and reward. As a proactive force in personal and social change, comentoring encourages professional learning among partners that enables organizational cultures to be reworked. Comentoring places emphasis on reciprocal, mutual relationships that value diversity in such areas as ethnicity, gender, status, age, ability, skill, learning style, and subject matter discipline (Bona et al., 1995). For the purposes of our work, comentoring is potentially an even larger force that infiltrates and reshapes the socialization process in leadership and teacher development, and higher education (Mullen, in press a; in press b).

Within the collegial network, the strengths and qualities of many partners are tapped, transformed, and transcended to promote new learning. A mentoring mosaic or network is indispensable for cultivating peer mentors; for compensating for the dissatisfactions of traditional mentoring relations; and for facilitating larger, team-oriented projects (Kealy and Mullen, 1999). Within mentoring mosaics, individuals interchange roles as mentors and protégés, optimizing the learning of all parties. In contrast, traditional mentoring relationships exclude vital aspects of professional and personal development; they can block the potential for synergistic relations that lead to such benefits as comentorship and coauthorship. Guided learning within mentoring mosaics requires a synergistic, flexible structure. *Synergy* expresses how a group's creative capacity beyond the individual level means that collegial friendship is redefined as collective purpose, identity, and enrichment. Networks that support synergistic comentoring guide, challenge, and inspire busy professionals.

In Giroux's (1991) terms, we in the PSG became border crossers. We "reconfigure[d] the boundaries of academic disciplines [and school-university cultures] in order to engage in new forms of critical [and appreciative] inquiry" (p. 508). Educators who commit to transforming relations across institutional differences must take risks and cross literal and figurative boundaries.

The inclusive support group structures that result from border-crossing accrue important socioemotional benefits as well. Within the PSG, emotional benefits included *self-affirmation* as a valued colleague and comentor within both the school and university cultures; *liberation* through the interpretation of hierarchy as a social and political structure that limits communication and research across status/rank; *empowerment* through the creation of a mentoring mosaic and reciprocal learning; *discovery* of one's misconceptions and stereotypes held about "the other" professional group; and *acceptance* as a responsible professional concerned about producing healthy communities of learners and alternatives to oppression.

Margins need to be addressed, negotiated, and changed "to effect change by bringing people from the margins closer to the centre" (Feuerverger and Mullen, 1995, p. 223). Where dreams of development have not been fulfilled, individuals can paradoxically live "on the margins" even when functioning at the activity center. This chapter is my narrative of how a book was birthed by professionals who "dreamed" differently about their own walkways. It is also a study of how comentoring is a process that can energize people and places, or those adjoining walkways of school-university cultures.

Rethinking authorship training

What are some critical authorship issues in higher education and publication? What changes can come from encouraging educational cultures to rethink authorship training practices to promote guided faculty authorship development? (It is worth noting that the Special Interest Groups of the American Educational Research Association include "Teacher As Researcher" but not "Teacher As Author.") In a later section called "The Invitation to Write," I set the scene for the work of the PSG through a formal invitation to the teaching faculty at FSUS. Finally, I outline some elements of working together that foster comentorship within the related contexts of storytelling, writing, and book-making. I have attempted to help prepare the reader for those chapters that follow and for our larger themes involving mentoring development, socio-organizational frameworks, and socialization processes. But this research story is primarily about how a shared identity and project can be created among a diverse group of professionals.

Authorship can be viewed as a vital source of professional growth, expression, identity, and knowledge – as well as of reputation, status, and power. This is probably one of our best-kept secrets in higher education. People can choose to ignore relations of power.

Scholarly publication is not a mirror that reflects social life and its knowable facets. Higher education institutions must confront the ways in which researchers and participants are socialized to think about authorship. One way to do this is to orient research courses to investigate conventional authorship practices and to propose field-based and inclusive alternatives. Generally, university faculty have not been prepared to work with innovative practitioners or for the demands of tenure and promotion within university laboratory schools. Professors often miss important resources. Teachers bring essential resources "to the table" as fieldworkers who understand that action research models need to empower local contexts and communities by supporting the learning of students, faculty, and administrators.

With respect to books (and journal articles), authorship must be appropriately determined, and yet conversations among contributors occur in private and sporadically, when they take place at all. Aspects of authorship include reputation and status; "ownership" or initiation of vision; experience with and familiarity of the topic; research and productivity efforts; specialized forms of knowledge and critique; claims of "expertise" based on former publication; and, perhaps most notably, quality written contributions. We, in higher education, are not prepared for discussions about what should constitute authorship or, importantly, about how to assess those specific contexts we may find ourselves in or wish to create.

Authorship negotiations require open dialogue with research participants that facilitate consciousness-raising. As a complex phenomenon, authoring practice is shaped by historical, cultural, political, professional, and personal influences. Issues of authorship are trapped in the status quo of social position, status, rank, and gender hierarchies. Authorship practices are further confounded by institutional beliefs and practices, human motives and desires, personal and social ethics, and positivist canons. These canons require that authorship be identified and ranked according to contribution, yet research participants are typically overlooked altogether. In the PSG, we worked against these social pressures. Decisions for identifying authorship and coauthorship on our book chapters were based on the quality of research and writing contribution, not on status or other privileged determinants.

Collaborating across cultures

The process of "birthing" books can prove rewarding where individuals across cultures participate in each other's well-being, negotiate openly, and contribute to the making of a work larger than their own chapters/pieces/parts. Life with the PSG has enabled me to think positively about these social aspects of writing, despite the unevenness of attendance and contribution at project meetings. In a general sense, our book became "an outlet for recounting experiences and documenting memories, ideas, reflections, and dreams for the future" (McCaleb, 1994, p. 49). More specifically, our writing process helped us to comentor across faculty lines. We used our own stories, histories, and analyses, combined with published theories and practices, to think about different kinds of mentorship. Book-making is an intensely human commitment of persons becoming larger than their institutionalized, isolated selves. We found that we had to make ourselves vulnerable and accessible to embark on this collective journey in comentoring identity transformation. Because of its joys and struggles, this spiritual-analytical journey has ultimately helped me to become more fully capable and empathetic.

Collaborators who become learners again

We felt a strong bond in our comentoring group. As we worked, laughed, and shared, I was reminded of the piano teacher in Adams' (1996) story. She felt exhilarated upon learning the cello as an adult, partly as a way of rediscovering mentoring relationships, and exclaimed, "I'm so completely involved; it just takes you out of your life" (p. 219).

We, the PSG, were taken out of our lives but returned to them as fuller beings. With a safe place to share, we explored our most significant mentoring relationships and emerging insights and themes. We did not directly reflect on our experience of oneness ("synergy"). Instead, powerful statements about who and what we were becoming would poke through our book-making ideas and tasks. On one such occasion, as we wrestled with yet another title for the book, one member suggested using "synergy because that is going on in this group, combined with the comentoring that allows the synergy to take place" (transcription, 11 February 1998). Based on our learning, it appears that synergistic comentoring relations question, confront, and transform prevailing norms of professional identity and practice.

Of course tensions can arise when it comes to "crafting" a collective identity where none (or only pieces) existed before. Always, individual identity must be valued and sometimes at a cost. For example, I felt psychic discomfort whenever I heard self-depreciating comments. The teachers would sometimes apologize for the quality of their writing as a prelude to sharing. I was also reminded of our status differences or deference when those without doctorates would address someone as "Dr. So-and-So," even though we had established being on a first name basis.

Another example of an unresolved tension in our partnership identity was evidenced in the development of our key terms. Such concepts as mentoring, comentoring, synergy, narrative, story, action research, and school-university collaboration were often flagged by the professors and published researchers, yet these were also openly negotiated by the entire group. Importantly, everyone made sense of these concepts in her or his own terms and through personal mentoring stories. Together, we worked through the concepts, mulling over their possibilities, sharing relevant readings, and then deciding the "fate" of each term. "Mentoring" was finally collectively cast as our primary concept along with new directions, which is not surprising as I had brought this term and its many forms to the project. "Synergy" was cast as our secondary concept and viewed as one that fueled a new mentoring culture and professional partnership.

My status as an affiliated newcomer helps account for why I was ironically able to freely "go-between" the university and school, and not feel stuck in, or overly loyal to, either place. According to the PSG group, which provided feedback on this self-perception, other elements were more important than my newcomer status. They helped me to understand that my credibility, approach, style, demeanor, direction, facilitation, organization, and collective goal all enabled me to function as a catalyst for change. Additionally, they expressed that their belief in me and the shared project I had initiated contributed to establishing positive conditions for growth.

As an adjunct professor, my uncertain institutional status had provided me with an ironic gift. It helped me to be a keen learner, to stay attuned to the localized, implicit perceptions of teachers, which in turn inspired this project. I came to believe that the teachers were thought of as service providers and that the school was viewed as an extension of the university – an unequal yet necessary counterpart in the academic enterprise. In the PSG setting, we dealt with this pervasive problem in a variety of ways, first by exposing it and then by developing strategies for learning from each other. We met in the teachers' space throughout the project; together shaped our agenda, dialogue, and chapters; shared abstract and local knowledge; used first names instead of titles (most of the time); provided feedback on everyone's research projects; and expressed uncertainties and questions about mentoring and partnership processes.

Collaborators as teachers who author

Teachers can be collaborators and coauthors. Collaboration itself involves synergistic relations steeped in ideals of equality and justice. The ideals guide practice, but they also must involve and inform human contexts in order to have value that withstands the test of time. Although scholarship is exhibiting sensitivity towards "others," or those persons traditionally spoken for, much of the writing is decontextualized. Split off from practice, the articulated vision – hope for change – is ironically removed from the opportunity to make a difference.

Teachers' voices permeate a few recent educational books, but this evolutionary process is in an early phase of growth. Teacher as researcher is a very popular concept these days. It has become a respected value orientation towards professional knowledge development, and its forms vary. In my estimation, the teacher-based studies function on a continuum from being supportive of teacher development, to problematic, even silencing. Regardless, few studies reveal a sensibility that demonstrates teachers as authors and as partners in participatory research. This is the crux of the underlying current of change in our book. I return to this point shortly.

As a participatory action researcher, I assume along with Elliott (1994) that teachers have the ability to conduct their own research and to represent their own learning. However, I have learned through this book project that this view of teachers may be insufficient. Many teachers in K–12 research laboratory schools, and throughout schooling systems, require the assistance of interventions aimed at writing, researching, and publishing with experienced others. This is also the case for many beginning administrators and also professors.

Comentorship is not a "compensatory" practice for those less capable or qualified. Rather, it is an opportunity for professionals to exchange feedback and gifts and to develop along a common path. For example, during our support group meetings we assisted one another to problem solve with respect to our research development. Here is an instance:

Speaker: The problem I have is that I don't have good data as to whether it was as effective as we thought the program was in terms of how many of the mentees were successful, and whether their success was a direct correlation of time spent with designated mentors.

Responder 1:   The concept of data has changed, it is now very much connected to story, lived impressions, memories, narration, and storytelling. For example, "significance" can be thought of as a relationship that is maintained over time. This may be the "hardest" data one can fine.

Responder 2:   You could interview a fair number of these people in your program and get their input, or at least their perceptions of what this experience meant in their lives.

Teacher-researchers have yet to constitute a life force in the educational literature. There needs to be a distinction between those who "author" on their own, and those who are "authored" as invitees in professors' books and articles. A finer distinction can be located in texts that teachers contribute to as invitees, and, even finer still, in those that they help shape. It is in this latter realm of negotiated coauthorship that this book seeks to make a contribution. My look at the "author phenomenon" in this project concerns books rather than articles. Examples of professor–teacher co-authored articles are beginning to emerge in such journals as *AERJ* and *Theory Into Practice.* Teacher-led coauthored examples are rarer still.

Taking this step forward as joint faculty-activists, professors and teachers become less stranded. Some educators feel "shipwrecked" when expected to author and disseminate research studies on their own. With this collegial move, teaching and university faculty generate intellectual and emotional support as well as skills enhancement. Coming together, they have the opportunity to rethink negative stereo-types held in earnest about faculty populations dedicated to theory or practice, whatever the case may be. As the "cultural go-between" and "project catalyst," I was exposed to views that pointed to intercultural investment in separateness and even exclusion. Several university faculty, nonmembers, shared with me that the teachers are not scholastically inclined or ready. On the other hand, a few school faculty shared that university researchers are not interested in joint work and re-wards. There may be shades of truth in both of these positions; however, I pro-ceeded from a hopeful platform.

Caring can be orchestrated and in some sense "designed." The PSG project produced strategies to promote caring, ranging from university faculty membership selection to reciprocal storytelling, appreciative critique, and research and writing guidance. Caring was also linked to responsibility for us. Most of the core members became invested in productivity that supported the entire book, not just our singular contributions.

When the whole of a book is being cared for, writers can become larger, more reflective selves. Functioning beyond their own immediate concerns, they perform not only as action researchers but as creative and caring partners. The PSG mem-bers sought to fill necessary gaps in knowledge; to relate the parts of the book to an overall sequence; and to share resources, including their own time. One of our precious resources was the custom-made artworks created by the art teacher-author and her students. The birthing of our book was partly the result of our symbiotic capacity to identity resources in our immediate environment.

Reinventing ourselves as collaborators

Professors typically cross over into schools to resource a data-gathering, accessible world. Indeed, a dual service-based mission of FSUS is

> to provide a setting where faculty and graduate students can design, demonstrate, and analyze the effectiveness of new instructional materials and strategies under controlled conditions [as well as] to serve as a vehicle for dissemination of re-search findings which have proven effective. (*Florida State University School, Research and Development Guidelines,* 1997–98)

Such mission statements can be used by faculty within school-university partnerships to forge joint (or needed) work on programs, research, and even publication and dissemination. Or, they can be used by researchers to justify accessing what can be easily construed as a service site to benefit one's own professional career.

As I read books based on joint experiences between educators in schools and universities, I see instances where work has been mutually undertaken. But often these teacher-authors are simultaneously graduate/thesis students of professors, or committed colleagues. When mutual work is made public, the product itself can get split off from the process, misrepresenting the very effort to collaborate. Why might this happen? What happens to teachers' contextual knowledge and contribution as texts develop a public identity? It is as though a force privately mocks: "Your worldview and energies are valued, and they will be publicly shared, but on our terms and without your voice or finalizing signature." This rather glaring gap between teacher as researcher and teacher as author represents a political milestone, requiring persistent inquiry by those of us for whom such issues matter.

Strategies are needed for reinventing authorship patronage systems if new mentoring life is to be promoted within organizational cultures. From this point of view, Goodlad (1988), a strong proponent of healthy interinstitutional arrangements, identifies three characteristics of partnerships: one, "a degree of dissimilarity"; two, the desire to mutually satisfy "self-interests," and three, enough selflessness "to assure the satisfaction of these self-interests" (p. 41). This leaves no room for a self-proclaiming "white knight" or "white goddess." Where the initiator of an experience in partnership, such as myself, creates symbiotic conditions for others' learning, professional losses and gains are foreseen. I empowered myself to give to, and gain from, others. Interpersonal conditions built around giving *and* getting can provide the impetus for group solidarity and productivity. Such a process should not resemble a balance sheet of calculated gains and losses, but rather a practice steeped in negotiation and lack of resentment.

Many current books are self-referentially collaborative, identifying principles of partnership, community building, learning, and more. The examples I am thinking of are founded on authentic dialogic practices that bring together teachers and professors (typically in graduate courses) and that value mutual reflections and analyses. Concerning the actual public signature, however, participants' names are anonymously identified. In such cases, the "invisible ink" syndrome has won out. Author-less, contributors appear selfless like giving trees.

I realize that some professors invest countless months envisioning, initiating, and managing book projects, and even writing the bulk of the material. And, they often give special attention to draft manuscripts belonging to others, without the same effort or interest expended in turn. Laboring as a "lone wolf," they may revise chapters, solicit the book contract, prepare the prospectus and book, and complete the production forms, all in an effort to facilitate the continued life, or dissemination and impact, of the work. Such a lopsided, singular effort within an otherwise collaborative endeavor can characterize even exemplary joint projects.

Books built on other writers' (invisible) shoulders is, thankfully, a less conspicuous scholarship practice. Nonetheless, there exist books that attribute authorship to very few, even though the project development and writing were essentially collaborative. Participants' ideas take the form of evidence giving, quotes, paraphrases, written reflections, materials, artworks, and more. These signature pieces are like baby's hands made miniature once inside an adult's hands. They are rendered almost insignificant when reduced in status.

While examining such pieces, I become alarmed if participants have provided extensive written contributions, especially in the ironic context of a collaborative project aimed at professional development. It is not always possible to establish opportunities for authorship with every vital participant and gatekeeper in all research contexts. But, it is at least possible to find out whether certain participants in specific settings desire to write and commit to the serious demands of publication. With guidance, contributors' pieces can be made into e-l-o-n-g-a-t-e-d signature works. A powerful transformation in professional identity and self-image can follow from pivotal writing endeavors. Some participants commit a great deal of time and energy to researchers' projects with only an informal or, at best, formal acknowledgment. Such a practice is politically compounded within joint facility sites like ours where teachers are required to write. Teaching faculty at research lab schools function, in part, according to the policy demands of universities. This means that they *must* undergo a modified version of the tenure and promotion process with its emphasis on research, publication, and dissemination.

We are accustomed, as qualitative researchers, to transforming the participants of our studies into data sets, narrative snapshots, and practical windows onto epistemological worldviews. Yet, the field of qualitative inquiry has a responsibility towards the ethical development of educators, and this most certainly includes what is done with participants' signatures. We need to find ways to distinguish between those institutionally "justifiable" projects that use teachers' ideas and settings, such as theses and dissertations, from those that require new framing. Paradoxically, all self-authored projects are born out of a "lone wolf" mentality that depends, in one way or another, on collaborative effort for survival.

University faculty are "caught" within the social/power structures of higher education and its tenure and promotion reward structures. This social reality helps to account for why the university school culture "is not so much, then, replete with failure as it is short on examples of carefully crafted agreements and programs accompanied by [what is] essential for success – namely, individual and institutional commitment on both sides" (Goodlad, 1988, p. 12). Collaboration is "messy," an intricate process that can function as a disguised form of self-authorship. Because of my (former) non tenure-track faculty status during this project combined with my own values, I was not "regulated" by the academy's socializing pressures.

Sitting knee-to-knee as collaborators

Unlike professors, teachers who publish books are in the minority. *Teacher* (1963) by Ashton-Warner is one such example. This New Zealander teacher has "made" books with her young students, based on their writings and her artful recreations, which became the basis for her own teaching story. What is the potential for teacher-authored books to help change the pervasive stereotypes in higher education that constrain the publishing potential of teachers?

The writing of stories by parents and their children is another example of book-making. McCaleb (1994), a professor, encourages teachers to use books to build relationships with parents and their students. The author describes the making of books by families. The role of the teacher is presented as facilitator rather than also as coauthor, editor, or publishing catalyst. The examples of data used in McCaleb's book are the unpublished life stories of families. What might a further development of this family book idea look like if it were to involve the teacher, parent, and child as authors?

Professors who invite teachers to contribute to their own books by authoring chapters are offering something new. Although this type of invitation hints at a new movement underway, it is still not yet a trend but rather an infrequent occurrence. Professors who reach out to practitioners often want to show the practical capacities or implications of their own abstract ideas. In such cases, the books have already been planned and sponsored, and teacher-writers develop those areas that are needed. Collaboration, in the form of a negotiated, mutually shaped project around unforeseen ideas and rewards, tends not to be fostered with this kind of invitation.

It does not follow that professors who work with school teachers (and graduate student-colleagues) provide space for their publishing voices. But for those who have supplied examples of teachers who author, various concepts have been demonstrated. Among these are teacher as researcher; teacher as storyteller; teacher as transformative educator; and teacher as artist. These represent major emerging areas in social consciousness development in education.

A new practice within the educational community is collaboration by professors and teachers who "sit cross-legged knee to knee on a mat" (Ashton-Warner) for the explicit purpose of constructing a shared project. Where examples of publication by school-university faculty support groups occur, these do not typically result by way of design. Moreover, these groups are usually small in number and they publish reports and articles. The current playing field of comentoring faculty partnership is wide open for many unanticipated forms of research.

Coming to this book

I came to this book as an outsider, a virtual stranger to the school and university – a Canadian immigrant with my first exposure to a university laboratory school culture. Wherever I go, I seek to belong to a community of diverse educators who write and publish (not just talk) together. But I find it difficult to locate such groups already in operation. So I originate my own. I have established collaborative publishing agendas and groups in Toronto, Texas, and Florida, and in all three places books have resulted.

In my role, I seek to create with different people whose energizing talents, skills, and qualities facilitate mutual learning. I look for those who are oriented less by institutional roles and external rewards and more by the promise of cocreation and care. For some members, our group served as a secondary support; for them, a primary mentoring relationship had already been formed. However, even these distinctions were blurred. Some primary mentoring relationships were part of our group, as in the case of the teacher–principal relationships.

For other individuals, our group was the primary mentoring network. In this sense, our PSG demonstrates a rethinking of the concept of "mentoring mosaic." The literature describes mentoring mosaics as a compensatory network that serve a secondary function of mentorship only. Yet, a collection of persons can come to mentor at different levels and in various dynamic ways across a platform of primary and secondary roles. Such a complex, growing network can come to be, as it has for us, a major transformative organism.

A book can grow from conversation with oneself, a new situation or colleague(s), or from efforts with those with whom one shares vision and core values. With *New Directions for Mentoring*, I have learned that a book can grow from a stranger's formal invitation, in this case, my own. In hindsight, this may be not surprising. Some school-university partnerships survive perhaps because they have been "creative in maintaining their integrity as knowledge-producers while establishing relationships with practice oriented to change" (Goodlad, 1988, p. 12). As a stranger, I may have had an advantage. Boyle and Boice (1998) have found that mentoring where strangers are involved instead of close colleagues can actually be beneficial. Besides, what matters most is how the facilitator functions on behalf of the group and its members.

To create pathways between school and university faculty, efforts need to be made and sustained in the areas of special invitations, working conditions, comentoring strategies, productivity, and public recognition. To craft a successful experience, there is a need for commitment, planning, creativity, leadership, sacrifice, and endurance (Goodlad, 1988). I would add the need for persistence, flexibility, empathy, patience, honesty, and enthusiasm. On a metaphysical level, many practitioners probably yearn to be guided in their professional dreams of becoming. I experienced success by tapping into the teachers', administrators', and even professors' latent interest in authoring their own visions and work.

Before meeting with the teaching faculty at FSUS for the first time, I'd known from my reading, writing, and practical work that comentoring among faculty is an area requiring development. Not much is known about faculty who mentor faculty, or even whether these relationships usually evolve naturally or through top-down policies and requirements (Sands et al., 1991). Deliberate forms of comentoring in schools and universities are considered seriously undernourished. As Sands et al. (1991) conclude from their research:

> those who are mentored by colleagues put themselves in an unequal and vulnerable position in relation to persons who, some time in the future, may be making decisions about their tenure and promotion. (p. 174)

Despite such socializing pressures that work against the establishment of university and teaching faculty comentoring structures, there are examples of joint projects.

One teacher–professor support group views their work as a "a mentoring project" aimed at "making it happen" through critical reflection and action (Beasley, Corbin, Feiman-Nemser and Shank, 1996). A second teacher–faculty group created a context for transformative multicultural learning where they "situated [themselves] in the system based on their gender, class, and/or ethnicity" (Saavedra, 1996, p. 275).

Innovative mentoring developments in this book include the creation of symbiotic relationships and activity settings; synergistic comentoring forms of teamwork; redirected learning and status relations within institutions; transformation of interinstitutional arrangements; and expression of teachers' voices, identities, and lives. I have attempted to capture aspects of these dimensions of the learning group experience throughout this chapter. The book itself offers a wider range of mentoring development within various relationships, sites, and projects.

The invitation to write

In May 1997, I interviewed Eileen McDaniel, the research coordinator/elementary principal at FSUS and learned about some of the cultural history of the school. An unexpected outcome of this interview was that Eileen joined the Partnership Support Group. She wanted exposure to a writing-for-publication process for her own professional learning. This internal mentoring support, at the level of administration, provided the teacher members with an "interface" between the school and university. It also gave them an advocate, someone they could trust and talk to privately about their concerns. And it gave me the same, an advocate who supported the project and who shared with me relevant aspects of the school culture. After the practitioner group met, I then invited a number of professors to join who we felt would be able to work constructively with the teachers. These persons had in common their energizing support for people and for ideas of reform as well as their commitment to innovation, risk, publication, and human development. Those who accepted shared the invitation with other faculty and administrators, some of whom also joined. For several months, our membership was in flux.

To encourage the establishment of the PSG, I did a presentation for the teaching faculty at FSUS at their first staff meeting of the year. Preceding my own talk, Dean Jack Miller of the College of Education at FSU spoke. He stressed the importance of research for these teachers of excellence and the value of publication, including with university professors. Just as Dean Miller had not known of my own plan to invite the teachers to participate in a comentoring publishing project, I had not known of his plan to urge this kind of motivation. It proved serendipitous that Dean Miller had energized this walkway for me.

I invited everyone to participate in the writing of a new book in which they would be authors of their own projects and chapters. I kept the concept of mentoring open, wanting those who might be intrigued to bring their ideas to the project group. But they asked anyway, "What do you *mean* by mentoring?"– to which they obviously wanted some kind of answer.

In a room heavy with silence, I talked about how mentorship is defined in the educational literature. Then I gave examples of how I have approached mentoring in my own teaching-research projects with graduate students (teachers) and professors. I depicted mentoring as a continuum covering traditional, expert–novice relationships as well as alternative forms of relationship. I avoided providing biased or limiting views of mentoring. My message was that mentorship is a complex phenomenon that needs further study, and that we could tackle this inquiry as a team committed to developing a book in which contributors would be authors. I encouraged those present to see the mentoring value in their work in school and elsewhere.

I held up my coedited book, *Breaking the Circle of One* (Mullen et al., 1997c), and described how it had been produced by a comentoring group of professionals. Later I jotted an entry in my journal but in the form of an I N, or "shape poem." (Figure 4.2) To read, begin at the top and move from left to right, across the three columns of the page, to the bottom right-hand corner.

Shaping a comentoring context

From 1997–98, I undertook the Professional Support Group (PSG) research project in which I recruited and led a diverse group of professionals in researching mentorship practices at a university and its affiliate teaching laboratory. This project involved implementing a comentoring or collaborative action research paradigm. At our first session, I asked members to develop our common purpose through a writing exercise. I used an introductory questionnaire that I had devised. It included the questions: "What do you think this mentoring support group is about? And, why do you think it is being formed?" Based on members' varying but complementary views, I was able to understand their expectations for our group project:

1 to collaborate and work together to achieve a common objective as a creative means of expediting getting a book published;
2 to become a productive comentoring group that will reflect diversity in mentoring experiences and that will draw upon those invaluable experiences that each of us brings;
3 to build synergy within a team of writers that will culminate in the publication of a book on mentoring from a school-university perspective;
4 to expose faculty to a broad definition of mentoring and to share vital information;
5 to describe and implement our individual mentoring projects;
6 to set and accomplish goals such as those involving students in mentoring other students, teachers in mentoring students, college professors mentoring education teachers;
7 to make a connection between the school and university, and to support the idea and practice of mentoring;
8 to gain ideas about how we can better mentor others and benefit ourselves from the mentoring process;

Holding "it" up	pround 'n glossy as can be,	my second ©hild,
energy breaking out	t e a r i n g at its own bubble.	A figure outstretched,
cycling in and out	in–between here and there	blurring borderlines
releasing itself,	tearing elasticized edges, self erupting,	the birth of a book.
Exhibiting its binding,	f \l \i \p \l \i n \g its pages, gives me a reality.	I am the book.
Another child yearned for?	the stranger-in-me wants the creator-in-you.	Must reach out
to belong somewhere	during these turbulent times of in-between spaces.	"Let me help you *appear*
in scrolls to be written".	Such strong words?! White goddess	evangelical,
sorceress, caster of lots,	calculator of profits,	Go-between?
W h o i s S H E	asking for our trust, but not saying *that*?	*Trust must be earned.*
Your dreams of tomorrow?	Guessin' and gamblin' it's a long shot,	but don't say *that*.
Researchers as gamblers?	sounds highly improbable. Faces suspended my way,	
can strangers merge?	become a mentoring mosaic? Have I made contact?	
How will I know?	And just then	widening of an eye/I
engulfed in hope.	Words stick, dreams t h u n d e r	written across cultures
I/thou reinvent	with steepled hands	sticky palms,
quivering temples,	Walkways inter X secting isolates	I pledge privately:
"At this time and place	where my feet now land	I give over
all that I can be	to you, fellow comentors.	Please let me I N."

Figure 4.2: Please let me I N (Carol A. Mullen, 1997)

9   to participate in a large study involving bringing together the collaborative efforts of professors and teachers to create a model of mentoring based on our individual and shared levels of interest, and

10   to conduct an action-based research project with publication as an outcome, and to form learning relationships across age, ethnicity, and experience. To document learning and research as a tool to help improve classroom teaching.

Clearly, like myself, members were interested in collaborating for the purpose of writing and publishing as well as improving relations within their community culture.

Getting to know participants

The university and school faculty were, generally speaking, respectively grounded in theory or practice but neither group understood the theory and practice of mentoring. The solution was to enroll both camps to serve as mentors for one another. Through this co-mentorship framework, I actively provided the guidance necessary to integrate educational theory and classroom practice.

The following areas of mentorship played a role in our conversations, in the mentoring logs that we kept, and in our chapters. Examples of mentoring experiences that had been formulated as such by members included:

- the elementary school principal's role as mentor for beginning and experienced teachers;
- a teacher's development of peer mentoring in various elementary classes;
- an administrator's directorship of a mentoring program for untenured faculty of color;
- a librarian's daily learning from experienced librarians;
- a French teacher's mentoring relationship with a minority college student;
- a professor's shaping of the preservice program at the school, and
- a professor's development of collaborative learning/writing structures.

Based on our experiences, readings, conversations, and writings, we came to "situate" or describe mentoring in these ways (see Table 4.1).

Developing comentoring strategies

The Partnership Support Group used action research strategies, some as a group and some by way of individual choice. For example, while some writers conducted interviews and shared data to develop insights, others opted for an informal approach, reflecting on conversations. Still others devised a theoretical framework derived in part from the mentoring and change literature. But most of us blended

Table 4.1: Group-based situational definitions of mentoring

Peer coaching model	School administrator provides opportunities for beginning and experienced teachers to learn from each other.
Supportive relationship	Established professionals assist those who are developing.
Area of enhancement	Mentee gains confidence and ideas about how to approach one's work and progress – "like a steady jolt of adrenaline."
Life-long learner	Two or more persons work together to learn from each other; share preliminary ideas; give critical and appreciative feedback; take risks with innovation; and share information and resources.
Form of assistance	Teachers help other teachers and students on specific tasks to expand knowledge, develop skills, and improve performance.
Collaborative learning, comentoring structure	Undertaken by teachers, administrators, professors, and students to achieve a commonly defined professional/ academic end (e.g. coauthored publication).
Leveling the playing field	Status and power are deemphasized (except where functionally relevant) and mutual learning is emphasized.
Form of protection	"Looking out" for mentees in areas of employment and academic/professional contribution, and well-being and negative gossip.
Support for major growth decisions	Transitions regarding career moves, research topics, publication strategies and outlets, and personal academic challenges.
Special form of friendship	Mentor is available to listen and provide guidance, if requested (or felt to be needed).
Collegial network	Made available throughout university and school systems and support activity within various professional networks.
Vehicle for opening doors	Establish synergy among key players who work toward shared goals to build individual, team, and organizational resilience. Vital tool for translating principles of teaching and learning into applied research and practice for the purpose of going beyond "what is" to "what could be."
Nurtures reformist energies and agendas	Support for questioning and working past organizational/ interpersonal barriers. Commitment to social justice, and writing and acting for desired change.

these three approaches. Table 4.2 lists the primary comentoring strategies that served to support our project.

Enlarging the conversation

Our doors were kept ajar. People were invited to join our meetings and the project even towards the end. This openness enabled us to participate in a larger conversation. We could see that educators are attracted to learning about mentoring, especially as a team. By sustaining this interdependence, the PSG was able to create an electronic-based family structure. This way, authors who worked at the school but who could not join us could still contribute. This accommodation included those who lived outside the state of Florida working in school-university settings. Some group members used the internet to collaborate with authors and even to collect data. Our academic "cousins" constituted a diverse membership.

Table 4.2: Strategies for developing comentoring support groups

1   *Introductory questionnaire*: An introductory questionnaire enables the group's research facilitator to identify emerging themes (e.g. members' perceptions of the goals of the project; familiarity with a particular literature base; background in research, writing, and publication; extent to which teacher education projects have been fostered). In the PSG, I created the questionnaire and compiled results to generate a group portrait of ideas about and experiences with mentoring. I compared members along similar dimensions, using a chart, to highlight levels of experience and types of expectation.

2   *Packet of readings*: Facilitators can assemble salient readings on topics of interest and participants can add to the reading packet. Members read and interpret studies to help foster an understanding of the relevant literature as well as perspectives useful to individuals and the group. In the PSG, members found the readings useful for generating their own ideas.

3   *Publishing works*: The actual process of publication of a joint project is worth sharing. In the PSG, I produced the book prospectus but shared my works to demystify the publishing process and to foster synergy. I also shared my correspondence to and from publishers.

4   *Local records*: Exploring a local culture and its history through recordings of events helps put the current study in context. The PSG teachers felt empowered when they shared material that had been generated in their school. This process legitimates the local context and keeps the current project in perspective, enabling comparison with previous projects.

5   *Mentoring/learning logs*: Members documented their own research ideas, responses to articles, and areas of interest. Mentoring logs provided a useful method for forwarding everyone's study, and for helping us to understand our "fit" with existing studies.

6   *Storytelling exchanges*: Storytelling and feedback offer a conversational structure for effective learning and analysis. The PSG members relied heavily on storytelling as a way of making personal sense of the literature on mentoring, support groups, and action research.

7   *Regular communications*: Follow-up and newsflashes keep everyone posted, motivated, and team and goal oriented. The PSG members appreciated being kept up-to-date on the goals of our project and its various phases. For example, when I returned from the 1998 AERA conference, members were informed of my various meetings with senior acquisitioners of publishing houses as well as subsequent responses to my book prospectus. With several book contracts soon offered and one secured, members became even more motivated, but the majority did not require this "carrot."

8   *Nuts-and-bolts tasks*: Ongoing reshaping of "items" (e.g. key terms, titles, and table of contents) keeps negotiations open and focused. In the PSG, we began each meeting by reviewing our emerging contents page for the book. Each time, we gained clarity of purpose and greater comfort as everyone extended and received help with chapter titles.

9   *Audiotaped meetings*: Transcriptions provide an essential record for everyone to draw upon for individual project work and purposes. As PSG participants conducted their own study, I produced transcripts of our sessions that they discussed and used in their writing.

10   *Interview research participants*: Members and nonmembers represent a rich resource of experience and material for case study development. PSG participants learned valuable action research strategies by identifying interviewees, transcribing tapes and notes, and working with quotes. Everyone appreciated articles that demonstrated participant quotation.

11   *Edited manuscripts*: Close editorial feedback on material prepared for public release is an important formal step in writing-for-publication groups. In the PSG, all chapters were edited numerous times by the senior and assistant editor, both extensively published authors.

12   *Members' publications/writings*: Members become empowered when their own writing is shared and their image as developing authors is reinforced. In the PSG most members had published something, however modest. They enjoyed receiving attention from the others who earnestly discussed their work(s) in the context of our comentoring project.

The group enlarged our own conversations about mentoring partly by incorporating the voices of other published researchers. We even included textual writers as "comentors." For each meeting, we read several publications, tapering off toward the end. Most group members kept a log, using it to "record" and share responses to the readings and developmental writings.

Synergy as an authorship process

We came to see "synergy" as an enabler of the comentoring process. The example that most captivated our imaginations, because we often returned to it, was Lori Franklin's. As the story by this beginning librarian goes, Lori and her immediate supervisor had moved rather quickly to being in a highly charged, comentoring relationship. One day they realized, while passing between themselves a computer keyboard, that they had the need for an extended one. Of course, no such collaborative writing tool has yet been invented. In Lori's own words:

> We needed two keyboards because we were finishing each other's sentences. We wished that there were some way to hook two keyboards to one machine, so that we could be typing at the same time. However, we managed well, switching the keyboard back and forth onto each other's laps. Thus our baby was born! Here was an event where we had worked as equals, and were so proud of each other. (PSG transcription, 28 January 1998)

I gained a new insight over time related to Lori's sharing. In an effort to offer a view of comentoring at another level, that is, as the synergistic production of a group reflecting on itself, I devised an exercise. First, I should say that my motivation was to show the group an action-based example of how we were ourselves developing synergy. As a second point, I wanted to demonstrate an example of my own case study research.

I initiated this exercise in synergy development by reading aloud from a transcript of our exchanges from the previous meeting. I had come to see the special ways in which one member's ideas had built upon, and evolved from, another's. This interdependent process had revealed, to me, highly textured moments of synergy in action. I speculated that it would be difficult for members to identify individual speaking parts. One person would sound like another in the transcript; our viewpoints echoed one another's, often becoming indistinguishable. I tentatively attributed my hunch to the idea that positive synergy involves a heightened experience of "oneness," which defies easy attribution of who said (or owns) what. Community might be about dismantling attribution/ownership in favor of synergistic selfhood.

Instead of simply offering my hunches to the group on that day, I attempted to demonstrate them. I initially threw members "off the scent" by pretending that the statements I was about to read were from a book. What follows is the climax in which we all alternated between experiencing confusion and understanding about how synergy is produced in a group.

Carol:	Can you identify the author of this statement? [Reads]:
	The concept of cascading change is that when you bring about change, it brings about other changes. And it would be hard to say which one made the difference. All you know is that you turned it on originally, something happened, and then some of the unanticipated things, like people baby-sitting for each other, followed from it.
Freddie:	Did I say a little of that?
Dale:	I said something about cascading changes.
Freddie:	The baby-sitting part came up in what I said about the mentoring program.
	(Dale had said this whole piece, and Freddie had provided context, but earlier.)
Carol:	Here's the next one:
	Preparing a series of in-depth questions in advance before the interview is very different from grounded research where the conversation produces the questions.
Freddie:	That last part was Sandy, and she was talking to me.
Carol:	And who said that first part about the prepared questions?
Overlapping voices:	Eileen!
Carol:	Strictly speaking, that was Dale again. Here's another statement:
	We're going to find that every relationship that we're having with a mentor and mentee is going to be different. It might be interesting to keep using the articles as a way to describe what our relationships are like.
David:	Carol, this was you.
Carol:	Strictly speaking, David, this was you! But you're right in another sense, if we were to consider how synergy itself develops. We're sounding like one another. Just listen to the resonance that comes across in our interplay of voices.
Lori:	Imagine! I'm having a hard time trying to identify who said what to whom and when. Maybe that's the point.
David:	This is hard to do. Even if you said something yourself, you don't necessarily know that you said it. You can't even identify yourself really. (11 February 1998)

Lori and David, both school practitioners, offer something important here. Maybe the synergistic comentoring experience is about changes in identity. We cease to be able to identify ourselves, at least in the usual ways, when we become involved in collective endeavor. So the question Who am I? might be, at a higher level, about what the group or team is becoming.

Growing new wings

We, the Partnership Support Group, created a new life in the form of a synergistic culture of comentoring. Our chapters tell about transformative learning through mutual activities, settings, and relations – construed as different kinds of gift-giving. These fibers of new life coalesce to write a new story about mentorship as a support group activity in which members sit "knee-to-knee" to conduct research about who we are and what we can become.

Those walkways that continue to separate/join our university and school have been traveled differently by us. Already a teacher who was not in our support group has proposed doing a new collaborative book. This is an example of the kind of spin-off that can happen when a group builds synergy, imparting gifts unknowingly.

Acknowledgment

I dedicate my poem, "Please Let Me I N," to she who let me in, Eileen McDaniel, Elementary Principal at FSUS and chapter contributor.

5 Creating Synergy in a Mentoring Relationship with a University Student Volunteer

David S. Greenberg

Figure 5.1: *Reaching in for a new life to mentor (Julie Johnson, 1998)*

Lè ou pran asosié, ou pran you mèt.
When you get/take (an) associate, you get a master.
(Haitian Creole proverb in Jeanty and Brown, 1976, p. 170)

In a mentoring relationship with a university student volunteer, how can synergy be created to enhance mentoring effectiveness, and what obstacles exist to this synergy? This research study sheds light on these questions by discussing a successful mentor–mentee relationship between myself, a French instructor, and a Haitian university student who volunteered to help me teach my French I/II class. In an effort to gain a better understanding of mentor relationships and processes, teachers can challenge themselves to grow by collaborating with university students (Figure 5.1).

A split-class scenario: my challenging new role

Although this is my fortieth year of teaching, it represents the first time I ever had to teach a split language class, that is, a class with two levels of language students, French I and II. One of my former superintendents and mentors, the late Charles D. Frier of Shenendehowa Central School in New York State, said it best: "If you stay around long enough, everything happens."

The mentor relationship

When I arrived in a new teaching situation at Florida High (the high school at the Florida State University School (FSUS)), in the fall of 1997, I had just completed my first day when a volunteer coordinator approached me. She said that a Haitian senior at Florida State University, who was a French major, would like to volunteer to assist me in teaching my French I/II class. Slightly overwhelmed, I suggested that we delay this opportunity for a while until I got myself more organized. A couple of weeks later, I did request that this university student volunteer come to meet the class and myself. Quite frankly, I found it challenging to teach a split class of lively and easily distracted teenagers, and so I welcomed any kind of help I could get. I shall call my assistant "Marc", which is not his real name.

Marc and the class took to each other right away, and so I put him to work. Because of his own busy schedule, he could only come to my Tuesday and Thursday classes, but even this provided me some relief with teaching both French I and French II in the same period.

Taking Marc on as my volunteer represented a definite risk on my part because here I was in a brand new situation agreeing to let someone unknown to me influence my students. Without realizing it at the time, I had also taken on a new mentee, a protégé. But as Zalezik (in Scott, 1992) writes: "This willingness to take risks is perhaps one of the most critical traits mentors can help their mentees learn" (p. 169), and what better way to do this than set the example yourself!

Now Marc and I were of different ethnicities as was the class itself. As much as I was able to relate to varying degrees with all of my students, I believed that a member of another ethnic group might better relate to members of a nonwhite ethnic group in ways I never could, thus providing a balance to my pedagogical approach. I anticipated learning directly from Marc how to improve my relationships with students of an ethnic group different from my own.

Learning from one another

In this effort to learn from each other, we could adopt an "inside-out model of mentorship" (Mullen, 1997a, p. 29) whereby Marc and I could enter into one another's cultural worlds as newly informed outsiders. Learning to mentor a minority university student who would in turn teach me would present unique challenges. In her research on Hispanic preservice teachers and professional development, Mullen (1997a) discusses how

> As marginal-insiders, minorities must find productive ways to thrive within accepted structures of university systems whose very history of marginalization produces a dialectic (or cultural site of struggle). A dialectical relationship between insider and outsider probably confounds, for minority students coping within bureaucratized environments, the evolution of an integrated cultural identity. (p. 15)

In this classroom situation, Marc was confronted with a bureaucratized environment within another bureaucratized environment – Florida High is an integral part of Florida State University. Marc was the outsider for me just as I was for him. The obstacles preventing a Haitian from developing synergy with outsiders can be seen in the description of "the Haitian mentality" by Jeanty, a Haitian himself:

> The Haitian is uncomplicated and complicated at the same time. You can live with him many years and still not understand him . . . He does not trust people, especially the outsider, until he finds out that the outsider is worthy of his trust. If you trust the Haitian, he'll trust you. Don't just tell him: "I trust you." But trust him, and he'll open his heart to you – he'll be ready to die for you! (Jeanty and Brown, 1976, p. 2)

Creating mentoring synergy

I attempted to reach into Marc's circle by creating a sort of synergy which would help us work together better. To develop this synergetic relationship, Marc and I would work on fostering "a caring support system in which [we] genuinely and openly cooperate with each other and provide creative sharing, assistance and encouragement toward our common goals" (Murphy and Lick, 1998, p. 89).

To build synergy, we would have to develop trust. But, achieving trust was also complicated in this case by our cultural differences. Willie, Grady, and Hope outline this situation well (quoted in Scott, 1992): "Trust, acceptance and support are necessary ingredients to all mentoring relationships, but are more of a problem for minorities. . . . Nonminority mentors were found to be less likely as accepting, trusting, and supporting with minority mentees than with nonminority mentees" (p. 174).

Marc and I are opposites in several critical ways that would prove to challenge, and even interfere with, our attempt to sustain trust. For example, I tend to be oriented in the direction of book learning and dependability whereas Marc is less so. Nonetheless, a mentor can be a catalyst to initiate some kind of change. But, just how much change would I desire to bring about in Marc and how would I change as a result of being influenced by Marc? In spite of our differences, we were able to develop a cordial business relationship which resulted in *quid pro quo* benefits for both of us – I could receive some badly needed help with my dual-level French class while he could gain experience teaching high school French.

Teacher mentorship roles and qualities

In an editorial in our town's *Tallahassee Democrat*, Green-Powell (1997) discusses the characteristics of a successful mentor. As these pertain to me, I have a successful track record having mentored many student teachers. I am also able to communicate and give feedback while passing on my "hard-earned" wisdom and experiences. However, while interested in Marc's personal growth, I could neither put his needs above those of my/our students nor of the school organization. Simply put, I was hired to teach students French. I could therefore support the development of my mentee only insofar as it did not conflict with my responsibilities, particularly toward my students.

Another very important point that Green-Powell makes is that "the protégés are the ones who are in control of the relationship because the wisdom can be imparted only when receivers seek it or are willing to listen" (1997, p. 3F). Smith (1998) of the *Seattle Post-Intelligencer* reinforces Green-Powell's point. Citing Jack Carew, author of *The Mentor* (1998), she asserts that "mentor relationships are two-way streets. A person seeking mentoring must be willing to try new things, take advice and be open to suggestions" (p. 13D). Fortunately, Marc was willing to listen and would try out new ideas to the best of his ability. On the other hand, Marc was hampered by his lack of exposure to teaching and learning through teaching methods courses.

Most valuable to my discussion in Merriam's (1983) article, "Mentors and Protégés," are the five categories she provides of the patron system: peer pal, guide, sponsor, patron, and mentor. Using this scale, I would classify my relationship to my mentee as "guide." I could help Marc understand the system, but I was not in a position to help advance my protégé, that is, to help shape his career. I could be his teacher, but not his strong advocate, because Marc was not hired to teach but rather volunteered his services. Moreover, as a part-time instructor, I had no power or influence to help Marc advance his career in teaching. Indeed, at that time, Marc had not even determined that he wanted to become a teacher.

Some principles of planned career mentoring, as discussed by Krupp (1992), also applied to our mentoring relationship. Particularly relevant to my research story is the view held of mentoring as a dynamic reciprocal relationship that feeds the career development of mentor and mentee. In my case, Marc had the opportunity of exploring teaching French as a professional option while I was given the opportunity of caring for, and hence nurturing, "a new life" (see Figure 5.1).

Another noteworthy principle from Krupp, applicable to my situation, is the need to trust one's mentee. For instance, if I were teaching one level of French and Marc, the other, I needed to trust that he was engaging the material in such a way that the students would be able to learn. Monitoring his teaching every conceivable moment was not possible, since I was busy teaching the other level, nor was this desirable to me anyway. I knew that I would later receive valuable feedback from Marc as well as from the students and the test results. I did gain a feeling of Marc's teaching from "out of the corner of my eye," what became for me a source of intuitive knowing gleaned from a kind of peripheral vision. My sense was that

Marc interacted well with the students, and in a friendly and relaxed manner. The students related to Marc more as an equal, a personal friend, while they related to me as their superior and disciplinarian. My learning from this underscored the value of treating students more as individuals and less as objects of classroom control.

What I grew to understand was that the building of a dynamic, reciprocal relationship can combine with the building of trust, thereby creating synergy. Inherent in this process, according to Lick (see Chapter 3), is that people really have to make themselves vulnerable to make the synergy work. That is, you have to want to know about the other's perspectives and ideas, and why they think and feel as they do. You also have to respect their thoughts, if you are going to build an interdependent, synergetic relationship. I tried to be mindful of these elements of synergy in my relationship with Marc, as can be seen from the examples below.

The unfolding of the mentoring relationship

Schein (in Zimpher and Rieger, 1988) designated the roles of the teacher mentor as "coach, positive role model, developer of talents, opener of doors, protector and sponsor, and successful leader" (p. 176). Of these, the coach, positive role model, and developer of talent are closest to the role I played for Marc. I coached Marc in developing and sustaining teaching responsibilities in a live teaching setting wherein accountability is crucial.

I imagine that I also empowered Marc to teach simply by not being constantly vigilant. According to Bird (in Zimpher and Rieger, 1988): [I]"suspended or deferred judgment in order to help [my mentee] adopt and display a stance of active curiosity and focus on the practice of teaching" (p. 177). As indicated, this was especially apropos to our situation because I needed to defer judgment while Marc taught. I simply was not able to observe the degree to which he was communicating effectively, or to what extent the students were paying attention to him or the task at hand. There was certainly no formal evaluation occurring, given Marc's designated role as volunteer, not paid employee or even student teacher. At the end of each class period, we shared what still needed to be accomplished. Marc also gave me feedback on how well he felt the students were responding to him. The following day I would ask my students if they had any questions about the concepts taught or reviewed by Marc.

On one occasion, while Marc was working with the French I's, and I, with the French II's, his group of students were failing to respond; in fact, they were deliberately *not* cooperating with him. The next day he urged, "We've got to do something about the way the students are treating me." In response to Marc's concern, I addressed the whole class saying, "Look, Marc is here out of the goodness of his heart, and he's trying to help you. I expect you to do as much for him as you would for me, and to give him just as much attention. If Marc should report to me that someone isn't responding appropriately during his teaching, I'm going to take off participation points from that person." This was the least I could do for my volunteer protégé. Protecting one's mentee in public is a vital part of mentoring. After that incident, the French I students were more respectful of Marc. They were even anxious to work with him. If I had Marc work with the French II's instead of with them, they were disappointed. I would then promise that Marc would teach them the next time.

Marc's most valuable observations to me were in the realm of my interaction with the students. On occasion, I could become most impatient with them and would raise my voice. One day he observed that my reaction to the students could have an adverse affect on my health. I have since made a special effort to deal with students by monitoring my voice. This exercise in self-control has proven to be a valuable lesson for me.

For each class, I would call Marc on the phone the night before and discuss with him the role he would play. Sometimes, as indicated in previous scenarios, his involvement would take the form of teaching a section of the class. At other times, he would serve as a resource, aid, or even as an assistant proctor during tests. During our phone conversations or face-to-face exchanges, I would tell him how a lesson in class had either turned out or how it had been followed up. These kinds of explanations would give both Marc and myself insight into what I did and why. This strategy proved to be a reflective opportunity for exploring my own pedagogical intentions, motives, and reasons. Thus, my mentee served as a sort of "mirror" into which I could reflect back on what was going on in my teaching life.

The mentoring gift

In Gehrke's (1988) article, "Toward a definition of mentoring," I especially like the interpersonal concept she provides of mentoring as a gift given to the mentee by the mentor:

> The greatest gift the mentor offers is a new and whole way of seeing things. This gift of wisdom . . . comes from having lived and thought deeply and it permeates all the mentor does with the protégé. It is, then, a way of thinking and living what is given. . . . Through the gift of self as philosopher, the receiver, the protégé is awakened. (p. 192)

Enhancing this gift requires that appreciative understanding be rendered in a nonjudgmental way (see, e.g. Chapters 3, 4 and 11). It is as if Marc and I were helping each other to move up Bloom's taxonomy to a higher level of learning, or comentoring.

Challenges to the partnership

Much of my chapter has focused on how I tried to create synergy with Marc. Now I must also outline some of the obstacles to the creation of this synergy. These tended to center around my concept, value, and practice of dependability. For example, I could not always discuss what was on my mind with Marc because he sometimes either arrived late or, on other occasions, he would not arrive at all. I would bring up this unpredictable behavior with Marc who would, in turn, promise to try to become more consistent. I asked that he call me beforehand so I could plan my class accordingly. But still the same behavior would occur. Nevertheless, the door was "left open" for Marc to join us in class. I valued the contribution he made as a member of an ethnic minority who was also a native French speaker. Thus I tried to empathize with him and delay negative judgment. Further, I invited him to lunch at a fine French restaurant in town to thank him for his contributions. We had agreed that he would call if he could not make it. But he did not call or show up! Later I tried calling him, but his phone was out-of-service. I thought that was the last I would ever see of Marc.

Our learning together

Overall, I sincerely believe that under these rather unusual circumstances I was able to create a meaningful synergy with Marc. Our mutual learning enhanced the effectiveness of our individual teaching, shared discussions, and mentoring relationship. In many respects, it was a pleasure working with Marc. He helped me handle a very difficult classroom situation requiring that I teach two levels of French during the same period. I also learned from being exposed to his relaxed, "laid-back" manner. I observed, first-hand, some of those difficulties a minority student has adjusting to bureaucratic expectations of a culture different from his own.

It is my hope that, in addition to taking away a better idea of what is involved in teaching high school French, Marc learned from the examples I tried to set for him. These mostly concerned the values of dependability, punctuality, and organization which are paramount to advancing one's career in the North American culture. I realize that I had wanted Marc to reach into my own circle of self while at the same time I was trying to reach into his. But the capacity for such a synergistic exchange has limits – we are both culturally fixed in many of our life-habits.

After Marc's departure, my students asked me what had become of him, but I did not know what to say. Perhaps I should have told them about the late Charles D. Frier's message that if you stay around long enough, everything happens. Working with this university volunteer in a split-level class has certainly proven this adage to have powers of truth for me!

Postscript: continuing mentoring connections

A month later Marc showed up suddenly. He had been in Miami to support his sister who needed an operation. I asked him why he had not called to cancel the restaurant appointment. He said he was sick that day and did not have my number while away. Anyway, he asked if I could use his help, and I of course agreed. Marc came to several classes after that, but I learned to plan with the possibility in mind that he might not show up. This relieved some of the pressure on both of us. Just as he did not have to feel obligated to come to my class, so I was not disappointed if he did not join us. Even though I was unable to treat him to French dining, I did publicly acknowledge his positive contribution to my class at a school banquet honoring volunteers.

During a telephone conversation near the end of semester, Marc revealed what he had learned from working with me. He talked about the way I organized my class, emphasizing structured lessons, and how I interacted with my students to encourage their learning. He said that he also learned an important point about classroom management – if you can get the "unofficial" class leaders to cooperate with you, then the rest of the class will follow suit.

In the final analysis, it may be difficult to completely merge as insiders into an unfamiliar culture. To some degree, Marc and I each remain as outsiders to one another, but have become better informed and certainly more empathetic.

Author's note

As my dissertation indicates (see Greenberg, 1997), catalysts, such as color, black humor, and dream, are used in literature to assist the reader to closure. I invite the reader of this chapter to find those catalysts that I have used to develop my main themes, bringing them to closure.

6   The League of Mentors: A Strategy Beyond the Faculty Handbook

Freddie L. Groomes

Figure 6.1:   Introductory handshake at program orientation (Bill Langston, 1992)

Having been born some x number of years ago to Negro parents living in a colored community and growing up to be a proud African American woman, life for me "ain't been no crystal stair." I've experienced the low roads and the high roads. As Executive Assistant to the President at The Florida State University with the responsibility for Human Resources including Affirmative Action and Equal Opportunity, I believe that I experienced high roads while providing leadership for the initiation of several innovative programs. These have been designed to enhance the status of people of color and women. One such program, The League of Mentors, is the focus of this chapter. As an action researcher and mentor to many, I am especially proud of the League of Mentors and its many benefactors, both mentors and mentees.

Mentoring in higher education

The mentoring phenomenon in adult growth and development is neither a fad nor a recent professional discovery. From Levinson's (1978) research we learn that one of the critical functions of mentoring is to support and facilitate the realization of people's dreams. Thus, it was a natural effort for the Florida State University professional mentoring program, the League of Mentors, to facilitate the success rate of faculty of color and women in their pursuit of promotion and tenure.

Despite the plethora of literature on the subject of mentoring, there is little that deals specifically with mentoring in higher education for the purposes of professional development and/or career advancement. Traditional sponsorship and advising fall short of addressing the personal or goal-directed support often needed by those nontraditional aspirants pursuing promotion and tenure.

A unique high road

Florida State University is a comprehensive, graduate research university with a liberal arts base. It offers undergraduate, graduate, advanced graduate, and professional programs of study, conducts extensive research, and provides service to the public in accord with its statewide mission. The university's primary role is to serve as a center for advanced graduate and professional studies while emphasizing research and providing excellence in undergraduate programs.

Consistent with this mission, the university pioneered the development of a comprehensive Affirmative Action Program to enhance the representation and progress of ethnic minorities and women. These result-oriented procedures addressed hiring, salary equity, policy reviews and grievance procedures. From the academic perspective of the university, it also needed to focus on promotion and tenure.

Although the university was becoming more and more diverse, it was evident that this diversity was not consistent at all levels, especially governance, in every area or academic unit. As a result of the underrepresentation of women and people of color in the tenure ranks, and allegations that these individuals were not as successful in the process, the League of Mentors was created. Ethnic minorities would often reach roadblocks on their pathway through a lack of awareness of an informal system of mentoring and, for female faculty, less peer support as well. The data on the status of the affected class at the university made this program practical and easier to promote.

The League of Mentors' program

At the university, all faculty had access to the *League of Mentors Handbook* (Groomes, 1982), which served as the documented guide for those seeking promotion and tenure. However, there was a perception that the campus, much like others around the nation, had an informal system operating in matters concerning promotion and tenure. Consequently, it has become important that one knows how to adequately interpret policy and understand not only the "essence" of what is stated, but also the culture within which promotion and tenure are critical stepping stones. In other words, there are strategies that can be adopted that are not necessarily formally recognized, but that can seriously influence the outcome of the formal promotion and tenure processes. Some would say that this is more perception than fact, but perception has a kind of reality all its own. Thus, the League of Mentors provided a much needed, and highly welcomed, strategy for learning, professional success, and socialization beyond the faculty handbook.

My examination of the academic workforce data in 1980 revealed that the rate of success for those women and minorities pursuing tenure was less than the rate for white males. Consequently, the Office of Human Affairs recommended to the president that the university initiate a program designed to augment existing efforts in the Office of the Dean of Faculties and the respective departments. With the cooperation of these groups, the League of Mentors was established in 1982. It lasted over 10 years.

The objective, to improve the success rate of women and ethnic minorities, proved very challenging to those institutional practices that had not been infused with formal mentorship structures and opportunities for people of color. The following steps were taken, at the university, to initiate, develop, and maintain the League of Mentors:

1 identify women and ethnic minorities currently in tenure earning positions;
2 identify senior ranked tenured professors who were willing to serve as mentors;
3 provide comprehensive orientation for all participants; and
4 execute the mentoring process.

The program was greatly enhanced by the cooperation of the Dean of the Faculties Office that remains a strong advocate of the League of Mentors process even though the League is no longer *formally* active. At the outset, the Dean made available a list of potential mentors and also helped identify new and continuing faculty with tenure earning appointments. Once these lists were compiled and screened, letters were sent to tenured faculty to inquire about their willingness to serve as mentors. The response was positive. A cadre of outstanding faculty indicated interest, submitting copies of their vitae to be included in an information booklet prepared to assist in introducing new faculty to potential mentees.

I developed a mentee reference booklet containing a summary of potential mentors, information on their research areas, length of service, and special interests outside of the work environment. It was anticipated that mentors who discovered with their mentees a shared research interest, Alma Mater, or previous work experience might make the mentorship more approachable, and the relationship itself possible and even durable.

Each potential mentee was sent an introductory letter explaining the league program. Interested persons were invited to attend a "get acquainted orientation." Figure 6.1 offers a view of the kind of mentoring connection that occurred at this event. Shaking hands, in the foreground of the photograph, is a potential mentor–mentee pair. I am the third person from the left and the second person from the right is Steve Edwards, Dean of Faculties at The Florida State University. This coffee hour had a specific agenda that was to acquaint mentees with mentors in a relaxed but professional setting. Subsequent events alternated between evening socials and coffees, each with an explicit purpose. Some individuals found the morning hour to be more convenient, while others preferred the end of the workday or evening.

On these special occasions, invitations were sent to mentors, mentees, and select university administrators. An attractive, convenient location was chosen and each person attending wore a name tag that identified his or her status. Mentees had the advantage of having been equipped with information on mentors while mentors were supplied with potential mentees' names, areas of specialty, departments, addresses, and telephone numbers.

Mentees who were not connected with mentors at the orientation were encouraged to approach mentors directly and request their service. Follow-up telephone calls were made to League participants to determine who the actual participants were in the formalized mentoring partnerships. Initially, a limited number had paired up, but with encouragement to mentees to take the initiative, participation in mentoring increased significantly.

Program structure and nuances

Regarding program structure, it should be noted that the League of Mentors was intentionally loosely structured to afford individuals the option to design their own personal mentoring opportunities based on mutually agreed upon needs and goals.

At the orientation, participants were advised to make the most of the mentor–mentee relationship through mutual trust, open and honest communication, and serious attention to issues and concerns related to agreed upon objectives. Mentors remained confident of the high potential for positive outcomes, and, with the agreement of their mentees, offered follow-up sessions regularly, or as needed.

Generally, mentors kept the mentees aware of submission dates and schedules for the series of steps involved at the departmental and college levels in terms of promotion and tenure. Some mentors also provided contacts, resources, and referrals for support of research and publication options. Mentees were also encouraged to be mindful of the instructions outlined in the *League of Mentors Handbook* (Groomes, 1982). Mentors often provided special assistance in interpreting, and being sensitive to, relevant tips and messages from others regarding their professional pathways. Additionally, mentors occasionally consulted directly with administrators to confirm the accuracy and completeness of the candidates' promotion and tenure folders. If there appeared to be an oversight in the mentee's preparation, which called for attention, the concern would be addressed in a timely manner. Mentors on occasion confirmed with the university Equal Employment Opportunity specialist, or suggested that the mentee do so, when questions regarding unique situations relative to the affected group surfaced. For example, the issue regarding the status of professional publications, comparable to refereed journals, arose for mentees.

Examples of success

One of my personal regrets is that the League of Mentors was not pursued as a research project, but rather as a result-oriented, professional mentoring program.

However, it did, in fact, result in a number of individuals successfully achieving promotion and tenure. To the surprise of many, a myriad of other accomplishments, that were not initially planned or considered, also occurred. Some of the results of the program, gleaned from observation and an informal survey, are addressed below.

A recent conversation with the dean of the faculties revealed that although the League of Mentors program no longer exists in its original form, there remain off-shoots of it. Persons who served as mentors continually make themselves available to new faculty, utilizing suggestions from resource materials provided by the program. The current dean encourages tenure aspirants to select an adviser/mentor to assist them in the tenure-earning process and/or to join a tenure faculty group led by a full professor. The dean, who has assisted numerous mentees himself, thinks that the League program and process of mentoring were highly effective.

Also involved in the League of Mentors were department chairs throughout the university. They were made aware of the crucial need to monitor the progress of affected-class promotion and tenure aspirants. As an example, there is the tendency for some new faculty to respond to all or most institutional pressures and invitations. They consequently become over-involved with activities that do little to advance their promotion and tenure efforts. Even though many such efforts have value to the university and its constituents, new faculty are cautioned to focus mostly on those endeavors that "count." One participating senior faculty mentor stated that she often wished that she had had the benefit of such a mentoring program when she was working towards tenure – such an opportunity would have served to eliminate some of the problems she had experienced. Along these lines, mentors generally advised mentees which projects or committee assignments would advance them toward their ultimate goal while making use of their professional resources and time. Some mentees had to be outright discouraged from pursuing particular interests and commitments.

Not surprisingly, the mentoring process took on qualities of personal advising and counseling. On one such occasion, a senior tenured faculty mentor had recently gone through a difficult divorce. Quite by chance, his junior faculty mentee shared that he too was, with hardship, going through a divorce. The mentor found himself serving as a counselor/supportive listener, helping the mentee to focus, during this personal struggle, in an effort to manage his psychic discomfort to achieve his goal. Not only did the mentee emotionally survive the divorce and subsequent life transition, he also realized his dream – the achievement of tenure. He partly credits this success to his mentor for having been such a timely, supportive "counselor."

This kind of deep, interpersonal support was not anticipated in the initial plan as such, but if one adheres to the premise that a mentor is a person who "looks after, advises, protects and takes a special interest in another individual's development," then this mentor proved to be more than on target. Such personal scenarios in academia are reflective of a holistic, caring approach that can find its way into faculty mentoring programs, such as ours, that assist in providing the conditions for human development to be nurtured.

For many mentees in our program, just having someone to talk with who understood the "trials and tribulations" of the promotion and tenure track helped to calm anxiety and bridge moments of waiting. Mentors proved to be great listeners. Great listeners are critical. Many times mentees were actually wanting a "sounding board" for their developing research ideas and projects. I spent many hours after work in informal telephone calls and meetings listening to mentees explore in these ways. I also learned the value of assisting by virtue of "meaningful silences." On occasion, I felt I could "hear" mentees reflect as I listened patiently, for however long was necessary. Some of them moved from "low roads" of personal insecurity and self-doubt to "high roads" of confidence and productivity as a result of such mentoring sessions.

Only one problematic mentor–mentee encounter surfaced, that I know of, but even it proved constructive in the end, providing an opportunity for refocusing. It concerned a particular mentee, who, after engaging in formal mentorship, decided that his professional interests would be better realized in a nontenure-earning position. He then assumed an administrative and professional line, becoming also a successful writer and motivational speaker.

Spawning a new program

Why does the apparently effective League of Mentors program no longer function formally? There are several reasons. Priorities at the institution have changed and a stand-alone, or specific mentoring program, was perceived as no longer required. That is, the rate of success among women and people of color, who obtained promotion and tenure, became more equal to their male and nonminority counterparts.

Further, growing out of this mentoring program was another, the Opportunity Leadership Enhancement (OLE) program. It currently focuses on support for ethnic minorities and women faculty, as well as administrative personnel interested in executive responsibility. The OLE program is supported by the Educational Leadership Enhancement Grant Program of the Florida Department of Education. Its three-fold purpose is to

1　enhance the status of faculty and administrative/professional personnel, including ethnic minorities and women who want to assume executive administrative responsibility;
2　develop participants' potential for key managerial level roles in higher education through intensive exposure in critical areas required for success; and
3　enhance diversity at all levels of the university workforce.

Florida State University's ongoing commitment to foster diversity and pluralism, as evident in its support of the League of Mentors program, was the catalyst for the development of the OLE program.

Success of League of Mentors' Program

Clearly, the League of Mentors' Program was effective and timely. Through a semi-structured format, it served its purpose. Now the university leadership generally encourages senior faculty to be supportive of promotion- and tenure-aspiring faculty.

As mentioned at the onset of this research story, not much has been documented about mentoring between faculty members in comparison to mentoring between faculty and students (Sands et al., 1991). However, a series of random telephone interviews with mentee participants indicated that they had been advantaged. As previously indicated, many mentees expressed their support of, and confidence in, the League of Mentors' Program. Nonetheless, the most significant consensus of the mentee-participants involved the attribution of their professional success to their synergistic mentoring relationships. They typically spoke of how they plan to continue such relationships, regardless of whether or not they are programmatically institutionalized. Such comments reveal that the university mentoring program had had a positive impact on many lives.

Forward-looking promise of higher education

Faculty mentoring faculty is becoming increasingly vital in colleges and universities across the country. Forward-looking institutions are, in a myriad of ways, providing support for faculty aspiring to promotion and tenure. Mentoring programs are growing in popularity and, in some institutions, they are formalized while others are semi-formalized, or even unstructured.

Both mentee and mentors can realize benefits from supportive colearning relationships, as in the case of a "helping hand and aspiring hands" metaphor. Senior faculty can, for example, benefit from new faculty who have technological expertise. The university benefits when promising faculty members are successful with promotion and tenure. Quality professionals bring credit, recognition, service, and unique research and resources to the institution. Mentoring also facilitates enhanced morale that makes for greater productivity throughout the university.

As established in this essay, faculty mentoring is, generally speaking, an inexpensive process that can yield a wealth of benefits for all concerned. Consequently, more formal research should be conducted to determine the extent of advantages of university faculty mentoring faculty. I contend that people who support others offer a socially important service that is difficult to "measure" in terms of its benefits – simply put, some of these seem more personal than pragmatic. In the case of faculty mentoring faculty, many mentees have a history of special challenges and "low roads," as did I. Clearly mentoring is a very effective strategy for extending special support to persons who are eligible for, and deserving of, promotion and tenure as well as the rights and privileges such status signifies within universities.

In the current wake of challenges to Affirmative Action and Equal Opportunity throughout North America, a program similar to the League of Mentors is a needed response in assisting universities to achieve the professional development and status of its diverse workforce. Mentoring is a vital pathway to reaching the "high roads" in higher education, and to connecting with seasoned travelers along the way.

Reflections on the Partnership Support Group

This chapter is a tribute to the value of mentoring in my own life. The comentors who represent the authors of this book served valiantly as mentors to me. During the 1997–98 meetings of our Partnership Support Group, they listened to me reflect on the League of Mentors. Their counsel, feedback, and suggestions proved indispensable as I began to conceptualize the worth of the program as an action-based study and positive example of mentorship in higher education. I felt special sharing my story about the developments and impact of the mentoring program. I also learned that I could use a narrative approach to this study, incorporating a point of view that reveals my own value for making a significant difference in the professional lives of women and people of color, particularly within the university context.

7 Profiles in Mentoring: Perspectives from Female School and University Voyagers

Fanchon F. Funk and Frances K. Kochan

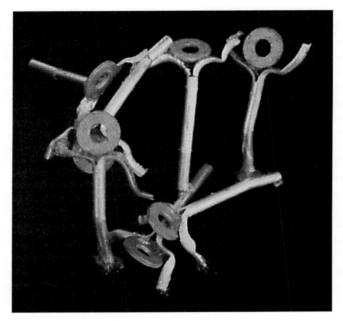

Figure 7.1: Dancing bolts connecting (Cara Delissio, 1998)

Mentoring opportunities in business and education worlds are very different. This is further negatively exacerbated for females in schools and universities. How should circumstances be changed and how can disparities be overcome? What can professionals gain from synergistic mentoring relationships and how can they successfully empower others through them?

In this chapter, we discuss our study on mentoring professionals in educational environments, including a collection of stories about personal journeys in mentoring from a female perspective. The study had its inception when, as comentors in the Partnership Support Group, we began sharing our experiences as mentees. Fancy's voyage occurred in higher education with side-trips to the K–12 setting, while Fran's trip consisted of lengthy excursions to both K–12 and university settings.

Reflecting on the impact of these relationships upon ourselves and our careers, we sought to formally gather stories about other experiences of female educators.

We now share our own experiences and add those of our fellow sojourners. In addition, we highlight our findings and include recommendations for creating synergistic mentoring relationships and progressively advancing careers and organizations through them. We hope that this study stimulates reflection and dialogue about the roles of mentoring in education for females.

Mentoring is education

The word mentor has been characterized using many synonyms: guide, counselor, coach, friend, parent, preceptor, teacher, and sponsor (Crow and Mathews, 1998; Zey, 1984). All of these words have their foundation in the notion of apprentice-ship, in which one, wiser and more experienced, guides and supports another. Some have suggested that such relationships are commonplace in the world of business, where senior management seeks out promising individuals and prepares them for advancement through mentoring programs (Clutterbuck, 1991). Others note that such mentoring opportunities are available, but only to a limited chosen few (Zey, 1984). Whatever the reality, there appears to be agreement that individuals who have mentors will more easily rise up the corporate ladder. Heidrick and Struggles (in Clutterbuck, 1991), a nationally prominent research firm, found that among 1,250 senior executives in competitive industries, the vast majority had had men-tors, particularly for the early years of their careers. Those who had been mentored had higher salaries. Mentoring appears to have a powerful impact on the level of success one achieves in business and industry.

Mentoring is a recognized force in the corporate world, not the educational world. Thirty states have policies formalizing planned career mentoring through induction programs for new teachers (Arin-Krupp, 1992). Further, some work has been done in establishing mentor–inductee relationships with beginning teachers (Zimpher and Rieger, 1988). However, apart from the intern experience few, if any, veteran teachers take responsibility for closely mentoring those entering the field (Brouch and Funk, 1987).

Mentoring programs

In 1991, the British government established a nationwide principals' mentoring program for England and Wales. This program consisted of providing each new school principal with seven days of mentoring from an established principal in the same area (Thody, 1993). The Danforth Foundation in St. Louis, Missouri has also funded an experimental program to stimulate structured mentoring relationships (Barnett, 1990). Singapore has had a structured mentoring program for its princi-pals for years (Walker and Stott, 1993). Although programs that formalize principal apprenticeships such as these exist, mentoring practices in educational administra-tion are "typically unintended and unsupported." Despite this, principals report that a primary source for their preparation and the strongest single influence on their leadership style was a field-based mentor (Crow and Mathews, 1998).

At the university level, there are a few formal mentoring programs such as those established through the Kellogg Foundation and the Kettering Fellowships program. However, in this culture it is individual accomplishment, not collaborative outreach that is valued, and there appears to be little formal mentoring occurring on a large scale basis. Although mentoring is recognized as valuable and perhaps even necessary to success in the administrative realm, it appears to remain on the periphery of education. It occurs, if at all, seemingly by chance, with occasional attempts to formalize the process, but mentoring is not fully incorporated into the heart and soul of the profession.

Case studies

We formalized our thoughts for this chapter by developing a set of questions (included at the end of the chapter) around four phases of mentoring, each of which includes elements of synergy that positively affect other relationships. These phases are *groundwork*, *warm-up*, *working*, and *long-term status*. We viewed these phases in the mentoring process as destination points in the trek toward development and growth. We created a broad conceptual area for each phase, and covered these questions: How did the mentorship begin?; What were some events that demonstrated that you were entering into a workable relationship?; How did the mentorship operate?; and What did the relationship evolve into? We then developed subsets of questions for each area (not listed here). Each of us, Fran and Fancy, wrote responses to the four questions and revised them based on our reactions. We then used the new questionnaire to interview six other female educators serving in administrative positions. Three of them work in higher education, three in K–12 environments.

We selected female administrators who had had formal mentors as our interviewees for three reasons. First, we are both female administrators who have been mentored to different degrees in our own careers and we wanted to compare our experiences with our counterparts. Second, females are a minority in administrative positions in educational management and thus lack role models at high administrative levels (Betz and Fitzgerald, 1987). Traditionally females have not been a part of the networking and mentoring systems available to males and have not been socialized to operate in their work environments (Angelini, 1995). We wanted to capture the stories of those who had been mentored in order to understand the process and the effect of that experience upon their careers. And third, little is known about women and their career experiences (Mullen et al., 1997).

After obtaining information related to personal demographics, job roles, and mentoring experiences, we asked the interviewees to focus upon the most important mentoring relationship they had encountered. We then asked them to respond to questions framed around the four mentoring phases listed earlier. The conceptual questions for each phase are embedded in the chapter as our stories unfold. We also asked some open-ended questions to allow the interviewees to add any pertinent information and insights from their personal journey. All interviews were tape-recorded and transcribed. After reading the transcriptions to gain an understanding of the whole, we identified some common themes. Next we compared our ideas and developed this chapter based upon our shared understandings.

The voyagers

Mentoring profile: Fran

I, Fran, am presently director of a college-wide center that facilitates the development of school-university partnerships and research initiatives. The focus of our endeavors is to strengthen university connections to schools, agencies, the community, and the state.

I have spent the majority of my educational career in the K–12 environment. I have taught children and adults, directed a number of projects which developed innovative programs, and have served as a principal and district office administrator. These professional experiences occurred in Micronesia, Guam, and in rural and urban communities. I spent six years as a principal and three years as the Director of the Florida State University School (FSUS), where I operated in both the K–12 and university environments. My entry into administration was a matter of having the right skills, at the right time and place, and was something I neither planned nor sought to attain. I had no political influence nor any formal or informal mentors who encouraged me to seek an administrative position. I was the second female principal in a rural community that had not had a female in that position for over 40 years. (The first female principal had been a teaching administrator in a one-room schoolhouse.) I was the first female director of the laboratory school. Although without female role models, I had a comfortable relationship with my male counterparts in the K–12 environment.

When I became Director of FSUS, a graduate student in educational leadership asked me to be her mentor. She was a middle school teacher who aspired to be a school principal. She explained that she was looking for a female role model who was a successful school administrator. She had been directed to me by a male administrator at the university. I accepted this responsibility and met with her for over two years. This relationship caused me to reflect on my own abilities, why I functioned as I did, and the areas in which I lacked confidence. It had a profound effect on my desire to seek out someone to serve as my own mentor.

While I was familiar with the K–12 environment, I was not at ease in the university culture. The traditional attitude of university faculty superiority toward K–12 faculty seemed to be a part of my psyche and training. As director, I functioned as a department head and attended collegewide meetings. Some university faculty and administrators were supportive of me, but I often felt inferior in status, power, and knowledge. I hesitated to share my real thoughts. Most of the university administrators I met with were male. Although I had functioned well in similar situations in K–12 environment, I typically felt invisible. My suggestions would be ignored until they were restated by someone else. I began to doubt my ability to communicate at times.

There was a faculty member at the university who had become a close colleague of mine. She was younger than I, but served as a mentor to me. She was a successful researcher who assisted me with the publishing role. While I appreciated her, I still felt the need to talk and share with someone who worked within higher administration to help me gain insights to operate more successfully. This led me to seek out a female administrator who had had great success as a both a university and a K–12 administrator. I closely observed her in meetings. She was dignified, intelligent, eloquent, and honest. When she spoke, people listened.

Mentoring profile: Fancy

I, Fancy, have been a faculty member and in administration at Florida State University for 28 years. Presently I serve as associate director and professor in educational leadership.

The first decades of my educational career were spent teaching biology, chemistry, and physics in a progressive high school in North Carolina. One of those years was spent on a Fulbright Teacher Exchange in England. My introduction to teaching in higher education was at the University of North Carolina where I designed the first compressed full year biology instructional program for freshmen. My high school biology teacher and college undergraduate adviser served as my first mentors, although I did not realize at the time the vital role they were playing in my professional development. Both were female administrators and teachers.

My doctoral adviser, a male, was chair of his academic department and also became a powerful mentor and role model. As a result of his encouragement, I applied for a position in teacher education at Florida State University. During my first 14 years of administrative assignments at FSU, no one served as a mentor for me, nor did I actively seek anyone. Most of the professionals with whom I interacted were male administrators. When I became Director of Clinical Education, I was one of only two females on the Administrative Council.

My first six years at FSU were spent in off-campus locations, so I had little opportunity to become familiar with the university culture. When I assumed the directorship and moved to the main campus, I found myself at a loss as to how to become integrated. And it was vital that I become so. Being responsible for a staff of faculty, support staff, and over 600 student teachers, I was riddled with moments of anxiety.

While I was eager to become involved with the traditional activities of teaching, research, service, there was something missing in terms of complete acceptance. Perhaps the tension between holding an administrative position, with only a portion of my time allocated to my department, promoted this discomfort. Again, most of my colleagues were male. If you allow yourself, it is easy to feel left out. When I developed a worldwide educational program that attracted thousands of educators and generated over two million dollars of revenue for the university, I finally had an opportunity for interaction in the decision making process.

In 1985, one of my colleagues in another program in my department began to involve me on doctoral and specialist committees. She encouraged her students to enroll in my already bursting classes. This person became my "booster" or mentor. I did not ask her to become my mentor, but somehow this knowledgeable, respected, and creative professor recognized something in me that inspired her to reach out. She gently guided conversations about the university culture, which often involved probing the "whys" of the politics that govern it.

Mentoring profiles: our interviewees

Rhonda is an African American who is an assistant superintendent in a rural southern school system. She has been an educator for 26 years. She is the only female and person of color in her upper level district administration. She also has been a classroom teacher and public school principal. During her career, several individuals have helped and supported her, but there was only one person whom she considers a mentor. This person, an African American female, was a principal and administrator in K–12 education. She was also a family friend and highly respected member of her community. Rhonda describes her as a "person of integrity who cared about others and who served as a role model for her community."

Rita is a white female who is serving in her second year as principal of a K–5 elementary school in a southern rural school. She has been in education for 21 years, having come from private industry. She previously served as a teacher in the same county in which she is a principal. The only person she considers to be a mentor is her former principal, a male who is currently one of her administrative colleagues.

Carolyn, a white female, is currently an assistant professor in the area of K–12 leadership in a research university. She has been a middle school teacher, the director of an innovative project, and a middle school principal, all in northern urban settings. Although she was not involved in any formal mentoring program, one of her principals served as her mentor, a male whom she describes as "exceptionally innovative, people-worker, not paper-pusher."

Grace is a white, retired educator who worked in the State Department of Education. She had had numerous mentors during her career, among whom were a female professor while she was a master's student, and a male in political office. The mentor that had the greatest impact on her though, was a female supervisor in the State Department of Education. She described her mentor as someone who was younger than she, as "having a very strong work ethic, a perfectionist, honest, fair, open minded, a stickler to the rules. She knew what she was doing in her job and was respected. She was honest in dealing with people."

Deborah serves as a department chair in a research university. She is a white professional who has been in administration for 11 of her 30 years spent in education. Three individuals have served as her mentors. One was a male administrator in higher education, another was a female teacher educator who was on her dissertation committee, and the other was a female who was a school administrator. The person who had the greatest influence on her was the female professor who she describes as "very caring and professional, easy to talk with, and well known."

Bridget is an African American associate professor in educational leadership at a research university. She has been in education for 26 years, having served as a K–12 teacher and university professor. She has had one significant mentoring relationship, with a female university administrator. Bridget views her mentor as an "open person, a creative risk-taker who is willing to try new things and learn just about anything she wants to."

The voyagers gathered

We, the eight voyagers, are women of color and white women, who collectively have been in education for many decades. Some of us have been in K–12 settings, others in higher education, and still others in both. Two of our primary mentors were males, six were females, one, African American. We have not had many mentors during our careers, but those who entered our lives have been professionally successful, well respected, competent in their field, people-oriented, and generally willing to share their knowledge – and themselves.

The groundwork phase

The *groundwork phase of mentoring* refers to those initial activities that occur in the mentoring relationship. It includes how the mentor–mentee relationship is established, goals to be pursued, and, in some cases, how strengths and weaknesses will be assessed. The conceptual question for this phase was, "How and why did the mentoring relationship begin?" One of the key elements of a successful groundwork phase is the setting of the goals for the mentorship.

Fran begins the process

I called my potential mentor and asked if she would have lunch with me. When we met, I told her of my admiration for her qualities, abilities, and accomplishments, and asked if she would consider serving as my mentor for a year. She immediately accepted. We agreed to meet, and when we did, I felt hesitant to share my feelings, so I asked her to share her career story. I asked questions about how she had overcome barriers in the academic environments in which she had thrived. She was so open that I felt encouraged to speak up. I shared how I wanted to make my voice heard in higher education administrative meetings, and to gain an understanding of the university culture and its politics. I wanted to become more decisive and to speak with confidence without being viewed as overly aggressive. Although we did not set formal goals, my wish to grow in these areas established a framework for our talks. I viewed her as a role model because her experiences and strengths were matched with my own professional goals.

Fancy's mentor reaches out

When I began my career in higher education, my mentor, a colleague, sought me out and offered to guide me. Although no formal assessment of my strengths and weaknesses occurred, I knew the areas that I needed help with, and my mentor knew them too. We did not set any formal goals, but our conversations focused on those areas in which I wished to grow. We discussed my involvement in committee and university activities that, over time, helped me to deal more effectively with the political structures within the university. I also sought her advice for designing two courses for adult learners. Since my mentor was strong in creativity, scholarship, human relations skills, and knowledge of the organization, her capacities were ideal for assisting me with the development of the knowledge and skills I was seeking.

Other beginnings

Rhonda's mentor was a family friend and their mentoring relationship was a natural outgrowth. They did not develop detailed goals for Rhonda's professional growth, but her mentor continually reinforced that it was important for her to do well academically in college and to become a school administrator. She was also encouraged to serve as a role model for others. Rhonda chose to accept these challenges and the mentoring relationship was crystallized.

Initially, Rita's mentorship was formal since her mentor was her supervising principal during her internship. He helped her set goals related to internship requirements and assisted her in meeting these goals. Of him she says:

> He sat down with me and helped develop my plans so I could complete my internship requirements, and he went beyond this. He also talked to me about career goals and encouraged me to seek a principalship.

Carolyn's mentor was also her first principal. He established formal goals with her on an annual basis. This was part of a standard he had set as part of his job as principal. She said, "He set personal and professional goals for every teacher in the building. At the beginning of the year, he would ask me what I would like to accomplish that year in terms of my own growth, and how he could help me be successful." Their mentoring relationship grew out of his role as her supervisor, but it was not something formally established within the organization.

After moving into educational administration, Grace sought out a mentor, a female who was her immediate supervisor. She viewed her as someone she wanted to model: "I realized that she knew what she was doing. I quickly felt that if I followed in her footsteps, I would be a very good facilities person and that is what I wanted to be, the best." As her supervisor, her mentor evaluated Grace and they worked together to develop specific goals and criteria for achieving them. They met on a regular basis to review progress and they both initiated these meetings.

In Deborah's case, her mentor was her former college professor. As a graduate student, she was seeking someone to assist with her dissertation: "I wasn't seeking

a mentor, but a committee member who had a community college background."
They focused on establishing goals related to the dissertation and later concentrated
on Deborah's future professional plans.

As a graduate student, Bridget was interested in establishing a research project
and her mentor, a faculty member, wanted someone to work with her on a project.
As Bridget says,

> It was a matter of timing. She had a good task going. She told me she had
> something I ought to get involved with. It sounded like a good thing to do, so I did.
> We sought each other out. It's interesting how folks come together.

Bridget said that they "had lots of talks about strengths and weaknesses" and found
that they "complemented one another." This healthy balance helped them as they
worked on the project. Initially, they developed goals for the project, rather than for
Bridget's own personal development, but later they addressed Bridget's needs.

A mentoring summary

None of our mentoring experiences were part of a formal program of mentoring
designed or developed by an organization. In most cases, we entered into our
various mentoring arrangements with a vague idea of what we wanted, and we did
not establish formal goals or a long-range plan for career development. Some of us
sought out a mentor or had someone extend a helping hand, while others stumbled
upon someone admired and trusted. Figure 7.1 captures our different but overlapping beginnings among our mentoring histories and pathways.

The warm-up phase

The *warm-up phase of mentoring* deals with the ways in which mentorship evolves
into a workable relationship rather than remaining a contractual or consensual
arrangement. The conceptual question for this phase is, "What were some events
that demonstrated that you were entering into a workable relationship?" A key
element of the warm-up phase of mentoring is the interdependence that evolved in
the mentoring relationship.

Fran's story

I was aware of the many responsibilities of my mentor and so I told her that I
would be mindful of her time. However, she seemed not to be concerned, and, as
time went on, I was less so. At first I was also cautious about delving too deeply
into things that might be considered personal. However, she was open and frank,
sharing details and experiences in a trusting way, and so I became open and trusting
as well. I willingly shared things about people and situations without fear of being

betrayed, judged, or abandoned. Our core values were similar, which may have accounted for the understanding we shared. After only six months, I found myself calling her on the phone, meeting for lunch, and easily sharing my thoughts and feelings.

Fancy's story

At first, I was mindful and even careful of my mentor's busy schedule, so I didn't request time with her unless it was extremely urgent. However, within a year our relationship as professionals grew as our personal relationship unfolded. We discovered that we share many of the same values, leading to an awareness of our joint commitment that became unshakable. Thus, it was easy for us to create a relationship that was trusting, open, and honest in its sharing.

Our sisters' stories

Rhonda's relationship is unique, as it was a long-term personal friendship that had developed professionally. Her relationship began when she was a child and it evolved over time. Despite this evolution, she cannot identify a specific "warm-up" period as they shared together and worked toward Rhonda's goals.

Rita believes there was a specific point at which her relationship with her principal changed from principal–supervisor to mentor–mentee. This occurred when she was appointed principal, moving from being a teacher he was supervising to a colleague he was supporting. They quickly began sharing more intentionally and openly at his initiative. She says, "I knew I could tell him things and no one else would ever know about them." They viewed their value systems as similar, which she says helped to make the relationship comfortable and enduring.

Carolyn is not sure how long it took before she and her mentor entered into a relationship. They worked together for two years and, as with the other partnerships, found their values and ideas to be similar. She offered: "He was a risk-taker like me. We started out as boss–subordinate. Then trust developed. We had joked about happenings in the building and a real bonding took place." She does not know what brought this about, but thought it was partially "his energy, caring, and willingness to spend time to help me develop professionally."

Grace also began her mentoring relationship as a subordinate. Initially she and her mentor talked only about specific job tasks she was given or had assumed. But with time, her mentor gave her more responsibilities and she realized that she was trusted. Perhaps, because of this trust, her mentor maintained an "open door policy" with her. Their values were similar, a strong work ethic and concern about quality. Their relationship changed after about four months when her supervisor began "supervising me less" and being more collegial. Trust, for the mentee, meant that she could share without feeling "put-down." However, this mentoring association remained primarily focused on job tasks without much attention on the personal.

Deborah's mentoring experience was professional and personal as revealed in her statement: "We did find time to play as well as to work." Their value systems were similar. She doesn't recollect when they came to a trusting relationship. She says, "I could discuss all types of questions and concerns with her. I really never paid any attention to boundaries between us. I just knew that as friendship and trust developed that our relationship became more meaningful."

Bridget reports that it did not take long for her mentoring relationship to develop. Both she and her mentor were keenly concerned with the success of the program they were working on. They had similar values, but different ambitions. When the mentor became a college president, she encouraged the mentee to do the same, but, as Bridget says, "that was not something I wanted to do."

Growing relationships

For all of us, the associations we began with our mentors became closer, more trusting, and less formal as we engaged in sharing problems, tasks, and ourselves. Except for Grace, our discussions often included both personal and professional issues. With the exception of Bridget, the mentor served as a role model for professional behavior and goal setting. The willingness and ability to openly share and mutual respect dramatically enhanced the interdependence of synergy in these relationships, helping to transform them into viable comentoring relationships.

The working phase

The *working phase of mentoring* denotes that a relationship has been formed. It focuses attention on how the mentor and mentee function together. The framing question for this phase was, "How did the mentorship operate?" Key elements of the working phase of mentoring, the functioning, are empowerment and participation.

Fran's perspective

I met with my mentor, the senior administrator, about every six weeks. I would also call her when I had a question or needed advice. When we met, I would ask questions like, "How did you deal with being the only female in an administrative environment?" I would ask her to share her personal experiences from which we would cull basic concepts and principles. I also shared what I planned to do in a particular situation to elicit her reaction. Although we did not formally observe one another at work, we would often be at the same meetings. Afterwards, I would ask her why she said or did something in particular, or I would ask for feedback on my actions.

It was meaningful for me to have someone I could turn to whose judgment and integrity I trusted completely. If I could have changed anything about this relationship, I would have formalized it more, asking for more specific feedback on what she saw as my strengths and weaknesses. I also would have discussed more actively our mentoring relationship. I tried to let my mentor know how much I appreciated her, but I wish I had done more of that.

Fancy's view

We did not set a formal time for meetings. As questions presented themselves, I would call or visit my mentor. I would seek her input whenever a sensitive issue or decision presented itself. She was able to give the broad view of situations, often drawing from her own experiences. We frequently observed each other teaching, and at one point she invited me to team-teach and administer a graduate class in a specialized, creative format. That experience provided me with skills that, even today, I use. Although we never formally discussed this relationship, we knew its growth patterns and objectives. It was one of those unwritten scripts in life that guides without drawing a lot of attention to itself. There was a feeling of acceptance and security that prevailed. It is an exhilerating feeling to know that a professional colleague had chosen to help me to grow as an educator and administrator, and was willing to *completely* accept me. I am deeply grateful to my mentor for her continued support. Even though my mentor shared suggestions for growth and was generous, it would have been helpful to have had more structured goal-related planning.

Our companions' perspectives

Rhonda's mentor was a part of her life. They shared at church, social and professional events, and at school. Whenever she had a concern or question, Rhonda would call or visit. Her mentor would advise her in a candid way, but often reminded her to "be professional, stand up when needed and remember to be a role model for others." She would not choose to alter this mentoring relationship in any way and claims that she owes much of her success to her mentor.

When Rita's mentorship began, she and her mentor would meet as needed to discuss what she was doing in her internship. He would share his experiences and answer her questions openly. Now that she is a principal, she often calls him for advice. He gives her his views on the structural and the political side of issues. He also helps her by asking procedural questions and reacting to her ideas. They talk about educational ideas as well as administrative and management tasks. She believes that this relationship has helped build her confidence in her leadership role. She would not change anything about this relationship which she views as part of a continual process of learning and growing.

In Carolyn's case, she and her mentor met on a biweekly basis. She tells this story:

> He used to give me feedback all the time, wonderful candid input. He would say, "Have you ever thought about?" or "Have you read about this?" or "Maybe you might want to talk to so and so."

We would sit together.

Carolyn claims that she wouldn't change anything (if she could) about this mentoring relationship. If there was anything she could have formalized, it would be the recognition her mentor deserved. He always encouraged her to become an administrator.

Grace and her mentor had offices near one another, which enabled them to call upon one another as needed. They also observed each other in the workplace; her mentor would provide feedback regularly and express appreciation for Grace's work. They never formally discussed their mentorship. She wonders about whether she revealed too much about herself because she is a very open person. This is one reason why she believes it was helpful to have had a mentor with whom she could relax. Grace developed a sense of security through this relationship, which translated into enhanced job performance. She would not change anything about it.

Deborah and her mentor met whenever either of them felt the need. They connected at the workplace and or at their homes by way of phone. They never discussed the mentorship itself. Powerful, for Deborah, were, "the good times of being with my friend and professional colleague, and the help and support that she provided. Her positiveness. I knew I could always call her." She says there is nothing she would change.

Bridget and her mentor worked together on a project, and met weekly to discuss it. They also spoke on the phone almost daily. The point at which the work and the relationship merged is something she finds difficult to determine. She says about her mentor, "She was very encouraging. For example, knowing that I do not seek out opportunities to speak, and still don't, she made sure that one of the things that I did was to serve as chair for a session at a conference." She added, "She pushed me out of my comfort zone." She found the relationship very satisfying.

Empowering our relationships

All of our mentoring relationships were informal even when they occurred within a formal setting. They grew out of needs we perceived and from the willingness of someone to help meet those needs. We met to accomplish tasks and develop our abilities. Some of us thought that a formal assessment of our relationship might have been helpful. Others believed that our relationships were satisfying as they were. Our ability to work with our mentors and to sustain the relationship was fostered by feelings of trust and security that extended beyond issues of competence and acceptance to empowerment.

The long-term status phase

The last phase, *long-term status*, considers the long-term effects of the mentoring relationship and its evolution. The question for this phase was, "What did the relationship evolve into?"

Fran's experience

My mentor retired and moved away, and I moved to another academic institution. As soon as I arrived, I found another mentor. However, I have kept in contact with my original mentor and I still view her as a significant role model. I don't have the same needs I had when we began our mentorship, but she is still a trusted colleague. Although we do not communicate as often as we did in the past, I call her when I need input. Now, we share a deeper comentoring friendship that includes talk about personal family issues. I have become more confident through this relationship and knowledgeable of how to operate effectively in higher education.

Having been an enriched and appreciative mentee, I now make a point of serving as a mentor to others. I feel that it is my responsibility, and even a special calling, to do this. I know how it feels to not have that special someone who takes a personal interest in you and your career. I also know how it feels when someone does. I want to make the journey along the road easier for those just embarking.

Fancy's view

My mentor retired from her administrative and teaching position several years ago. We still live in the same town. I call her about three times a week to connect and update. We have a deep friendship and I cherish her input on those questions and situations that I initiate. She is my guiding light. I recently asked her to travel over 100 miles to speak to a graduate class I was teaching. She willingly did so and the class responded with: "She's awesome!" She uses all modes of communication to share information. I am thankful for the time and interest that this special person has taken in my life. She helped me to be more effective in how I used and presented materials, whether for teaching a class or speech-giving. My mentor also encouraged me to understand facets of the administrative role in higher education; how to interpret political signals within the culture; and how to grasp more fully the political structure of the university. I still grow in these areas.

I can now see how the "political tables" are turning as I mentor those who seek answers to similar questions that I once asked.

Relationships of the others

Rhonda's relationship with her mentor continues to be an important part of her life. Her mentor has retired, but she continues to be someone Rhonda turns to, particularly in times of trouble. She values her wisdom, experience, and achievements. Rhonda says, "I try to mentor others in the same way and thus pass on what she has given to me. She is my hero."

Rita's mentorship is still "in the making," so she does not know how it will develop. Recently, she was able to help her mentor deal with some finance issues, and hopes to be able to provide him with more assistance in the future. She sees them becoming more like equal colleagues than mentor–mentee as she grows in experience and knowledge. She is still struggling with becoming an administrator, although it is "easier now." Rita is an informal mentor to another new principal who is having difficulties and hopes to be able to serve as a mentor to others because she views it as vital "to have someone you can trust to talk with and learn from."

Carolyn has lost physical contact with her mentor, but remarks that he is with her in spirit. She says, "He touched my heart in many ways and on many different levels. I would never have become an administrator without him. I had no interest, but he believed in me." She has been a formal and informal mentor to others, and says she feels it is "part of my job and responsibility." One of her mentees is now a principal. She is "doing beautifully." She thinks the most important aspect of being a mentee is the ability to use feedback constructively.

When asked about the present status of her mentoring relationship, Grace responded:

> Friends, but I guess the real answer is there is no relationship. Since my retirement there is really no need to continue in a mentorship relationship. I will always respect her. I look back on that particular mentoring experience in mixed ways. The positive aspect had to do with her skills in teaching me to understand departmental formats for writing reports. The negative aspect is that she never shared the inner workings of the political side of the organization.

Grace has mentored several females to whom she gives career advice. She says a mentee needs to be able "to be humble and eat humble pie."

For Deborah, her relationship evolved from a professional one into friendship. She shared that it is an "everlasting friendship that I cherish. And, of course, I completed my doctoral program." She says the experience taught her about the culture and politics of the organization, both of which helped her tremendously. She has not formally mentored anyone, but when she sees those with potential she tries to broaden or strengthen their abilities.

Bridget says that her relationship is "at a different level now because we are not working together and she cannot give me specific feedback." However, they are in touch and her mentor asks questions like, "What's going on with your life? Are you accomplishing what you want to accomplish?" She offered that "I did not have a sister. I talk with her like I would a sister. She provided me with opportunities and challenges to do things that I would not ordinarily have done." Bridget believes that "Mentoring is a give and take relationship. You have to be ready to learn some new lessons and ways of doing things that you are not comfortable with." Having such a relationship has become important in her life. She has been involved in a woman's mentoring network to assist others in higher education.

Lasting effects

The relationships we established at a professional level became long-lasting friendships both professionally and personally. For the most part, these former mentoring alliances developed into highly synergistic comentoring relationships. For all of us, these relationships provided vision, goals, support, guidance, mutual dependence, empowerment, and knowledge. They enhanced our competence, confidence, and ability to understand the cultures within which we were operating. We learned to be open to feedback, more conscious of our working environment, and appreciative of mentoring experiences. We value our own mentoring experiences and passing the legacy onto others, especially young professional women.

Reflections and musings

A final question the participants responded to is: "Is there anything else you might like to add about this experience or relationship or about mentoring in general?" The responses and themes drawn from them provide an avenue for reflection and further dialogue.

Fran speaks first

I believe that organizations should have formalized programs for mentoring in order to help people survive and thrive. It would have saved me grief if I could have entered into such structured arrangements early in my career. Women do not have the strong networking systems of their male counterparts, and may consequently leave too much to luck, talent, and positive thinking, particularly at the beginning of their careers. Women (and men) in positions of authority have a responsibility to reach out to women and mentor them.

Next, fancy speaks

This opportunity to reflect on my mentoring experience has reinforced for me the importance of mentoring at all levels. I shudder to think of the potential disasters that were averted because I had a mentor with the intelligence to suggest another path. It seems that all women entering higher education would do well to seek a mentor as they begin their careers. The business world is full of stories of males mentoring males as they move up the career ladders, but where are the success stories about females and how they develop?

Other travelers' insights

Rhonda is deeply appreciative of her mentor and hopes that she can be as effective a role model for others. She says her mentor made a lasting impression on her; she even summons forth advice she had received when faced with new challenges. She believes that it is because of her mentor that she has reached the senior administrative level she now holds.

Rita believes all administrators should have a mentor, "particularly when you are starting out, you need someone you can turn to." She believes all principals should ensure that they mentor their teachers to help them become all they can be.

Carolyn says, "It's hard to put into words the value of these mentoring relationships. I was touched on a personal and professional level and it was a gift these people gave to me. Because of that, I feel I have a gift to give to others also. It is difficult for me to see other people who aren't willing to do that for other people."

Grace agrees with the value of having a mentor: "We are fortunate to find a mentor in our lives. There are a lot of mentors out there but most folks don't take advantage. I think most people don't ask people who are 'over them' for advice because they think this reflects a lack of knowledge or self-confidence."

Deborah focused on what she learned about herself, "One of the most important things that I learned as a result of being a part of this mentoring project and relationship is that I need to talk through major issues before making a decision to clarify my thoughts." The mentors in her life are people whom she has talked with about major decision points in her career.

When reflecting upon mentoring, Bridget confides: "This relationship has been essential for me and I think everybody should have a genuine mentoring experience. A lot of places have mentoring programs, but they can be artificial. What can come out of that?"

Reflecting on our reflections

The experience of being mentored has had a positive impact upon our careers and development. Although all of us gained job competencies through our mentor–mentee relationships, it was in the political–cultural realm where we appear to have benefited the most. Understanding traditions and structures of organizations and their political workings can translate into powerful tools for achieving success. This knowledge is usually acquired through trial and error. Our mentoring relationships served mostly as enduring shortcuts.

None of us had experienced mentoring as a formalized operation within our organizations. The mentoring that occurred resulted from the efforts of individuals who reached out to aid us, or who accepted the invitation to do so. It appears there are many individuals who are willing to mentor others, if asked. There are also successful professionals who willingly seek others to mentor. However, mentoring with a goal of supporting newcomers or potential leaders is not something that appears to be an everyday part of the organizational culture. This helps to explain why many people do not ask to be mentored. As demonstrated in *Breaking the Circle of One* (Mullen et al., 1997), even experienced mentors often do not outgrow the need to be mentored in some capacity. Likewise, novices should seek out mentors.

We invite our readers to join us in initiating dialogue and action to ensure that mentoring becomes an integral part of education. We salute our mentors and thank them for their trust and empowerment. Our closing thought about mentoring is simply to "pass it on."

Author's Note

Authorship of this chapter should be considered equal; name order is alphabetical only.

8   Becoming Seamless: Dynamic Shifts in a Mentoring Commitment

Lori L. Franklin

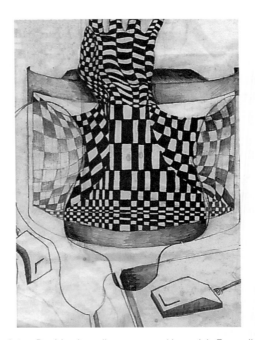

Figure 8.1:   Dual keyboarding partners (Jeremiah Foxwell, 1998)

How many times in life do we form an instant bond with someone we meet? Because it happens so infrequently, I have learned to recognize that unique moment when two people "click" and make a connection. This can happen in any number of ways. Something in common is discovered within moments of a first meeting. A quirky sense of humor can be shared by both. Some spark ignites and, before you know it, a relationship is forming. Such events are special ones. In my life, they have been rare, meaningful, and life-changing.

Beginnings of synergy

The initiation of a relationship can be symbolically likened to the beginning of a "marriage" – even if that connection takes place in a work environment. In my case, my "courtship" with Donna Shrum started even before my first day of work at the Florida State University School (FSUS) library media center.

When I first met Donna, I was a graduate student doing work in her library; she was in her ninth year as the high school librarian. One day I approached Donna to let her know I had completed my job. It turned out we both had three children, with approximately the same number of years between their ages. We also learned that we had both worked on graduate degrees in library science while raising young children. And, we had both delayed entering the workforce until our youngest children were in their last year of preschool.

Donna later remarked that during our conversation she felt that we shared personal values and life priorities. Indeed, the beginnings of synergy were taking shape at our first discussion, although I was not thinking about our potential to learn from one another at the time.

Partnership support group

Two years after that first meeting with Donna, I was able to reflect upon our connection. The catalyst that made me realize the special mentoring situation I shared was the formation of the Partnership Support Group. Teachers, administrators, professors – all fellow colleagues from Florida State University and Florida State University School – came together biweekly to discuss our personal mentoring experiences and those observed or investigated in classroom and research settings. We all met in a private room in the school library.

At the time that we congregated, I had had some familiarity with the term "mentor." I knew that people often turned to wise adults and leaders in many different cultures and situations in life. My own mother had been my first and most powerful mentor. Throughout my childhood, and even today, she has provided me with a role model for honesty, support, and love. I often think of her when I have important decisions to make and catch myself asking, "What would mom do in this situation?" Her examples of using humor to diffuse tense situations provided me with some powerful ammunition when I became an adult, and later a wife, parent, and professional.

I also had a mentor during my first job after finishing my undergraduate degree. Robert was the editor of the weekly newspaper where I worked as a reporter. His style of mentoring was, in contrast to my mother's, one of intimidation and sexual innuendo. An older, foul-mouthed man, he made me uncomfortable. In spite of this, I stayed at my job, gaining experience while trying not to let Robert's comments affect me. He resigned from the paper about six months after I began working there. Strangely, Robert reached out to me with sensitivity after he left, even revealing vulnerability. He became supportive of me through letters and phone calls. Robert even championed my growing success in the newspaper business. I was able to feel sadness when he died suddenly of a massive heart attack two years after his resignation.

My relationship with Robert was hardly an ideal mentoring experience. I experienced other mentoring influences during subsequent years, but it wasn't until

I began working with Donna that I realized something new – what it was like to cocreate a mentoring relationship rooted in collegial friendship. Joining the Partnership Support Group allowed me to take the time I needed to reflect on, and explore, the special qualities of our mentoring union.

The support group provided an environment where storytelling was endorsed and enacted, and so it became our major vehicle of connecting. Elementary principal Eileen McDaniel told us of the invisible barriers surrounding relationships with teachers – should she encourage close mentor ties, or instead hold back and let the teacher decide whether to initiate or sustain the connection with a school administrator? One teacher spent time in our meetings describing the close comentoring attachment she shares with her sisters. The French teacher, David Greenberg, shared many of his difficulties and successes with his student volunteer. Like myself, he regularly updated the group as his own mentoring plot thickened.

These discussions, as well as others shared by group members, helped me to see just how unique and important (even magical) is my relationship with Donna. When I would describe everyday events where we had, yet again, "clicked" the others would suddenly become very quiet, listening carefully. They looked spellbound. At each meeting, they would urge me to share more details about the comentoring partnership I share with Donna. I have to admit, I enjoyed the attention that my own "storytelling" received and I even enjoyed telling my own story! I liked disclosing aspects of the many ways in which Donna and I have worked so well together. I became part of this story after having been hired as the elementary media specialist at the school. Or had I become part of this story even before then? – at the very moment that Donna and I met at the interview.

Under her mentoring wing

After I was hired as the school's media specialist in 1996, I thought I'd have to wait until the beginning of the school semester to learn about my new working environment. However, Donna called me three times during the summer, offering me insight into the workings of the library and familiarizing me with my new colleagues. At her suggestion, I came in one July afternoon and began learning how the library's computer network was set up. While I didn't feel ready to "take off" at that early point in terms of expertise, I did become comfortable with the technology and password procedures.

Unfortunately for Donna, she severely burnt her foot in an accident that prevented her from coming to work that first day in August 1996. Indeed, her injury was very serious. She spent several months on crutches, going through physical therapy and coping with pain. In spite of her accident, she had immediately called an elementary teacher, asking her to take me "under her wing" during the first week of teacher meetings and preparations for returning students. I really appreciated Donna's thoughtfulness. I could have had a lonesome experience at the welcome-back teacher's breakfast. Instead, I had Adele Smith by my side, an experienced teacher who introduced me to everyone and who also shared information about the school.

A mini-mentoring relationship

What is fascinating to me is that as the school year unfolded, Adele and I formed our own "mini" mentoring relationship, even as Donna and I were working on extending the parameters of ours. Adele was a former media specialist and my peer teacher. She had stimulating ideas about how we could use library materials to support her students' research efforts. During the past two years we have jointly developed several lesson plans. Once, I introduced her students to a new computer resource called *Electric Library*. In order to demonstrate it, I used a scan converter to show the computer monitor enlarged on a television screen.

As most educators and parents know, children will really get involved with something they see on television. In order to get the fifth graders excited about this new program, Adele and I agreed that I would locate photos of, and information about, giant squid. The students loved learning that although giant squid have never been captured, their tentacles, measuring more than 26 feet, have washed up on beaches. Their mouths dropped open when I explained that the eyes of a giant squid (as evident in the computer-generated picture I showed them) are as "large as dinner plates." Adele and I followed through by having the kids research other "unsolved mysteries" such as the Loch Ness Monster and Bigfoot. While teaching this lesson, I was observed by the elementary principal for my year-end evaluation. I received positive comments when we talked about how the lesson had progressed and its obvious impact on the students.

Adele and I often collaborated on research ideas. Most were successful; some required modification upon realizing that changes needed to be made. In the spring of 1998 we asked her students to find information about various careers. What we didn't realize was that the students would have difficulty reading "between the lines" to grasp certain concepts about job performance, working environment, and skills development. The students wanted to be able to instantly find the information we requested. We, on the other hand, wanted them to search for subtleties embedded within several paragraphs. This was a lesson that probably needed more explanation about, and demonstration of, our expectations for such discovery learning.

It is no coincidence that Adele acted as a mentor for me. Not only had she been a school librarian in the past, but she had an ideal audience for using the library tools that we had at our disposal. And, she had been recommended to me by Donna, whose advice I quickly learned to value and appreciate.

From courtship to engagement

After my very first day of school in 1996, Donna called me to see how things had gone. She wasn't worried about how well the library was functioning. She was genuinely interested in how I was experiencing my new position, the people around me, and my immediate surroundings. During the first few weeks, Donna spent *hours* mentoring me. Besides training me in the various library procedures and rules, she also helped me understand how the school itself operated. There were many forms to fill out, meetings to attend, and decisions to be made about retirement plans, health insurance, and automatic payroll deposit. She proved to be a tremendous resource in providing me with an orientation in learning to cope with multiple tasks. When I began this job, I really had no idea about how much help I could expect. I anticipated getting along well with Donna, but I didn't know what to expect in the way of "extra care."

As it turned out, I came to learn about the difference "extra care" makes in one's professional development and joint work. Donna was always supportive and quick to brainstorm solutions to the many questions I asked. I remember thinking, "What would another newcomer do in a position like mine if there was no one like Donna to act as guide?" I quickly realized that I was lucky to have a partner who was looking out for my best interests, in accordance with the rituals and expectations of the school culture. I remember as a young mother feeling overwhelmed with my new parenting duties. It was when I joined a support group for mothers that parenthood really started coming together for me. I needed that advice and support – in many ways, the mothering–mentor group validated my very existence. I experienced similar feelings as I worked with Donna, whose knowledge of the library and school environment provided me with a foundation in understanding how to constructively work with others.

During this first year, there were many times when I was asked questions by students or teachers to whom I needed to provide definitive answers. I quickly learned to approach Donna for help. She was never abrupt or dismissive of me, but always shifted from what she was doing to assist me in finding the best solution to the question posed. Donna was always able to switch gears, discuss an issue, question, or problem and then go right back to whatever she was doing. She provided me with many mentoring examples through her capable actions.

While Donna was a valuable resource, our library technical assistant was very unapproachable and would actually snap at me in front of library patrons. The contrast was striking. I realized that Donna, besides providing job guidance, was also providing something more essential – human communication that was simultaneously knowledgeable and caring.

Much to my surprise, the technical assistant provided an impetus for the synergy that flowed between Donna and myself. When two people are "thrown into the trenches," so to speak, they learn to help each other and to survive, making the best of the situation. I have entertained the thought that if I were stranded on an island with Donna we could manage to devise some type of shelter; develop a communications method for attracting rescue attention; and enjoy a gourmet meal from the sea! This says something to me about the highly synergistic relationship that we were evolving.

I never expected the incredible depth of understanding that Donna extended to me in terms of my "other life" as a working mother. When I had to arrive late because my four-year-old son had an ear infection, she was relaxed. "We've all been there. Don't worry about it," she'd say. Donna and Kathy Broome, the school's publishing center worker, became an invaluable source of parenting information and advice for me. Because their children were older than mine, they had already faced many of the parenting issues that I was encountering. Given that our core parenting values were similar, I was open to, even eager for, their suggestions. I often felt lucky that I had hooked into this wonderful synergistic network of mothers who mentor and work.

As my first year continued to unfold, this relationship with my primary mentor deepened. For many reasons we quickly entered into what I call the "engagement" phase. Our relationship was strong during the "courtship." There were no arguments or misunderstanding which can frequently derail a deepening relationship. A benefit of this trust and acceptance was that as the mentor–mentee bond strengthened it also became a flexible two-way communication system, allowing comentoring to flourish. We were becoming seamless, embodied in two as one.

Knowledge center construction

About five years previous to my arrival at FSUS there had been a Southern Accreditation of Colleges and School (SACS) visit which resulted in identifying areas for school improvement. One recommendation was that a new library media facility be constructed. The existing library at the time was small, cramped, and unable to accommodate more than a single class at a time.

The responsibility for forming a committee for new library construction fell into Donna's lap. She told me the story of how she was suddenly required to learn about new areas of education which she'd never concerned herself with in the past. There were policies to be considered, bids to be examined, proper protocols to be followed. Through the years that followed, and with assistance, Donna's plan for the "Knowledge Center" evolved, taking shape. When I arrived on the scene, the physical groundbreaking for the new building had already occurred. I joined the construction committee and helped choose furnishings, brick colors, lighting fixtures, technology equipment – even the color of the wastebaskets.

My entire first year involved a great deal of time managing construction issues. For example, at one point Donna was informed that choices needed to be made about where and how many voice (telephone) and data (computer) boxes would be installed. This alone involved drawing a color-coded map; visiting the skeletal structure of the building; making phone calls to ascertain those services available through the university; meeting with university telecommunications representatives; and finally sharing our decisions with concerned parties. And that was just one "little seed" in the whole "tomato"!

Development of comentoring

Every day brought with it concerns about the new building. Donna frequently asked for my opinion and also asked me to confirm her note-taking during the decision process. During this phase of our "marriage," a great deal of comentoring was forming. Various seasoned school employees would laugh about my having to live in the old library for just *one* year (the building had been built in the 1950s) before enjoying a brand new facility. But during that year I was immersed in both the old library and the new one being constructed. I knew that Donna was relieved to have someone to share ideas with, much the same way an experienced parent yearns for the fresh perspective and input of a more recent parent.

I think that when a mentor takes that step into the background something new develops, changing the formality and quality of the mentor–mentee relationship. Collaboration or comentoring becomes possible at that point, if both parties are willing. This calls for some initiative on the part of the mentee, who may still be overwhelmed with job duties and "learning the ropes." The mentor, in turn, must be open to new suggestions, while seeking new input from a less experienced coworker. While comentoring is occurring there continues a level of original mentoring that is infused throughout the metamorphosing relationship.

All of this defined, for me, my evolving layers with Donna. When I began working with her, she was ready for some dynamic, coworker input. She had been shouldering the load in the library for several years. She was searching for someone to share the concerns of running the library. Although I don't think she fully realized it at the time, Donna was, in my view, intellectually and emotionally ready for, and open to, "fresh blood" and invigorating ideas.

This phase of our working partnership can be imagined as a synergistic marriage. When a couple is enjoying their early years of marriage they are often flexible and open to change. With more togetherness, people tend to get set in their patterns of response. When I began work with Donna, we were both ready for change.

Several factors in particular played into the development of the "marriage," and the creation of synergy and even seamlessness. We had agreed that our common goal for the year was to be able to perform the other person's job duties nearly as well as our own. If a teacher approached me about buying textbooks, for example. I needed to be able to discuss ordering procedures. If an elementary student asked Donna a question about the latest book contest I was running, then she needed to be up-to-date on my activity.

So, between Donna's foot injury, the new construction, the technical assistant's attitude, and our mutual readiness, several factors merged to solidify our comentoring relationship. It was in our "marriage" that the most powerful synergy was created by us.

From engagement to marriage

I suppose that a successful marriage can simply "be." But for a relationship to become dynamic, change must occur, not in the status of it so much as in the expression of it. Donna realized the importance of a mentor knowing when to step back to allow the mentee to step forward, even though mistakes will be made. Mentors often have a protective instinct, but they should spend time facilitating degrees of freedom in addition to structured forms of assistance and guidance.

When I began preparing for the Sunshine State Young Readers Award program in 1997, I had some ideas about how to present this contest/event to elementary readers. The program promotes the reading of literature during the school year. Books in the program have been nominated by fellow Florida librarians and media specialists. At the end of the contest, students vote for their favorite author who is later recognized at an awards ceremony.

Donna had been the one who, for many years, introduced this reading program. She actually had several bulletin board plans and cut-outs ready for me. But I wanted to try out my own idea of using sunshine rays to recognize readers, instead of the individual construction paper seagulls which had been used before. She suggested several other ideas, but when I seemed less than receptive she stood back and said, "I guess you are ready to do your own thing. That's fine. You can use your own ideas, but I hope you'll come to me if you need help." I did use my own ideas and they proved highly viable. They were also warmly received by Donna. When the contest began the following year, I again used a different approach. Donna again stood back and let me "take off", all the while giving me encouragement.

Dual keyboards as image of synergy

A particularly noteworthy example of Donna stepping back to allow comentoring to emerge evolved around the creation of our first library newsletter. A lot was happening that year and we wanted to spread the news to the faculty, especially to those who didn't visit the library often. We could have performed this task in a variety of ways, but realized that a newsletter would allow us to reach everyone at the school with the most important information – updates on the construction process, names of winners from library contests, addresses for new websites with teaching lessons and strategies, and library policies which needed explanation.

Separately, we both wrote several articles for the newsletter. Donna also played around with getting a graphic to work on CorelDRAW, and I looked for different fonts to use. We agreed to call our newsletter the *Information Builder*.

At this point I could have turned my part of the project over to Donna, letting her put it all together at her desk. After all, she was the more experienced partner and I'd never written a newsletter. However, I did have experience as a newspaper reporter, and with text and graphics layout. I also did not hold back on pitching my readiness, for this project, to Donna.

Donna then made what I would later interpret, with the help of the mentor support group, as a symbolic gesture of acceptance and openness – she sat at my desk and let me do the "driving." Looking back, what we really needed were two computer keyboards attached to one another (see Figure 8.1). However, we managed well, switching the keyboard back and forth on our laps. Thus our synergistic "baby" was born, and we were so excited! Here was an event where we functioned as equals and glowed with genuine pride of each other. I respected Donna's knowledge about which articles would be of most value to the school, and she respected my viable newspaper strategies and intuition.

This probably constituted my favorite mentoring story for the Partnership Support Group. The others loved the idea of the dual keyboards – a symbol of two minds working together as one, the ultimate in synergy and comentoring. And, while I realized what had happened between us with the newsletter was very special, I didn't realize just how well it embodied our comentoring relationship until the other group members, having heard my story, shook their heads, exclaiming, "That's incredible!" And, they remained fascinated whenever I would reveal new insight into my image of partnership as a dual keyboard, or whenever someone else would do this from his or her own perspective (see Chapter 4).

I find it necessary to add here that Donna and I are not always in complete agreement on every issue. Even on the surface, we are, in many ways, different. She is petite, wears tailored outfits, and loves country music. I am tall and large-boned, apt to wear sandals year round, and absolutely despise country music. I feel deprived if I don't have onions on my pizza; she avoids them at all costs. I have to be the driver on car trips; she is content to sit on the passenger side and navigate. Obviously, these differences do not matter in the larger picture of our relationship. And, in an odd and magical way, they even played into the development of our comentoring relationship – Donna as content navigator, myself as committed driver, and vice versa, depending on the situation.

Construction helps promote marriage

As my first year at FSUS wrapped up, it never really ended. It was decided that I would work during the summer of 1997, as the building construction was nearing completing. We faced some challenging stresses when we were prematurely moved out of our old facility to a small room in the front office building. All of our books, machinery, equipment, and desk belongings had to be temporarily stored in a technology lab.

Once we set up camp in the front office, Donna and I focused on wrapping up building details. How many data boxes would be combined with voice boxes for greater efficiency? Why had the contractor installed the wrong color of carpeting in the group projects room? What type of telephone options would we have installed in the different offices in the building? How, exactly, would the library be wired for security?

Donna and I worked through such decisions that summer. Crammed into a small room along with us were boxes and computers, all lying around. I remember complaining one day about how sick I was of being in such cramped quarters. "Now Lori, you're whining. And you just can't whine, you know," remarked Donna, with a grin. Well, I had to laugh. Here she was underscoring the fact that our front office situation really was only temporary. Once again, Donna helped me look at the "big" picture by virtue of not focusing on minor inconveniences. Many times she served as my role model of an energetic person with perspective and good humor.

Our work environment brightened considerably when we moved into the new library. It was beautiful and spacious, with soaring ceilings and tile floors. Of course there was some chaos while all of our belongings were moved, for the second time, to our new home.

I had spent some time earlier looking up information about how to physically transport the contents of a library. I shared with Donna and Kathy one of my findings, that books could be easily moved in shopping carts, and they loved the idea. We all met at the local grocery store early one morning to load up shopping carts in our vehicles. The carts really did help. Our student assistants didn't have to bend over as much to pick up stacks of books, and the carts moved easily along the sidewalks between the technology lab and our new library. Of course, I enjoyed having my "shopping cart" suggestion valued and appreciated. Throughout our mentoring marriage Donna always gave me credit for my ideas, both interpersonally and publicly.

Perhaps a good test of synergy is how well a group functions when members are absent. During the 1997–98 school year, with the opening of the new library, Donna, Kathy and I (after the difficult employee resigned, Kathy had been awarded her position) have been scrupulous about work attendance. Between the three of us, we serve more than 1 000 students, and 90 faculty and staff members, daily. We manage the same workload that four people performed the previous year.

Testing of self and seamlessness

During my second year at FSUS, Donna injured her back and was "out" for nearly an entire week. This was an excellent test for me, to determine how comfortable and knowledgeable I had become with the library, procedures and policies, and various school personalities. I had a heavy teaching schedule that week – second graders were going to learn how to use multimedia software; third graders were going to be shown how to locate materials in the library; and fifth graders were going to be taught how to use encyclopedias to do research – all activities that I had not been prepared for during my preservice teacher preparatory work years before. A tour of the new library also needed to be conducted, and there were high school students as well as college work study students to supervise. I obviously anticipated being overloaded.

That week proved even busier than I expected: I had to load a new software program that all of the elementary classes would be using, both in the library and classroom. Teachers wanted information about textbook orders for the fall. A second grade teacher wanted me to ensure that the Winter Olympics program would be piped into her room via our television distribution system.

I got through the week and the work got done. Although I missed having Donna with me, it felt terrific to have everything I'd learned the past two years "gel." Without Donna, I was like a machine with an important part missing that could function until the part would be replaced. I didn't want to be on my own indefinitely, but still it felt rewarding to be managing well nonetheless.

Every evening I would call Donna so we could together review how life in the library had gone. When I was working, I would have to often surmise how she would have handled a request or issue. It felt good to learn that I was right on target in most cases. For example, upon sorting the mail one day I noticed a request for Donna, from the school director, to write a thank-you letter to an alumna who had donated $50.00 for the acquisition of new library books. As I had been typically assuming the "thank-you letter" writing duties, because I enjoy writing and communicating so much, I suggested to Donna that I write the letter. She agreed, and I e-mailed her the product. She had no suggestions for changes, just thought that the note should appear on letterhead. The director was pleased with the letter as well.

I know that during her absence Donna was relieved that I was capable of handling the various facets of our joint work. Upon returning, she was able to quickly resume her responsibilities.

Because Donna and I had invested the time, caring, and effort into our work relationship, we have a strong "marriage" – one with peaked expressions of synergy. We had become nearly seamless. Our mentoring relationship had changed from one of dependence, on my part, to mutual dependence and independence. I think that the week Donna was absent was when I realized that I can "make it" anywhere. Donna had given me a tremendous amount of helpful information and advice which I have not only internalized but shared, in new forms, with her and others. We had a special circle going between us.

More transition, yet hope for the future

I expect the shape of our comentoring circle will be altered in 1998 because I am undergoing a tremendous personal and family change. Midway through the 1997–98 school year, my husband accepted a job in Kansas City. What a change from Tallahassee, a place that after 10 years of my life felt like an "old comfortable shoe." Telling Donna that I would be moving at the end of the school year was not only difficult – it was one of the hardest things I've *ever* had to do. I deplored having to "break up" our wonderful, seamless marriage.

As always, Donna was understanding towards me. She didn't like to think of me leaving, but she told me not to worry and to have faith that everything would work out. She added that people have different places in their lives where they need to be at different times for mysterious reasons. As my second year at FSUS drew to a close, I began to disengage from the workaday routine. Projects were on the go that I wouldn't be around to finish. It was hard to get excited about the new library cards planned for next fall (they would have special stickers showing which students had Internet permission) when I wouldn't be here to see them.

I also had my own personal challenges after my husband moved to Kansas City in 1998. I was faced with parenting our children, making moving arrangements, and showing our home to prospective buyers. I tried to maintain perspective and not let my personal situation intrude at work. However, as the end of the school year coincided with our moving date, I couldn't help making a "mental move" as well.

But still, something very special between Donna and me is holding steady. Our magical glue continues to adhere. I still finish some of her sentences before she even does. And she knows the best ways to handle frustrating situations that suddenly crop up.

Before I left, Donna asked me hopefully, "Couldn't you get a 24-hour chat line on the Internet?" That way, she reasoned, we could regularly keep each other posted on what was happening in our lives. This way she could also get instantaneous feedback from me on issues and concerns that arise with regard to the library. We laughed a lot while imagining the things we'd be saying during such electronic conversations.

Acknowledgment

This chapter is dedicated to Donna Shrum whose advice, suggestions, and support shape my present and future. The new challenges in our relationship suggest what an ideal marriage can become – two people who encourage each other to pursue their best self, secure in the knowledge that a shared foundation exists despite the flux.

9   The Principal as Mentor:
       From Divergence to Convergence

Eileen L. McDaniel

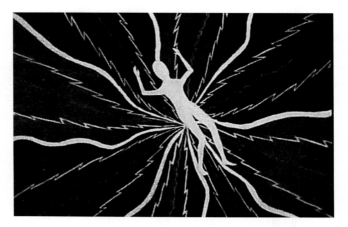

Figure 9.1: Creating synergistic relationships (Katrina Kittendorf, 1998)

How does a school principal function as an intentionally practicing mentor to bring convergence from divergence and improve student and teacher relationships? In this chapter, I, an elementary school principal in a university laboratory school, share my reflections on the value of mentoring in the context of my professional life and service. I share how the role of the principal in a K–12 setting like my own provides a rich environment for creating mentoring opportunities.

Personal mentoring influences

A lifetime goal of mine was to be an educator of some significance. From my years in school and finally a doctoral program in educational leadership, I have focused on my lifetime dream to be the best educator I could, not only for children but adults too. Each phase of my educational journey has led to new positions and exciting opportunities to interact with students, parents, and colleagues who have helped shape my future. From the early years of my career as an elementary teacher, to new challenges as a resource teacher and counselor, and my current ventures as a school administrator, I have encountered people and events that have helped me to grow not only as an educator, but as an individual. Significant others have mentored me with far-reaching impact on my life, leading to my present position as an elementary principal at the Florida State University School (FSUS).

Several of my mentors have chapters in this book. From their writings, aspects can be discovered of who they are, as well as an impression of why they have had such an impact on me. For instance, Ed Vertuno, who served as director of FSUS, shared his gift for saying the "right thing at the right time," even in times of dissonance. Additionally, Frances Kochan entered my life in 1987 at a critical point in my development. As the new director of FSUS, she had a gift that I had rare privilege to encounter – a vision of schools as a community of learners. Frances was both a mentor and friend who provided constant encouragement and role modeling which I still attempt to emulate. Sandy Lee, a family counselor at the school, also helped to shape my life in ways I thought unimaginable. With her forthright manner in "telling it like it is," but with respect and a steadfast belief in accountability to others, I am learning to hold myself accountable for saying and doing what I feel is best for children as well as for those whom I supervise.

I would be remiss to not also include, within this mentoring network, my major professor in educational leadership at Florida State University who has offered me intellectual and moral support throughout my doctoral journey.

A mentoring culture

The Partnership Support Group resulted from the efforts of Carol Mullen who, as Principal Investigator of a self-initiated mentoring project, brought together FSUS faculty and administrators with The Florida State University faculty. This comentoring opportunity has also greatly influenced my role as an educator. Bi-weekly meetings, selected professional readings, and, above all, communication and synergy between the two worlds of K–12 and postsecondary educators, have all impacted my thoughts and actions as a school principal. The greatest gift this group brought me was the time to reflect and write on my role in a university climate that has shaped various mentoring connections for me.

While exploring those synergistic relationships that have resulted during my principalship, I have come to see that some of these relationships were initiated with differing, or divergent, philosophies. Yet, these particular relationships eventually converged, moving me toward a common focus and purpose. In contrast, I have also experienced interactions where an immediate connection was felt, and a meshing of educational philosophies established. Each synergistic encounter of mine has provided an opportunity for a special form of mentoring as collegial friendship, or as "comentorship" as Carol Mullen refers to it.

The Partnership Support Group has given me a structure for reflecting on these varying kinds of relationships and particularly how I mentor others within the school-university culture. Figure 9.1 represents my need to promote synergistic relationships within learning organizations and communities. It captures my various mentoring roles and synergistic connections among university and teaching faculty within our shared but also different educational culture.

Functioning in close collaboration with the university community, the principal experiences an increase in teaching/learning opportunities. In this atmosphere of collegiality, the principal regularly encounters both beginning and master teachers who sometimes welcome the work of the principal as instructional leader. Moreover, the laboratory school-university connection provides unique opportunities for the principal to mentor preservice teachers and to communicate with university researchers who aim to conduct research at the school. These mentoring relationships can be applied, to varying degrees, to other educational settings.

Mentoring role of a principal

The educational literature provides numerous examples of mentoring relationships within university and school systems (Lieberman, 1992; Little, 1990). For the instructional school leader, occasions frequently arise to provide mentoring to the many stakeholders invested in education. The principal acts as overseer of the school's programs and enforcer of the student code of conduct. Students are often sent to the principal for counseling to help steer them away from transgressions that could interfere with their learning.

As a frequent visitor to the classroom, the principal is seen as an *encourager* who is interested in students' progress through a particular curriculum as well as teachers' expectations. Teachers, parents, and other family members consult with the principal for guidance in their child's development. Principals may perform as a mediator between the teacher and student in assuring the best educational program for a child.

The principal also provides advice to parents in what seemingly is "common sense" skills. But, in today's world with the changing role of the family unit, school personnel are providing parenting education for family members who lack the experience to raise youth as responsible, capable citizens. On a daily basis my appointment book is filled with requests from parents who seek my advice in assisting their children to learn in a challenging environment. Faculty and staff members seek out the advice of the principal as well. Whether it is to gain insight into a student's particular learning or behavioral problem, or to implement a beneficial learning method for students, the principal offers guidance to those who seek it.

The principal provides the link among the school, the home, and the community. At a recent parent–teacher conference, I assisted the parent to see her child through the eyes of the school as a troubled youngster who was in need of professional support outside the scope of services the school could provide. With the assistance of the classroom teacher, counselor, and anecdotal records, a picture was painted that helped the parent to see the need as we saw it. Unfortunately, conferences such as these are becoming more commonplace as more demands are placed on the shoulders of public school systems. As schools continue to link with social agencies and resources available with the community, the burden will be lessened. Students and family with reap the benefits.

Laboratory school context

The role of the principal in a public laboratory school setting is unique. Not only is the principal a key figure in the instructional program of K–12 education, he or she is also liaison to the university, community, and other public schools. Teachers and administrators are expected to be master teachers as well as capable researchers who do committee work and sponsor student activities. More experienced teachers are also expected to provide service to the university through membership on college committees or leadership in professional organizations at the state or national level. Dissemination of innovative and best practices to public schools is also a common goal.

Each public laboratory school in Florida (there are a total of four) also serves as a separate school district. Being under the auspices of a university, such schools must comply with the State University System's regulations. However, because all funding for the laboratory school comes from regular public education dollars, the school must also comply with state and federal regulations with the Florida Department of Education. The two governing agencies have different sets of regulations that have been known to clash. Although conflicts are few, it can be a "juggling act" to remain in compliance with both postsecondary and K–12 regulations.

Leadership role

Seven years ago I was offered the opportunity to become the elementary principal at the Florida State University School. With this role came many other "hats to wear" and the rush against the clock that I experience playing many mentoring roles each day. Finding a balance between these necessary duties and responsibilities and my role as the instructional leader for the elementary program provides me with a constant challenge. However, each role I play carries with it mentoring opportunities with regard to some facet of the school-university culture.

As Research Director, it is my responsibility to carry out the two missions of FSUS. First and foremost, the mission of the school is to conduct research projects that will enhance educational processes and programs. The great majority of the research projects come from the College of Education and other colleges at Florida State University. These research requests are reviewed within the school by myself to determine if the project in consideration meets the criteria for research as determined by FSUS policy.

I meet with each researcher – graduate students, university professors, and teachers – to assess the appropriateness and benefit to education of proposed projects. In many instances, I make suggestions to the researcher to improve the research design model. For instance, the instrument (i.e. survey) may be too long or too difficult to read for the targeted population. Generally, researchers have complied with my recommendations and have even found them beneficial.

In addition to research projects, I also coordinate all assistance/service requests, which are wide and varied. They range from simple requests to do classroom observation to conduct instructional design projects as part of a course. On any given day during a college semester, FSUS has as many as 50 observers in our school, providing preservice teachers with hands-on experience. After I meet with each person who requests the services of the school, I match the individual with the most appropriate teacher or group of students, and follow up with notification to office staff and faculty.

Strengthening comentoring links

As a result of my research directorship role, I have had the opportunity to collaborate with many university students, faculty members, and staff. One of the most challenging functions of this role is to provide "the bridge" between K–12 education and postsecondary education. At Carol Mullen's initiative as Principal Investigator, faculty in the school and university collaborated in serious discussion of selected readings on mentoring and their connections for, and impact on, each individual. Through this dialogue, we became a synergistic learning group that more fully understood the concept and practice of mentoring and its many roles and complexities. I grew to know university professors and even my own FSUS colleagues in ways I had never imagined. Through our reflections, I could see my work to be one of professional mentoring, a status and perspective that had previously eluded me.

Something even more important resulted from our regular gatherings. A synergistic relationship developed among the members, one in which Carol Mullen described as "two people coming together and being much larger than any one being." Indeed, all members of our support group were winners, regardless of status, preferences, and aspirations. After each session, I felt good about myself as a contributor as did the teachers who shared with me. But much more resulted from these interactions. A sense of *oneness*, a culture of synergy, developed among this diverse membership, with each of us sharing our mentoring encounters, relationships, programs, and research. Indeed, we learned more about ourselves as both mentors and mentees.

University relationship outcomes

One outcome of this school-university collaborative effort was my desire for increased contact with those College of Education faculty who would be willing to take an active role in our K–12 setting. I currently seek a "win-win" situation in which our preservice teachers gain exposure to current research and practices being studied and taught by university professors. In return, university students gain practical experiences to help prepare them for their chosen career. I seek expanded participation of the university students at the school; additionally, I would like to see College of Education curricula modified to include more practical experience in interactions with FSUS students, particularly those who need individualized attention.

With an increase in students at our school who are not proficient in the subject areas of reading, writing, and mathematics, it is imperative to locate additional resources to assist them. Providing tutorial services to students needing remediation would not only benefit them, but would also provide valuable teaching experience to preservice teachers. My preliminary proposal has been met with a positive reception from university personnel.

New mentoring relationships

Probably my most challenging and rewarding role as a mentor has been as a principal. In 1981 I completed the graduate program in educational leadership and met the requirements for school principalship. Within a year, a vacancy occurred in the elementary principal position and I was selected. In my new role, I continued the K–12 responsibilities and took on the additional role as coordinator of the Beginning Teacher Program and teacher certification responsibilities.

Becoming the instructional leader among one's own peers is certainly not an "easy row to hoe." Moving from the role of peer to administrator was difficult for myself and the elementary school faculty. However, my previous experiences combined with my learning in the doctoral program served me well. Opportunities for mentoring arose as a result of my many roles in the professional lives of the faculty. For example, I served as a mentor for new and veteran teachers, including out-of-state experienced teachers pursuing a Florida Professional Teaching Certificate.

Florida High (the high school at Florida State University School) also became engaged in major restructuring efforts, as well as the innovative practice of block-scheduling. As part of my own professional growth, I participated in extensive work in cooperative learning. I used this preparation to assist secondary teachers in adjusting to longer instructional periods. One of these teachers, a renowned veteran foreign language instructor, embraced the cooperative learning model and revolutionized her way of teaching. This same teacher, who had successfully taught for over 25 years, found herself in the position of having to seek Florida Certification – a requirement that came about as a result of laboratory schools becoming "public," removing the exempt status that some laboratory teachers had exercised for years. Even though she was an experienced teacher who had published and written national and state-level curriculum, this teacher needed to demonstrate the same competencies as novice teachers seeking state licensure. I assisted her in "jumping through the hoops" of state bureaucracy to attain certification status. Our relationship deepened as a result of these combined efforts, continuing to this day.

Mentoring successes

My mentoring relationships occur with faculty new to the elementary program at FSUS. Even though our teachers are all members of a grade-level team, I invite new arrivals to chat with me at least once monthly. Most new teachers embrace this invitation and a regular appointment is established. Some teachers have met with me weekly, making use of my "open door" policy. I also make myself available after the regular work day to teachers who wish to share concerns and seek advice.

One such elementary school teacher joined our faculty five years ago. Although she was an experienced teacher, she was new to the public laboratory school culture. Upon my invitation, this teacher formally met with me once weekly for three months, and then biweekly until the end of the year. She shared stories of student success and under-achievement. She also expressed facets of her relationships with her grade-level team members and ideas about new projects she wished to implement. This teacher relied on my advice, often seeking affirmation for new strategies she might attempt.

Because 4th graders in Florida are annually administered a statewide writing assessment test, this same teacher had a keen interest in improving the writing capabilities of her students. I encouraged her to experiment; as a result of her efforts, her students made significant gains in their writing abilities. She was also completing a master's program in educational leadership, and so I encouraged her to use her leadership skills by sharing her teaching strategies with colleagues at FSUS. While her aide supervised and taught her classes, this teacher would share her developing knowledge with other 3rd, 4th, and 5th grade classes by role modeling effective teaching strategies for developing student-writers. She also conducted workshops for her students' parents to assist them in improving their children's writing abilities. Consequently, the writing scores of her students and other 4th graders rose even higher that year.

Presently, with my encouragement, this same teacher is investigating exemplar writing programs across the nation while making arrangements for K–12 teacher workshops. She has become a member of our School Advisory Council, elected by her peers to represent the faculty on school improvement issues, as well as department chairperson for her teaching team, a facilitative role she plays well. To this day, this teacher shares with me her joys and concerns as well as her desire to grow. As a result of her applied efforts in a number of areas, she has become a mentor for others, readily sharing her developing expertise. Yet, she continues to publicly identify me as a significant mentor in her teaching career.

Another person, whom I also mentor and who attended meetings of the Partnership Support Group, is a second grade teacher at FSUS. During several group sessions, she described the mentoring relationship between us. She told us about how she had come from another school in which the "administrator did not want to hear about her teaching and came into her classroom only two times. It was special to have Eileen call me at home, treat me as a colleague, and 'come down' to be a friend and encourager."

Despite such mentoring opportunities, not all teachers are receptive to the role of principal as mentor. As a reflective practitioner, I have attempted to understand why it is that some teachers wholeheartedly seek a teaching/learning relationship while others avoid a close alliance. I query veteran teachers in regards to this perplexing issue, and the responses vary. For example, one teacher responded that she is "private" and feels uncomfortable seeking the advice of administrators unless there is a problem she alone cannot resolve, while another indicated her fear I might disclose the nature of conversations, despite my assurances that this would not be so.

Reflecting on my mentoring relationships with teachers over the years, it has dawned on me that those teachers, who had *not* formerly been my peers, were more readily amenable to my mentoring functions. For some teachers who had been my colleagues when I was a teacher, the mentoring relationship has been more difficult to establish – if at all. While some veteran teachers resisted the development of mentoring relationships, others, with increased efforts on my part to connect, responded over time. Others respond differently – they have become dependent on my advice. I have had to work at assisting some teachers to make independent decisions and to develop leadership skills in their classrooms and with their colleagues.

Despite obstacles, I continue to practice what Reitzug (1994) described as the empowering behavior of the principal as an instructional leader. Daily, I spend quality time considering how I can facilitate teachers' examination of their own practices for the purpose of better serving the needs of our students. According to Reitzug (1994), "principals should spend more time asking questions and suggesting a variety of alternatives that expand conceptions of how organizational tasks *might* be accomplished, than telling how these tasks *must* be accomplished" (p. 304). My role as a mentoring principal needs to be one in which I engage in behaviors that stimulate openness and critique of practice and that provide alternative frameworks for teachers to consider.

Final reflections

The Partnership Support Group provided an opportunity for all faculty members to participate in a collegial atmosphere of reflective practice on mentoring relationships. From the perspective of an administrator, I found this group to be facilitative in developing self-awareness of mentoring opportunities and prospects for the future.

The title of principal conveys both meaning and function for a community of learners. With this title come assumptions about the role of the instructional leader as someone who, for example, initiates new programs; motivates others to become risk takers; inspires experimentation with new ideas; and facilitates solutions to educational concerns. Little, Galagaran, and O'Neal (cited in Galvez-Hjornevik, 1986) describe a study of teacher advisers wherein the notion of assisting teachers demonstrates a respect toward colleagues as professionals rather than "charges" to be led. In considering my role as a mentor for teachers in combination, I similarly see myself as employing a facilitative leadership style that I have learned from my mentors and mentees as well as from my varied practical experiences.

I am happy to say that each mentoring opportunity has become a comentoring experience for me. I have gained new insight into the individuals with whom I interact which I, in turn, use to refine my skills and to grow personally. I have become a more empathetic listener, interspersing leading questions to get at core issues. I encourage others to foster a sense of on-going learning in which every event in our lives can be reflected upon and possibly improved. Above all else, I now see my role of principal as a nurturer and role model for others. The principal-mentor needs to, I believe, anticipate and understand others' concerns; celebrate their accomplishments; and offer just enough feedback to promote reflective forms of practice.

The Partnership Support Group framework could be used schoolwide in any educational setting. Establishing teams of teachers and staff interested in mentoring relationships and inquiry could facilitate the reflective-analytic processes needed to initiate and implement change in educational practices. From my own personal experiences, I am not certain that every individual is suited to this intensive growth role. In my attempts to provide mentoring to teachers, I have found that not all teachers are receptive to, or are ready for, such a learning relationship with an administrator or even someone else. Some teachers resist personal and professional change. Does this make either them or me an ineffective instructional leader? I dare say, no.

The mentoring relationship must build upon mutual agreement, one in which synergy and union is formed so that mutual benefit can be reaped. Should principals feel a sense of failure when synergy is not present in every relationship with teachers in their school? Definitely not. Synergistic relationships take time and desire, and they need to be promoted through encouragement, support, and, above all, a feeling of trust. Can principals foster synergistic relationships within their school? Most assuredly, yes – through consistent role modeling of reflective and caring forms of practice.

10   Spiritual Mentoring: A Synergistic School Therapy

Sandy R. Lee

Figure 10.1:   Spiritual tree of life (J. J. Fenno, 1998)

How do a spiritual foundation, academics, and therapeutic efforts come together for an effective approach to helping others in a university laboratory school? In this chapter, I discuss the transition in my life from early spiritual development to becoming a professional therapist and how mentoring served as a common empowering vehicle for all three realisms of my life, spiritual, academic, and therapeutic. In addition, I explain and illustrate how synergistic comentoring provides a practical, powerful process for growth, learning, and development in schools, churches, and in families.

My journey

A spiritual foundation was enabled for me by my parents and broadened by my life with, and observations of, my father, who was and still is a pastor. One of the highest priorities my father had as a pastor was to 'mentor' and provide guidance to different "teams" of people, such as elders, deacons, various church groups, and other committees. My spiritual foundation was further strengthened as I became interested, at a young age, in helping people. Friends came to me for advice and told me they appreciated the guidance I provided. This form of identity and connection progressed into my choice of profession and career. Currently, I am a counselor for families at The Florida State University School (FSUS) where I have opportunities to "mentor" and guide different groups of people – students, parents, families, teachers, and administrators – just as my father continues to "mentor" groups of people within his congregation. The comentoring group discussions have made me realize, to a great extent, how my spiritual, therapeutic, and academic experiences are not counterpoints of one another, but in fact have become integrated within me, and have even come full circle.

As we discussed mentoring issues in the PSG around the questions what does mentoring mean; how does it take place in school and university settings; how has it developed in personal lives; and what impact does it have for and on us as educators, I realized that I had heard and seen the terms and processes under study by us in my own life. As we explored the terms and processes within the group, they were familiar because of their similarity to the spiritual terms and processes I had internalized, observed, and practiced as I grew up. I carried them deep within me even then, and in the PSG discussions my experiences of spiritual, academic, and therapeutic mentoring coalesced.

One of the first questions that the support group tackled in September 1997 was, What does mentoring mean? This was an important question for me then as it is now, as I wondered about the meaning of mentorship within and across spiritual, academic, and therapeutic realms. I also realized that I would need to be cautious in how I defined mentoring in each of these areas so as not to negate or weaken their fuller range of meanings. In other words, therapy involves more than mentoring, as is teaching, or pastoring/spiritual guidance. It is with this concern that I wondered whether I should write about the similarities of the three realms. As we further defined and refined mentoring in the support group, we all agreed that it is a complex concept and that it has various meanings for people in different areas of life. However, there is something that allows mentoring to have a distinctive quality despite its complex nature. In this chapter I examine the meaning of mentoring in key areas of my life to further its understanding and use.

The spiritual circle

First, the *spiritual circle* or *realm*. This is, indeed, the foundation and overall frame of who I am and the area from which I approach the therapeutic and academic realms. It is the domain that is most personal to me, and one not always easy to speak about or articulate. When, in the comentoring support group we came to discuss how mentoring is a way of telling stories, and of passing on our lives and creating legacy, this was when I perceived similarities between spiritual and academic realms. At first I was hesitant to share with the others because of the sensitivity to "spiritual" topics in an academic setting. Then a teacher made a comment about how in the scriptures there are examples of older women mentoring younger women, and older men teaching younger men. At that point I felt more comfortable about entering into the discussion and committing to this chapter.

As I previously indicated, my father had served as a pastor. I observed how he lived what he preached. He integrated the spiritual into his everyday experiences. There was a continuity, within him, among his roles as the husband, father, and pastor. We, as a family, watched him struggle and question his relationship with God, and then experienced him applying the very things he taught from those struggles. Over time, he built a deep relationship with God, and his story was a powerful life lesson for his children.

My father's role as pastor had many responsibilities, but a main priority was the mentoring of new and potential leaders of the church. The term mentoring, as defined within the spiritual realm and my father's own practice, means to provide a model that can be imitated by others. In scripture, the Apostle Paul states to the followers of Christ: "Whatever you have learned or received or heard from me, or seen in me – put into practice. And the God of peace will be with you" (in Phillipians 4:9, *The Holy Bible*, 1973). This orientation toward, or value placed on, mentoring brings with it a high accountability. Mentors need to understand that if they do not hold themselves accountable, and to a high standard, then the potential for others, in their way of thinking and behaving, will be lessened. Mentors should be able to say to their mentees, look at how I live and learn from what you see, so that you too can become Christ's example of a model mentor. McPherson (1995) states simply, "To mentor is to model," and quotes St. Francis of Assisi: "Preach the Gospel at all times. If necessary use words" (p. 28). What is most important is what we do and how we live: "Being a model is being an example for someone else to follow" (McPherson, p. 28).

Mentoring is also about responsibility. Mentoring defined in this way becomes an essential part of personal and communal growth, and of the healthy functioning of our entire life-system. Like these three domains of growth, the personal, communal, and global, the three branches of the tree of life (see Figure 10.1) are all rooted in the same source for me, spirituality. Similarly, our readings in the PSG support this vision of mentoring – it is something passed on through a primary source that widens the circle of who and what is influenced (Gehrke, 1988; Merriam, 1983; Mullen, 1997c; Zimpher and Rieger, 1988). My father taught the congregation that mentoring exists on other levels, including sharing one another's burdens and growth in a personal relationship with Christ. For example, older women who embark on mentoring relationships with younger women can guide them with their wisdom, using their own life experiences to help others to strengthen their relationships with God.

Another area from my father's congregation that I later engaged in, was that of discipling others. *Discipling* is defined as having a one-on-one relationship with another person who is probably at a different phase of growth in his or her relationship with God. The intent here is to develop a relationship where trust, confidentiality, and accountability are established and one's relationship with God is deepened. This learning process might require consistent spiritual meetings; specific growth goal-setting; and work compatibility alongside each other with encouragement toward insight. It also entails being honest and reflective, and discussing areas that need work and adjustment, even correction. The mutual goal to be met is that each person will be able to go forth and disciple two additional people. Thus, church mentoring takes on a very intense and serious meaning, one in which the healthy functioning of individuals, families, and the church as a whole depends. The comprehensiveness of a mentor's responsibilities, combined with the length and intimacy of a particular relationship and what gets passed onto others, are of great significance. Like a pebble in water, a spiritual connection is made through the ripple effect of deepening relationships over time.

The academic circle

Second, the *academic circle* or *realm* is where my experiences and foundation grew as I matured. When I was in junior high school, I unexpectedly discovered that "helping people" was "natural" to me. Even though I was quite shy, my friends would seek me out for advice on a range of problems in their lives. The unexpected part came when they actually returned, telling me that my advice worked and they appreciated my input. That feedback served to boost my self-esteem and shape my sense of self. I enjoyed "helping" people problem solve. My career choice was decided at this early age, and it has never fluctuated during my college and post-graduate years when I refined my abilities and talents to help others. The refinement occurred over time as professors, peers, colleagues, and even clients encouraged, guided, and supported my aspiration to become a practicing therapist.

The therapeutic circle

The *therapeutic circle* or *realm* was shaped during my eight years of work in agencies as a therapist. My role as a therapist at FSUS is unique, since most schools do not have a therapist on site. I provide therapy to students' families as well as to the faculty and their families. I provide short-term therapy, including referrals for emergency food, shelter, and health services, and give referrals for long-term therapy service. Additionally, I coordinate the crisis plan at the school and provide crisis intervention therapy for families and individuals.

Being in a public school setting has indeed broadened my perspective on, and approach to, therapy. Also, I am involved in many other activities, such as being coordinator of the sports model program. This mentoring activity entails matching high school athletes with elementary students who teachers feel need a "big-brother" or "big-sister." This work was appealing to me because of how a sports "model" was defined, that is, as one with the following characteristics: responsive to athletes and having good academic grades; positive thinking and constructive behavior; and responsible citizenship. Each high school mentor had a sponsoring teacher who met regularly with him or her, advised on possible approaches with mentees, mentored progress, and answered questions. This teacher–student relationship presented a kind of mirror of what the high schooler was to do. This modeling worked well when there was follow-up from the teachers. This type of mentoring could work well in the academic setting, especially at any K–12 school, and it could also be adapted to a teacher-buddy system, one whereby seasoned teachers mentor new teachers to the system. However, it only works well if there are clear, mutual goals and dependable follow-through procedures.

Another role that I have played as school therapist was teaching a peer counseling course. An unexpected outcome of this course was that it provided the students with a "safe harbor" to discover more about themselves; gain in new communication skills; and learn about human issues on a personal level. As trust and confidentiality developed, the group became closer and were empowered to share deeper feelings. They scarcely shared in this way outside the room, but in this room they felt safe with one another. There were older and younger students. The older ones provided wisdom and guidance to the younger, and the younger ones listened attentively. In response, the younger students also taught the older ones, reminding me of the spiritual commands to share one another's burdens and to encourage each another. Comentoring can produce a strong bond regardless of the length of interaction, as I also experienced occurring in the PSG project: "Trust, acceptance, and support are necessary ingredients to all mentoring relationships" (Scott, 1992, p. 174). I would add "confidentiality" as a necessary ingredient to mentoring relationships. These elements all worked to bond the group of young people into a synergistic team in the peer counseling context, and opened them up to the potential for meaningful communication in school and in other parts of their lives.

Murphy and Lick (1998) indicate that synergistic teams have common goals that involve such processes as interdependence and appreciative understanding. All of these characteristics have been an integral part of the mentoring experiences which have shaped my life. For me, the spiritual, academic, and therapeutic learning that people gain from each other, and pass along (a form of synergistic comentoring) has been a powerful source of life-energy. This understanding has confirmed for me that we all have something valuable to pass onto others, no matter what realm (spiritual, therapeutic, or academic) may be more prominent at the time. It is a necessity, for the healthy functioning, growing, learning, and educating of the future generations that we all attend to what we can pass along. I agree with Merriam (1983) that "clearly how mentoring is defined determines the extent of mentoring found" (p. 165). Kealy and Mullen (1999) point out that "insights gained from interpreting [our own] examples [can] include recognizing existing and new mentoring roles, increasing the awareness of one's academic lineage, and mentor–mentee participation in meaningful joint activity" (p. 379). No matter what field we are in, we need each other at some fundamental level, at some intensity, and for some length of time.

Because of my unique role as an on-site therapist, known for holding confidentiality as a high priority, the school's administrators have come to trust me. They would discuss with me the best ways to handle difficult or delicate interpersonal issues and situations. Through my seven years at FSUS, I have had the opportunity to observe several administrators, particularly with regard to how they balance their role while keeping the primary purpose of our school in mind – the education and well-being of the children. One person has stood out, for me, in the way that she has balanced her role with the school's purpose. With integrity and respect, Eileen McDaniel has consistently demonstrated sincere concern. Her example of how not to turn away from difficult situations and issues, even if it meant standing alone, was most profound.

Eileen was in a difficult position as she progressed from teacher to program specialist, and from elementary guidance counselor to, most recently, elementary principal within the same school. While having these different layers of experience would be advantageous for a principal, it would at times work against Eileen as her colleagues had become her employees. Eileen was mindful about how she worked through these differences and how she balanced this delicate line between colleague and supervisor. Her example in caring about this delicate balance was most exemplary, especially when still confronting resistance and difficulties. Eileen was, and continues to be, the person everyone goes to, especially when solutions were needed to resolve problems. Eileen treats everyone with equal respect and assists to the best of her abilities. Eileen's special capacities are her patience; care for meeting teachers' needs; desire that teachers be the best they can be; and, most importantly, care for the children. She pursues her capacities and skills as goals to be nurtured, in practical ways, on a daily basis.

I have observed Eileen over the years – she has grown in confidence as someone who is her own person; who has an important role to play as elementary school principal; and in her ability to keep children as the priority while, at the same time, helping teachers become the best they can be. I have become more and more concerned with how one works within a school organizational system to make it function more effectively and sensitively to meet the educational needs of young children and adolescents. Through observing Eileen's example of day-to-day striving to balance the needs of faculty, staff, facility/maintenance, and the organization, in addition to her many other responsibilities, I now have a new area of interest to pursue. As indicated, I am becoming intrigued with how organizational systems can function more effectively, efficiently, and healthily. I have seen, through Eileen's example, that there exist administrators who are willing to work hard at accomplishing the broader goals of the system while assuring that the practical goals and needs of the organization are met in a way that is best for the whole system.

I now realize, through this PSG opportunity and chapter writing, that Eileen has been an exemplary mentor all along. She has not only encouraged my new area of interest in organizational systems but, more importantly, has shown how one maintains a sense of integrity, respect, consistency, accountability, and sense of humor while carrying out the many responsibilities of an administrator. These same characteristics are also important in spiritual forms of mentoring.

Because of my spiritual foundation, I view the therapy I do very seriously. Therapy is not only a profession, but an opportunity for me to pass on important life principles that will hopefully bring about healthy relationships, making a difference to others. Passing on healthy patterns of relationships is a vital form of mentoring. In my therapy, I encourage individuals and family members to tell their stories. It is often in the hearing of their own stories that people will see a lesson or direction for their lives, bringing about healthy, sometimes lasting, change. With families, I try to create an environment whereby members listen to each other's stories and, by virtue of carefully listening, perhaps hear how they can encourage each other to become more reflective and caring. It is with this synergistic comentoring storytelling process that families heal by lending much needed supportive assistance to each other. The questions I ask help family members to reconsider their own stories and the lives they wish to lead. I am careful to formulate my questions to fit each family's circumstances, but also to give members a different way of looking. Like Gehrke (1988), I believe that "the greatest gift the mentor offers is a new and whole way of seeing things" (p. 192). To me, this gift-giving is the essence of the lessons of life I hope they will learn, and then practice and pass onto others. This is where therapy has a spiritual mentoring application that matters.

A new understanding

Finally, while struggling with how to complete this story, I happened to be sitting in a parent meeting at my church where our youth pastor was presenting his perspective on where our youth group now needs to go. The youth group has grown in numbers and is progressing toward the goals established for the group's development. We had "hit a ceiling" in the youth ministry due to size, growth, and limited adult involvement. We now needed to go to another level, and in order for this movement to be realized, we had to have a serious commitment from adults/parents in the congregation. They needed to become more involved by becoming mentors/ disciples to our young people. This "topping out" phenomena is simply the result of not having enough shepherds and lay leaders to disciple students. This is not just a matter of growing in numbers; our youth are missing key benefits of discipleship and mentoring. A paradigm shift is now required for restructuring of the ministry towards mentoring and discipleship. In the words of McPherson (1995):

> No longer can relationship-building be viewed as an optional add-on to youth ministry. The primary objective of youth ministry should be to support parents and families by providing young people with adult mentors who will walk with them through their adolescent experience. It must happen one kid at a time. (p. 51)

The whole congregation is needed. The community is needed. As Rice (in McPherson with Rice, 1995) states, "I am now convinced that the dominant *modus operandi* of youth ministry, which continues to separate youth from the significant adults in their lives, has got to go" (p. 15).

While the youth pastor discussed the necessary paradigm shift, I smiled, realizing that I had an ending to my chapter. I felt that I had come full circle. This meeting enabled me to reflect differently upon the those discussions we were having in our book mentoring group meetings. This, in turn, brought me full circle to better see the academic realm in the spiritual, and the spiritual realm in the academic. How magnificent and powerful for me! The discussion in the parent church group meeting evolved into an attempt to define mentoring; who should do mentoring; how long does it require; and who will decide who mentors whom. The agreement among us was that mentoring may mean something different for each young person and his or her family, but that, at the same time, it means a serious commitment to providing guidance, wisdom, accountability, encouragement, responsibility, consistency – and hope – to our youth.

The mission statement of the church youth group is aimed at finding ways to equip students to serve. Thus, through mentoring, an avenue is created for these young people and adults to pass on their experience/stories to the next generation. Our youth pastor realizes that this important generational work cannot be done by him alone. Nor ought it be. Mentoring provides a model which endorses the responsibility of living and being alongside our youth. There is a place for youth workers in a mentoring program, but it should be one of support and facilitation, rather than domination and subservience. Everyone needs to be part of a team.

All of the terms and processes being described during the church group meeting were, to me, similar to those discussed in the PSG. This spiritual-academic linkage reminds me of Adoue's (1997) research story of a Professional Development School and the comparison she makes with "com[ing] full circle from the mentoring of one to the mentoring of many" like a "a pebble thrown into a pond. The pebble creates a circle in the water, and then another, and another. It's effect grows and expands" (p. 115). Downer (1998) calls this the principle of the "power of one. Changing the world one life at a time" (p. 54). For teachers, youth group leaders, parents, and adults, the child is the focal point of the ever-widening circle.

Coming full circle

My worlds have come full circle via a powerful theme of mentoring during this journey of sharing and writing my story, and being part of the Partnership Support Group. In the PSG, we attempted to function as part of a "life-systems approach to mentorship [that] could create healing and lasting relationships between people and within cross-cultural communities" (Mullen, 1997c, p. 172).

I am coming to realize the gift of mentoring in all of us. According to Gehrke (1988), this gift "should capture the giving and receiving, the awakening and the labor of gratitude. And finally, it should capture the passage to another that immortalizes the gift, and extends humankind toward the omega point" (p. 194). This was the very message of Christ, which enables me to function with synergistic renewal in a university school environment.

11 Coloring Outside the Lines: Portrait of a Mentor-Teacher

Debi P. Barrett-Hayes

Figure 11.1:   Coloring outside the lines (Amelia Allen, 1996)

All teachers in their professional work mentor on numerous levels and in a variety of ways. But what is that special mentoring approach that makes a teacher a mentor-teacher, one who generates opportunities and communities for students and self to creatively nurture and synergistically comentor each other to new and unusual horizons and pinnacles? In this chapter, I discuss and illustrate the various aspects of a mentoring teacher, especially the powerful role of the mentor-teacher.

Blurring the boundaries

It is Friday afternoon and school is out for the day, but a few students remain hanging around in the art room. Amelia approaches Debi, "Have you got a few minutes? I would like to show you that encaustic (hot wax) painting technique I have been working on. You said you always wanted to learn how to do it – now is your chance."

The two meet at a counter where supplies are out and work is in progress. Amelia begins a running dialogue as she prepares the material. She demonstrates several techniques for layering and applying hot wax for encaustic painting. After Debi asks several questions, Amelia smiles openly, "Want to try it yourself?" Debi hesitates and Amelia encourages her by saying, "Oh come on. Look, I will help you." Amelia reaches over and carefully places the hot iron in Debi's hand and guides it to the canvas. "See, that is one technique. Now look what happens when you do this. Now try this." The lesson continues for a while as Amelia helps Debi explore the various ways to apply the hot wax pigment.

This seems like a typical scenario in the day of a teacher, one experienced many times in classrooms across the country. But, this is actually a rare and valued moment in a teacher's career; it is that precious moment when the teaching-learning roles are reversed. Amelia is the student and Debi the teacher in this scenario. The student has assumed the guiding role. This is one of many rewards that can be fostered when genuine colearning develops between a teacher and student. The results are a collaborative learning environment with a blurring of the boundaries and a reversal of formal roles. Debi and Amelia have developed a synergistic comentoring relationship.

As author Herman Melville reminds us: " [w]e cannot live for ourselves alone. Our lives are connected by a thousand invisible threads, and along these sympathetic fibers, our actions run as causes and return to us as results" (in Clinton, 1996, p. 7). These invisible threads bind us to the past and connect us to the future as we continue to weave the fibers of life's fabric.

Reflections in the mirror

When I look in a mirror, I see many pairs of eyes looking back. I see that creative child inside, the one who still loves a new box of sharply pointed crayons and the feel of wet, shiny paint from the palette to my finger tips. I see the teenager with tireless energy, a quick, off-beat sense of humor and the need to be different, a unique individual. Another face reflects an image of the committed college student determined to succeed and acquire the knowledge and skills for success. There is also the responsible adult and teacher who strives each day to plan, organize, and implement challenging goals and objectives that meet or exceed educational expectations. The administrative chair of the Art Department is also looking back from the mirror with long-range plans for the school district and knowledge of K–12 curricula and national standards. Also reflected is an image of a community activist and volunteer committed to issues related to art, education, and human rights, especially those of children. Close to the community activist is the view of a mother and wife who loves and is loved more deeply than imagined.

Appearing in the mirror, but at a distance, is the frantic face of the artist. She yearns to find the time to create, translate the world through uniquely personal visual expressions. The artist-specter is not central in this reflection but rather is essential to the creative forces that hold together a complex collage of roles. Amidst all of these images are the forces and contributions of students, teachers, and role models who have contributed strong fibers of invisible thread to weave the complex composite image looking back – this is *the teacher*.

As an artist, teacher, friend, and mother, I recently had reason to deeply examine my purpose for being in the classroom and my role as teacher. Most teachers hope for that rare occasion when the relationship developed in the classroom becomes a significant, life-changing event. Although unusual, this life-altering occurrence is what keeps teachers in the classroom. It sustains us during dry periods in our creativity and rejuvenates our commitment to education.

A shining star

The loss of a child or student from an untimely death is one of the most difficult tragedies to accept as a parent and teacher. One can feel no greater pain. I recently experienced not only the loss of a star student but also the loss of someone who shone brightly from within a field of 20 years of shining student stars. Amelia, the one whose light reached far beyond our classroom walls at The Florida State University School to illuminate the lives of her family, teachers, classmates, and those fortunate to call her "friend."

Amelia was brilliant, committed, and passionate. Additionally, she was selfless, compassionate, and spiritual. Although she left us with many stirring and inspiring memories and an amazing creative legacy, I feel her greatest contributions had yet to be realized. Amelia had decided to become a teacher. She was my student, protégé, friend, and mentor – as I was hers. This was a duality rarely achieved at the high school level.

The depths of my loss caused me to reexamine my motives and purposes for staying in the classroom. Had I ever, or would I ever again, experience a student–teacher relationship that rivaled this one? Would my enthusiasm and energy be compromised by this tragic loss? Could I still find other student–teacher relationships fulfilling and challenging?

In my imagination, Amelia has taken wings but is still grounded. As her piece I call "Grounded with Wings" (not shown) conveys, we become transported to another place through our art. But, we must find ways to remain connected to the people and places that surround us. These two ways of viewing the world create a dynamic struggle within the artist–teacher.

Returning home

Despite my metaphysical views, it was not easy to return to *that* classroom. A once welcoming messy but creative atmosphere became suddenly foreign and hostile to me. It was a space filled with reminders of Amelia, her energy, her spirit, her corner

135

of the room still filled with "works in progress" and creative plans for a future of unrealized dreams. I wondered what was left to say to these students, her friends left behind to deal with this loss. How could I continue on with the journey without her by my side? Her senior class had lost a leader, their friend, their National Honor Society President and Valedictorian. But, I had lost my comrade, my student, and somewhere along the way, my mentor. When the boundaries among these roles had blurred, I could not quite remember. Perhaps it was gradual, like osmosis; through a slow metamorphosis Amelia had become my special colleague and friend.

I returned to school on the Monday following her death in 1997. I got to school early to deal with this passage on my own terms. I was still unsure that I was ready for this challenge. For some reason, I parked as far away from my classroom as possible. Perhaps I figured that I would be unable to traverse the long trek to deal with *that room* where, only three days earlier, Amelia had taken my hand to show me her newly acquired technical skills as an encaustic painter.

It was difficult. I experienced waves of emotion familiar to anyone who has dealt with personal tragedy. I still don't know how I managed to stand before my students and deal with their loss, my loss, our loss, but I do know that, at some point, not long after my return, I felt a calm. It was as though Amelia were there with me; I had made the right decision to return. I realized then that she continued to inspire me to reach beyond my comfort level to mentor.

I was able to reach one difficult, distant student by recognizing her pain and sharing Amelia's desire that we meet each other half-way to resolve our differences. I realized a depth of mentoring as I sat outside comforting this hurt, young woman. It was that rare moment when, as roles and boundaries are blurred, we stand as synergistic comentors or equals. In this moment, we contribute essential parts to the mystery of life, an instance when the whole is greater than the sum of its parts. I placed that encaustic art experiment that Amelia and I had created together next to my office telephone. It commands my attention daily, reminding me of our journey together, the togetherness and separation, but also those invisible threads that remain strong.

Amelia was diagnosed in her senior year with bipolar manic depression. To those who knew her only on the surface, they would never know the depth of her strength and courage, of her drive and motivation, and also her fears and frailties. She died just days prior to her eighteenth birthday, and my fortieth. We talked about the sharing of milestone Piscean birthdays in the days preceding her death.

Another major milestone was in the plan. Amelia had helped me as the local chair to plan a community art auction. Amelia had donated one of her best art works to benefit the arts in education programs. Amelia's classmates came to me after her death to protest the selling of her work. I expressed that it had been her desire to contribute. The senior class was incensed: how could I sell her work, one that was priceless and emotionally valuable!

The class began a nickel-and-dime campaign and, in a matter of days, were prepared to attend the community auction. The auction organizer and sponsor, the local GFWC–Tallahassee Junior Woman's Club, decided that the funds should be given to a scholarship in Amelia's name. Other students began to contribute works of art for the scholarship fund. The senior class sponsor, who was the school nurse, attended the auction with students. The senior class selected a representative to bid on the work. The bidding was fast and furious and, in the end, the class purchased the Amelia assemblage for $1,300 which became the seed money for a scholarship in her name. The senior class presented the artwork to Amelia's family, and it now hangs, on loan, in our school's media center. My mind still reels at the events following this day. Each year as we present another student with the coveted scholarship, I realize that Amelia continues to mentor her peers through an academic-artistic scholarship that proudly bears her name.

My new goal as a mentor is to create a wide variety of situations and opportunities which foster the ability to create, strengthen, and weave these invisible threads into a resilient fabric for future mutual growth and stability, that is, to become a mentor-teacher.

Mentoring relationships

What is a mentoring relationship, and how is it different from other teaching relationships? In Homer's *Odyssey* the wise teacher was Mentor. He was purposeful about teaching, loving and supportive, guiding and nurturing, as well as creative and insightful. Most teachers strive to be mentors in their classrooms. They use relevant and engaging activities and learning assignments. But, mentoring really needs to be manifested in a multifaceted and dynamic role that needs to be filled. Teachers can reach out far beyond their classrooms to make the community their learning environment and the world a resource for mentoring opportunities with students. The role of learning institutions and of educators has expanded. It is no longer appropriate to say that the teacher is a role model in the classroom and that others in the community are responsible for modeling everything else that assists children and adolescents in becoming successful. We, the community, the students, teachers, parents, community and business leaders, are all responsible for the development of our future citizens and leaders.

Mentoring relationships do not simply happen overnight and without effort. They require sustained development, motivation, planning, and orchestration. A comentoring relationship is always in the process of change and development. As the individuals concerned learn and grow together, their relationship changes to meet new needs. I have categorized mentoring relationships and projects fostered in the Art Department, and within FSUS as a whole.

1 *Artistic and creative mentoring*: Artist-teachers set an example by helping students to realize the value of creative thought and innovative problem solving. Students are encouraged to explore their unique solutions to visual problems. This requires a number of components: a respectful atmosphere; time for incubation and experimentation; freedom of experimentation without fear of failure; and respect for the individual and his or her unique contribution.

2 *Teaching and learning mentoring*: Teachers help students to see and recognize the connections between art and the more traditional academic standards as well as achievement across the curriculum. Students are exposed to a holistic approach to how knowledge and learning is connected which contributes to the education of well-rounded individuals.

3 *Community and citizen mentoring*: Teachers provide opportunities for students to meet and work with members of the community as valued contributors to community events and development. Students see that their hard work makes a difference and that community members have relationships with schools that they recognize as vital.

4 *Work and career mentoring*: Teachers provide opportunities for skills and technique development related to work experience, demonstrating how classroom experiences and academics apply to career expectations and demands. Career mentoring requires continual knowledge and updates about current trends in the workplace.

5 *Personal and group mentoring*: Teachers provide opportunities for individuals to develop, demonstrate, and mentor accomplished practices and to improve performance among teachers, administrators, and university colleagues. Opportunities are provided for the exploration of one's natural interests and aptitudes in order to maximize strengths and minimize weaknesses. Modeling includes management of time, stress, and conflict resolution. We need teachers who model the process of becoming part of the solution.

6 *Professional and collegial mentoring*: Mentoring of colleagues on numerous levels and in a variety of ways is an important role for all teachers.

Mentoring benefits

Mentoring programs have a number of benefits that I have derived from examining our school's projects at FSUS.

For the student, benefits ideally include enhanced self-esteem; strengthened relationships; higher job aspirations and educational enrollment; and elevated Grade Point Average (GPA). For the teacher, benefits include improved relationships with individual students, and broadened cooperation and assistance in the classroom. For the school, benefits are greater involvement from student mentees, broadened involvement of students in school events, and development of partnerships in varied arenas.

For the university, benefits include reality-based experiences with students and teachers; increased knowledge in teacher expectations and student behaviors; new research that reflects practitioner and student concerns and issues; and innovative applications of theory and practice. For the community participant, there are opportunities to give back to schools and get a "reality check" on what educational demands are like; there is also the potential to develop long-term relationships with members, workers, clients, and patrons.

A mentor-teacher

Teachers are leaders of the community demonstrating what educational commitment involves for our students, ourselves, and others. We need not forget that while we serve as role models for children, we also are important models for parents and members of our community. First Lady, Hillary Clinton (1996), says that "children should be encouraged in all sorts of ways, not just scholastic . . . helping kids to identify and explore their passions will prepare them to get the most out of not only school but life" (p. 103).

A mentoring teacher has the opportunity to develop many different mentoring styles. Mentors serve as experts and provide a sense of potential to both students and peers. They have the opportunity to demonstrate the difference between the idea of a teacher as "sage on stage" and "guide on the side." Tracy Bailey, the 1994 Teacher of the Year, has commented that teachers come in one of three types: a speedboat, barge, or rock. On the other hand, I have always seen my mentoring role more like that of a captain on a tall ship, and my comentoring role as a partner on a learning excursion. These then for me lead naturally to a special kind of mentoring teacher that I call a *mentor-teacher.*

I define a *mentor-teacher* as a teacher who not only mentors in the typical ways discussed above, but who also fulfills two other specific key mentoring roles:

1   nurtures creativity in others and self, and
2   uses mentoring occasions, where practical, to generate synergistic comentoring opportunities.

My relationship with Amelia, described earlier, is a special example of my striving to be a mentor-teacher. In that mentor-teacher role, we not only nurtured each other's creative spirits and talents, but also synergistically comentored each other to new heights and vistas.

Mentoring creative thought

Teachers can mentor creativity by taking educational risks themselves. They can model various scholarly approaches and learn new techniques and technologies. Experimentation, "playing around," and making mistakes can all be beneficial to the creative process. One of the ways to promote risk-taking, creative problem solving in a class is by demonstrating it yourself. Allow yourself to say, "I don't know, let's try this," or "Let's see if this will work." One of the exercises we do in my class is draw the majestic oak outside the art room on the FSUS grounds. This subject, one of Amelia's drawings (not shown), serves as an opportunity for developing students' observational skills in order to prepare them for creative work. This is not a unique drawing exercise but, like playing scales as a musician, it is necessary as a developing artist to keep one's eyes and hand working together.

Ernest Boyer, former US Commissioner of Education, loved to tell a story about a college student who watched his five-year old niece color one day. The child leafed through the coloring book and selected a blank page. The uncle asked her why she had chosen a blank page instead of an illustration to color, to which she responded, "Outside the lines, you can do anything you want." As the opening artwork to this chapter shows, mentor-teachers need to provide these opportunities for students to explore "outside the lines" with sensible risk-taking (Alexander in Donohue, 1997).

Creative mentors can model how to reflect on ideas and solutions that were successful as well as ones that were not, but that may have played an integral part in problem solving. There are many situations that teachers can model and assess as part of the classroom experience. But teacher–learner peer assessment requires that teachers give up or share power and control with students. The reward of having students help with critical reviews of classroom events is crucial to learning for everyone involved. In my classroom, we often reach the end of a learning excursion to find ourselves in a new place. The process of learning takes on a life of its own. This is the wonderful benefit of power sharing.

This reciprocal mentor role means that the teacher can play student. When this happens, my students know that I too am a "work in progress." As I allow opportunities for them to witness me as a learner, our roles become blurred in a safe and nurturing collegial environment. Mimsie Robinson, the 1998 New York State's Teacher of the Year, offers these words of wisdom: "We're not born good teachers, but have to evolve into one. If you stop learning today, then you will stop teaching today" (Abernathy, 1997, p. 15). It is important for mentor-teachers to seek out opportunities for their students to see them as learners as well as teachers. This and other forms of mentoring for a creative, open environment can be quite challenging because students can surprise teachers with their candid expressions.

Partnerships in mentoring

Teachers need to lead the way and provide models for getting others meaningfully involved with schools. Mentoring through partnerships, a powerful form of comentoring, can be one way of helping our overcrowded schools and overwhelmed teachers. In a report to President Clinton, a committee on the Arts and Humanities recommends that action begin at the community level where innovative partnerships have been forming among schools, universities, and other institutions. Across the nation new cultural institutions have developed programs that provide teachers with resources they need to promote student learning (President's Committee on the Arts and the Humanities, 1997).

Teachers can and need to be the initiators of these partnerships. Mentoring experiences can help to bridge the gap between isolated content knowledge and practical knowledge, skills, and experience needed to succeed in the workplace.

These are precisely the goals of FSUS's PLUNGE (Practical Learning Utilizing New Gadgets in Education) initiative. The PLUNGE team consists of a science/technology teacher and visual arts teacher joined with interested students. The goal is to find work opportunities for students to learn new knowledge, integrate technology, and produce innovative learning materials and products with practical applications. Students find opportunities in the real world of work to *comentor one another, learn together, and show what they know.*

The Florida State University School seeks partners that can provide valuable experiences for students and teachers as well as unique opportunities for career mentoring. One such relationship is our partnership with the National High Magnetic Field Laboratory (MagLab) at FSUS. The art department functions in the capacity of art and graphic design consultant. My students and I work alongside the researchers engineers to develop an interactive CD ROM, teacher/student guidebook, and classroom manipulatives to teach middle school students about magnets and magnetism. The results for the students include an enriched comentoring experience, an expanded integration of new technologies, and the application of innovative learning materials.

Bridge to a new pathway

Mentoring relationships, partnerships, and activities create those threads that weave a complex image of myself as a mentor-teacher. This unfolding composite of people, places, and events has influenced my life and career, my bridge to a new pathway. Similarly, author Kazantzakis has defined teachers as "those who use themselves as bridges, over which they invite their students to cross; then having facilitated their crossing, joyfully collapse, encouraging them to create bridges of their own" (in Canfield and Hansen, 1996, p. 113).

A further development of this metaphor involves sustaining the bridge by adding or leaving a footbridge, or an anchoring thread, to allow students to return for a visit, often a reminder as to why they crossed the bridge in the first place. Many of us are superstitious about burning or destroying those important bridges in our lives. We know from experience that a day may come when we need *that bridge.* As someone once said: "Some people come into our lives and quickly go. Some stay for a while and leave footprints on our heart and we are never the same" (source unknown, in Canfield and Hansen, 1996, p. 134).

Amelia, my protégé and mentor, was the rare one that entered and was quickly gone but her impression on me will remain for a lifetime. The "bridge to new pathways" that we built for each other are enduring. FSUS has established a student scholarship in Amelia's name so that she may continue to touch the lives of others. My relationship with Amelia reminds me of one of her favorite poems by Robert Frost about how "I took the [road] less traveled by/And that has made all the difference" ("The Road Not Taken," 1916/1971, p. 223).

The role of mentor inspires students and teachers to color outside the lines in search of the road less taken.

12 Discovering Mentoring Relationships: A Secondary Teacher's Reflections

Margaret L. Ronald

How can a language teacher use the concept of mentoring as a vehicle to better understand students, to improve classroom effectiveness, and to progressively evolve as a professional? In this chapter, I explore new classroom meanings and nuances of mentoring. I apply these to help me develop enhanced relationships with my students and to learn more about their readiness and capabilities to learn. New learning approaches are also introduced, including a "culture wheel" which allows me to improve the teaching of culture as part of a language class.

A student's insightfulness

Several months ago, while shopping in a local supermarket, I ran into a former student who was stocking the dairy section. He remembered me before I realized who he was. It had been 12 years since we had crossed paths, and now he was working in Tallahassee, some 600 miles north of his childhood home.

"Hello. Ms. Ronald?," he broached tentatively.

I peered across my shopping cart.

"Remember me?," he asked. "You were my Spanish teacher in Okeechobee."

I went back over my years of teaching until I recalled my first year in Florida. "Yes, but I don't remember your name," I admitted.

He reintroduced himself and added that I had been one of the teachers who had made a lasting impression on him. "You always used to walk the aisles. When we were taking a test you'd stop and point out something that needed more work," he said.

"I used to feel funny about that," I admitted. "I knew it was a test, but I wanted you to do as well as you could."

"No. That was nice. I learned more that way," he said. Then he laughed and commented, "at least I learned to take my time and think things over." He paused and added, "You made us feel like we were all important. I was sorry when I learned you'd taken another job and weren't coming back."

We talked more. Later it struck me that it was not what I was *supposed* to have taught him – Spanish – that he remembered with fondness, but rather my treatment of him and his fellow students. Reflecting on my life as a student, I too recalled that it was not the subject matter that I mostly learned, but rather bits and pieces of advice combined with how well I had been treated and the ways in which teachers had acted. These all left lasting impressions on me. Those that were favorable impressions were "gifts" (Gehrke, 1988).

Joining the comentoring group

These reflections might have just come and gone had it not been for Carol Mullen who spoke at one of our faculty meetings in September 1997 about her interest in forming a group to explore mentoring relationships at The Florida State University School (FSUS).

"I am too busy," I argued with myself as I contemplated joining the Wednesday group sessions. In addition to teaching full time; serving as the foreign language department chair; working on several school committees; and trying to complete my doctoral course work at Florida State University, I was a single parent of two teenage daughters. "Another commitment would be one too many," I convinced myself.

Several days later I sought out Eileen McDaniel, the school's elementary principal and group member of Carol Mullen's new comentoring, writing, and publishing team. Though I teach in the high school, Eileen is someone I have frequently turned to for advice. She listens thoughtfully and has always been helpful. This time, I was concerned about a group of students who had been scheduled to take Spanish I in 18 weeks instead of the traditional 36-week period. Many of the students were 9th graders, academically weak, and not highly motivated. Several were enrolled in the drop-out prevention program at the school.

"How can I ensure these students' success?" I asked Eileen.
Her advice to me was to join the comentoring group to find some direction. I was reluctant, so I sought a second opinion in Lori Franklin, one of the school's media specialists who had been attending the group sessions. Her enthusiasm for the group's project was as contagious as the smile she shot my way at the next meeting.

I left that session feeling uplifted but also somewhat overwhelmed as I contemplated the much greater role that it appeared I had been playing as a teacher – that of mentor. I reflected on the many "gifts" I had received from mentors as well as having given as a mentor. I saw that I had in fact been thinking too casually about these special gifts. Only then did I realize that the course of my life had involved a mosaic of mentoring relationships (Darling-Hammond, 1986) with fellow teachers, graduate students, graduate professors, my own students, and, most recently, the Partnership Support Group. I decided to further investigate the potential of the mentoring process, hoping that a deeper understanding of mentoring would allow me to benefit more from my own teaching and learning relationships.

To explore mentoring in the classroom I studied my teaching during the 1998 year at FSUS (commonly referred to as Florida High).

Learning about mentoring

To start my own action research project, I wanted to know more about mentoring. I read articles that dealt with peer mentoring, and mentoring in the graduate school setting and the business arena, but few touched on the secondary classroom teacher's relationships with students. I searched for clues to what I might uncover about the mentoring relationship between myself and my students.

Certainly, Merriam's (1983) discussion of mentoring as a powerful emotional interaction between an older and younger person fit my situation. My first year of primary teaching in Brazil had made me all too aware of this phenomenon. I recalled many nights when I had lain awake worrying about how I could successfully reach a particular student.

Erikson (1950) has approached mentoring as a way to resolve the issue of generativity and stagnation. This researcher defines generativity as an interest in guiding the next generation. I have seen this advocacy for students expressed by those colleagues whom I most deeply respected. This concern was also something I felt I should investigate in my own teaching.

Levinson (1978) views the mentor relationship as one having characteristics of both the parent–child relationship and peer support, without being either exactly. This definition was meaningful for me. I recalled several of my students who had inadvertently called me "Mom" in class before asking a question. They had made me realize how closely my parenting relationship with my own daughters was tied to my teaching. On the other hand, I have observed many teacher-interns and beginning teachers who were having difficulty leaving the student role behind to assert themselves as teachers. The peer-like relationships these younger teachers had established with their students were fraught with confusion and difficulty.

Levinson (1978) also appreciates that mentoring is multifaceted. He said that mentors are teachers, sponsors, developers of skills and intellect, guides, and exemplars. As a secondary teacher, I readily saw myself playing all of these roles. And, as I reflected more upon my life as a teacher, I began to wonder just how much of it was teaching and how much was mentoring, and whether the two can even be separated.

The first step, I decided, was to determine what types of mentoring relationships were occurring in my life and, as Merriam (1983) suggested, to investigate them in their totality. Her comment about the ongoing quality of these relationships directed me to look both in and out of the classroom, and even beyond the school arena. Merriam (1983) further suggested that the research focus might be on the "dynamics of the relationship itself, the motivations behind the formation of such relationships, the positive and negative outcomes, [and] the reciprocity of the relationship(s)" (p. 171).

As I continued to read, I realized that my teaching/learning relationships represented informal mentorships. I had never been told that as a teacher I would mentor. I recall a time when an administrator where I had formerly taught had explicitly counseled teachers against providing emotional support for their students.

"This was the role of the guidance counselor, and a very shaky area for the untrained professional, the teacher," he had said.

I remember shaking my head. That year I was teaching a Spanish IV/V class to a mixture of Latin-American students who had been assigned to me in desperation. Few of them spoke English well enough to academically succeed in other classes, and support for their English language skills was just being developed. As I looked back, I discovered that most of my time with this group was spent counseling. One boy had impregnated two girls; all three were desperate for advice but none spoke English well enough to find help elsewhere in the community. One girl from Mexico had no place to sleep and no shoes to wear. Another was looking for health care for her sick mother. Besides working with the students' English skills, I provided shoes, located health care, and visited families. I was welcomed to *quinceañeras* (15-year old birthday parties) and other fiestas. Looking back I realize that I was primarily a mentor to those students. Now I am aware that mentoring implies imparting values, socializing individuals, and providing emotional support (Blackwell, 1983).

Since then I have realized aspects of my mentoring of many other students, but the role of mentor has never been made explicit to me. It is certainly not included in the current Sunshine State Standards that guide curriculum in Florida. Still, if mentoring is essential to success in the academic environment (Merriam, 1983), what mentoring is, who will be a mentor, and who is to receive mentoring, should be more clearly defined.

Mentoring in the secondary context is not even available to all students. Some qualify for special assistance, drop-out prevention, or tutoring, and accordingly are assigned mentors. Other students, especially those gifted and motivated, search for mentoring relationships with an adult or teacher. But there are many students, who neither qualify for special assistance nor are assigned advisers, who do not search out mentors. They probably experience less academic success than they might under different circumstances. Possibly these students lack the skills needed to relate with adults comfortably enough to form alliances across status differences. Perhaps they are unable to find a suitable mentor, especially if they are minority students and/or female. Some of these students may establish a peer-support system, or a "mentoring mosaic," but others may be unable to initiate or maintain any system of support.

When I read that mentoring enhances job success and advancement, I knew that my role as a mentor was particularly relevant to my new students. I began my investigation.

Research and reflection

My first job was to limit the scope of the research. I decided to look only at my first period – the first-year Spanish class that was scheduled to meet for only 18 weeks, 80 minutes each day. At that time, I was teaching two other first-year classes.

Next, I looked at how I would go about the research. I determined I would keep a daily journal; occasionally ask students to keep a journal in response to questions; analyze all the materials I used for teaching and assessment; and reflect upon student notebooks and assignments. To further aid my study, I would use a tape-recorder, and the observations, both verbal and written, of two colleagues, one a fellow Spanish teacher and the other an experienced substitute teacher. I also made use of a number of college students who observed me as part of an education class at FSU. Since I regularly speak with students and parents, teachers and counselors, I decided to jot notes during conversations to aid my reflection.

The school setting

At first I regarded a description of the setting as frivolous. I had worked at Florida High for five years and felt that while a description of the setting may be of value to my reader, it would not be of much use to me. But, I was wrong. Writing contextually made me more aware of my surroundings. As I talked about my writing with the comentoring PSG I was intrigued by one observation in particular: "It really gives you the picture of an inner-city school." These words appalled me at first. I had never thought of Florida High as an inner-city school. A school in downtown Tallahassee, yes. But an inner-city school, with inner-city problems? Well, no!

"Florida High" is situated south of the College of Education. Visitors find parking a scarce commodity. If they have a university parking decal, jokingly referred to as a "hunting license," they can legitimately search for a space. A glance to the east reveals new landscaping and the fresh brick of a new media library building – the Knowledge Center.

As visitors walk south, they pass a new sign that reads "Administration, K–12 Classrooms, Auditorium" in garnet and white, the university school's colors, and looking up they will see a larger, rather faded Florida High sign atop a brick, concrete, and paneling sign, again in garnet and white. (This sign is visually depicted in Chapter 14.)

As visitors continue their walk, they will discover three major wings running east to west. The northernmost wing is the primary level; the second, the middle school; and the third, a two-story wing, is the high school.

Diary entry: 14 January 1998

It's 7:05. I parked to the north of the school. At this early hour, students huddle with sweatshirts pulled over their knees. (Although students are not supposed to be on campus before 7:30 am many are dropped off much earlier.) Older students have already found places out of the wind while some younger ones crowd the cafeteria door. If any of the support staff has arrived, the front office will be open. I will check my mailbox before heading to the computer lab for coffee and conversation. (I treasure this time, as some days it is my only chance to speak with adults until the school day is over.)

At 7:45 I head to the classroom where I teach my first period. Middle-school students, with their orange crossing-guard bands, are raising the US and State of Florida flag on the central flagpole. Children are walking the covered cement corridors, clustering around picnic tables, walking in and out of the front office, and huddling against walls. The grass is worn in sections but crepe myrtles, podocarpus, and other child-resistant plants are surrounded by mulch in railroad tie-edged beds.

With my paper load I try to avoid the crowds by walking through the corridor of the middle-school wing. Going east, I skirt ballplayers and clusters of students who do not spread apart for the flow of traffic. When I get to the end of the corridor, I veer south. The pavement slants before reaching the soda machines that students are plying with quarters and punching. Though the machines are supposed to be on timers to prohibit their use until after lunch, many times these are not functioning. Sodas become breakfast.

There is the usual crowd in front of the girls' bathroom. It parts and I walk around the corner to the stairwell. Midway up the stairs I meet the "F . . . Y . . ." greeting scrawled in chalk on the brick wall. (As many times as this sign has been washed, it magically reappears.) On my way back down the stairs to run an errand, I am greeted by obscene drawings etched in the dust above the red metal middle-school lockers located on the ground floor.

Once upstairs again, I see Andy and two of his buddies, Hank and Joe (three of my Block I students). They have been hanging out in front of the classroom door, their heavy backpacks stacked against the wall. My office and the language laboratory are located one door down. I head there to unload paperwork. I scramble for my keys, unlock the room, and then my office where I begin to organize. I grab my attendance and grade books, the Spanish text, and other materials I need for the Block I class. I check the office passageway between the lab and the class and, finding it locked, I head back into the corridor.

Andy and Joe greet me. "Buenos Días. ¿Cómo está Ud.?" (Good morning. How are you?) I unlock the door and turn on the lights. The boys go in and Hank runs to turn on the heat. It is cold.

The room is large, dirty, and disorganized. There is not enough storage. Older textbooks, desks, and broken materials have accumulated in corners. There is a large picture window that looks out onto the FSU campus. To the south there is a high row of windows and several are broken. There are two chalkboards, a smaller and a larger, older and pitted one – the front of the room for students. A large table sits parallel to this chalkboard. It is usually cluttered with work from the previous day. Against the front chalkboard there are four pull-down maps of Hispanic nations. To the back of the room, there is a bulletin board and an office. There are 6 rows of desks, 6 to 7 desks long, and about 10 more desks and chairs, in various states of disrepair. I teach in this space one period a day.

Teacher as researcher

Teachers and administrators at FSUS typically wear a number of hats not needed at other public schools. One important function required is to conduct research and disseminate results throughout the state. FSUS refers to this work as "teacher as researcher." We pilot new programs; stretch to bring new materials and technologies into the classroom; and assess how well new innovations work. This aspect of teaching at the school is the one that most intrigued me when I interviewed years ago. I find my role as researcher to be the most demanding, but also highly reward-ing. Research, the accumulation of data, and ensuing analysis are time-consuming. Writing, presenting at conferences, and publishing are even more so.

I constantly find myself facing new issues as a professional. Even now, as I turn back to my description of FSUS, I find myself facing issues of mentoring that would have been more comfortable for me to ignore. It would appear that if I am an "exemplar," so is the setting where I work. This proposition puts me in an awkward situation. As a teacher without a classroom, I am frequently placed in uncomfort-able situations in which I have little control. Where I have been able to stretch myself, I have made some changes. After rereading the section about the middle-school lockers, I dusted the tops to erase the obnoxious "artwork." I also have washed the brick wall in the stairwell. Within classrooms I have borrowed bulletin board space when possible and even changed the seating arrangements.

Developing relationships with students

Introducing myself

How do I go about establishing relationships with students? To find out, I examined my journal reflections and materials used for class.

Though Block I meets for 80 minutes, I used the first two meetings for organ-izational matters and introductions. One of my priorities at the start of a term is to have students begin to know who I am and for me to know who they are. I use a number of tools to help me. The first handout I used is a short autobiographical statement of my educational philosophy. I let students know that Spanish was not my native language, and that I learned it as a second language, beginning just like they, in school in the United States. I shared my experiences with migrant students in California where I was fortunate to have Spanish twice a week in 6th grade. I emphasized that I only learned how to communicate in Spanish once at a college in Mexico. There I had the opportunity to hear and speak the language daily. Later, I realized that I felt it was important for my students to understand that successful second language learning can *begin* in the high school classroom. However, fluency develops only when a person has the opportunity to become immersed in the language.

I also talked about my family's emigration from the US to Brazil in 1970. This experience, I explained, gave me an opportunity to learn Portuguese. I discussed the process of acquiring both a second and third language – of learning how to learn a language. I believe that my students needed to realize that learning a lan-guage is not something impossible, like climbing a glass mountain, and that speak-ing a second language is the norm for many people.

As I talked about myself, I added that while a high school student in Hawaii, I had been one of the only "haoles" (white people) in my classes. In retrospect, it dawned on me that I had added this point once the ethnic diversity of the group became apparent. I probably shared in this way because of my feeling that there exists latent racial suspicion in Tallahassee. If the teacher is white, many black students seem to assume there will be a bias against them; if the teacher is black, many white students seem to feel the same way. At the end of the semester, when I analyzed my data and spoke with some of my fellow graduate students at FSU who had conducted research at the lab school, I found they observed the same pattern. Like myself, once they had successfully developed relationships with students, racial suspicions would disappear.

Analyzing student data

On the third day, I asked students to answer questions on index cards. Questions included their full names, nicknames, social security numbers, parents' names (first and last because of divorce and stepparent situations) and telephone numbers. In addition I ask them, which parent would you prefer I call?; why are you taking Spanish?; what is your 5-year goal?; and what is your 10-year goal?

In this class, five students had nicknames and one student preferred spelling her name differently than it appeared on the school roll. Nicknames are a good place for me to begin looking at how students regard themselves. It is also a good time for me to talk about the use of diminutives in both English and Spanish. One student, a large football player who was one of the oldest in the class, had written "Johnny." "In Spanish the "y" or "ie" becomes "ito," I explained, and "it is used as a term of endearment or to indicate smaller size." Johnny quickly decided he preferred to be called "John."

Knowledge of a social security number sometimes gives me insight into a student's maturity level. In this group, 37 per cent did not know their social security numbers. Most of these students were in the 9th grade (18 in total); only four of the 27 had outside jobs. Realizing a student has a part-time job is important; it explains why someone has insufficient time to do homework and feels tired in class.

Parents' names can give me some insight into complicated family relationships as do home and work numbers. Realizing there is a single-parent relationship can help to explain behavior. One student wrote, "Father dead." With investigation I later found out that the father is alive, but evidently not for that student. A different last name on the part of the mother sometimes indicates a new marriage, divorce, or return to a maiden name. I always ask which parent the student would prefer me to talk to when I do call home. Four students, though living with both parents, had distinct preferences. These preferences were evidence of tension between students and their parents. After talking with some teachers and the school counselor, I decided to honor their requests unless a situation arose where both parents needed to be informed. In the case of two students, I found mother and father had different home numbers. These students rotated households which is why they came to school somewhat unprepared. In one case, a student lived with her grandparents, one of whom was frequently on campus.

Only five students (19 per cent) were highly motivated to take Spanish. Another five students were somewhat motivated, realizing that two years of a foreign language is a college prerequisite. The remainder would rather have been taking another school subject. When this information was coupled with responses to the questions about their 5- and 10-year goals, a more accurate picture of academic motivation emerged. More than half of the 27 students responded, "I want to graduate from high school." Only four students indicated having a long-term goal. Writing goals is a big step for 9th and 10th graders; yet, highly motivated students are usually looking ahead. After examining the student profiles, I saw that less than half of the students were motivated to study Spanish.

I had to pass out report cards during the first week that contained the final grades for first semester classes. The overall grade point of this group was 2.2. There were three honor roll students. The students readily passed around their report cards. They seemed nonplused about the high numbers of Ds and Fs. This gave me the impression that the students with low grades were accustomed to receiving them. In fact, only one student complained, "You shouldn't look at our grades!" I explained that it was important for me to know how they were doing in other classes, even though grades were not the only criterion I used for assessment.

The culture wheel

Becoming familiar with students is crucial to the formation of an informal mentoring relationship, but this is difficult in the secondary classroom where teacher and student may work together for only 18 weeks. To speed up the process, I used another tool, a culture wheel (see Figure 12.1), which I adapted from one in use at The University of Michigan. The wheel allows me to teach about culture, an important part of a language class. This mentoring tool also enables me to learn who my students are individually and as a group. It helps me to encourage students to realize that while they are different they share many similarities. The culture wheel activity centers the individual within his or her culture. Once completed, a student can see that he or she belongs to different subcultural groups within a larger culture. When several cultural wheels are finished, they can be interlinked to show similarities among students.

I modeled the process by placing the class as a whole on the wheel. We completed the outside spokes where possible. All agreed that we were English speakers, members of the same school, state, nation, and geographic area. We went further to explore our race, religion, ethnicity, images, possessions, preferred foods, and social relationships. We found that while we varied, we had many similar values. "These variations," I explained, "are the subcultural groups we find ourselves a part of. These impact our personality and change over time."

Completed wheels allowed others to look at how we saw ourselves, to see who we thought we were. As a teacher and mentor, I find this mentoring tool is extremely valuable. In the past, I typically learned about my students gradually, never becoming aware of some vital things. Having everyone make a wheel allows me to glimpse inside each student, and each person to see another. The culture wheel activity enabled this Spanish language class to talk about who we were and what was important to us. I feel this tool had the effect of uniting us into a more cohesive

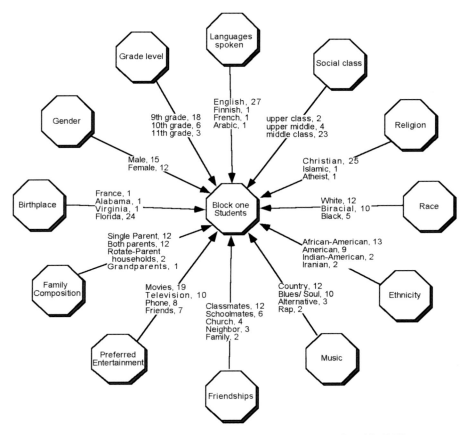

Figure 12.1: A culture wheel mentoring tool (Margaret Ronald, 1998)

group. This proved crucial for later when I was to struggle to understand some of the students' disagreements.

When the wheels were completed, I discussed them with the FSUS–FSU comentoring group. Later Carol Mullen reviewed my results. She was able to suggest further ways for me to investigate my mentoring role. Carol has written on the concept of "cultural identity development" in her work with mostly white university students. In her former preservice teacher classrooms, Mullen (1999) used personal ethnic maps and student performances to encourage identity construction and transformation.

Evolving as a teacher

Mentoring requires a constant conversation between the mentor and the mentee. Reading over my journal entries, I saw that as I became more involved in assessing students' knowledge of Spanish, I had lost touch with them as individuals. I had allowed the subject matter to become a barrier. Realizing this, I changed how I presented material. For instance, instead of relying on my "tried and true" method of introducing *gustarse* (to be pleasing to someone), I changed my assessment to group interviews and oral introductions. This allowed students the opportunity to talk, experiment with language, and learn more about each other. I can see that my reflections and changes improved my teaching – and my mentoring capacity too. When I was a beginning teacher, I had constantly reflected on my work, but this lessened over time.

I was relearning that my evolution as a teacher had to be on-going. In Pollard and Triggs' (1997) book, I found "recipes" for getting to know my students better. One tip seemed simple, and it required that I record my students' names without looking at the roll. "Okay," I said to myself, "27 students, 27 names." I quickly wrote 23 but couldn't remember the last four. I wondered why. The next day I discovered that two of them were quiet, but this did not explain the other two.

The student in the front whose name I had forgotten was quiet. He never volunteered an answer and did not talk to anyone. Despite his ostentatious hairstyle, I had allowed him to melt into the background. I thought about his hair. I had not known how to treat him and, as a result, had just ignored him. The next day I asked how he did his hair and how long it took. This seemed to relax us. From that day on, he was very much part of the class. The other, a girl, was a hard worker but was having difficulty. To cover this up, she was quiet. After I reviewed her work I took her aside to suggest she attend the after-school laboratory help sessions. She did so regularly, with struggle, but I had at least opened a door for her. She began volunteering in class.

I was realizing that the better I knew a student, the more effectively I could teach and mentor that person. Looking for other means to discover who my students were, I discussed related issues with a colleague of mine. "Who are your students' friends?," he asked me. He recited a Spanish proverb, *"Dime con quien andas y te digo quien eres."* (Tell me who you hang out with and I'll tell you who you are.) At his urging, I began studying the relationships my students had developed both in and out of class.

I found that two students, Andy and Hank, were frequently together and talked before class. Andy had been at FSUS since Kindergarten while Hank was new to the school. Hank appeared to have few other friends at school; though highly motivated academically, he was struggling. By the 9th week of class, I did not see Hank and Andy talking together before class. I ran into Hank later and asked him where Andy was. "Andy's mom drops him off at school at 8:00 in the morning," he answered. "I just hang around with anybody," he added, shrugging. Apparently his relationship with Andy had hinged on Andy's early arrival. Concerned about Hank's apparent lack of friendship and progress, I called home. His mother recognized that he was needing a Spanish and math tutor. She was a strong parent-mentor. With her help I felt Andy would succeed, despite his lack of peer mentors.

Another friendship I recognized was that of four students in my class who socialized constantly in class, at lunch, at the mall, and during extracurricular activities. They supported each other in both constructive and problematic ways.

All were freshmen and all but one, Clyde, were new to the school. Only one of the three new students had chosen to go to Florida High. Two of them, both girls, did not want to be here. Their parents had made the decision. Josephine, one of the followers, wanted to be at another high school. She was the only one in the group who had established a relationship with an established Florida High student, Bartholomew. Bartholomew was a highly motivated, honor roll student. Josephine told me, "If it wasn't for him, I wouldn't stay here. All my friends are at Godby" (the "other" high school).

Both Josephine and Bartholomew were from racially mixed backgrounds. Josephine was part Hispanic while Bartholomew was part black. Josephine's mother was upset by her choice of friends, saying "I don't want to appear biased but Josephine thinks she's black. She always hangs around with blacks. I don't think she knows who she is." I consulted with Carol Mullen (1997a) and read her article on the professional development of Hispanic preservice students. I learned that Hispanic students sometimes associate and identify with other nonwhite, ethnic students. This insight enabled me to better work with Josephine.

Rebecca was the leader of this group. A tall girl of mixed racial background, Rebecca was loud and disruptive. When she was not able to control her friends' behavior, she became more disruptive. The two boys in this group were Clyde and Stevie; Clyde was resentful in class. Instead of taking out his books, he would grab his backpack and place it on the desk under his head.

When I called home, his mother said with hostility, "Clyde says you don't care about him." Determined to make a difference, I continued to involve Clyde in activities even though he did not respond. He began arriving tardy. When I again called home, I encountered his mother's despairing voice: "I don't know what to do. Clyde's acting this way in all his classes."

Unfortunately, Clyde's behavior had begun to influence the others in his group. Rebecca stopped doing homework and acted out more in class. Occasionally, Stevie would refuse to do homework, and would walk around when others were working. Even when I placed Stevie, Clyde, and Rebecca in different corners, they continued to be disruptive.

When I called Stevie's parents I learned that they were aware of the negative attitude their son was developing. They wanted to help me. After reflecting on my students' journals, my own journal, and those of observers, I realized that John, who sat next to Stevie, needed help. John, the football player introduced earlier, was having great difficulty in school. One day I took Stevie aside. I explained that John was too proud to ask for his help but that I had placed Stevie where I did with the hope that he would take on a gentle leadership role with John. Days later, Stevie was going over John's work with him. A peer mentorship was being established.

After this incident, I was fortunate to run into Stevie's brother who echoed the concerns of his parents. He also admitted that since he had married, moved out of the family home, and had had children of his own that he rarely had time to play the "big brother" role. This sibling relationship was an obvious source of a potentially powerful mentoring experience for Stevie. He promised he would speak with his brother. It was about mid-semester before I noticed any changes. Stevie had turned around; his grade had jumped from 56 per cent to 93 per cent. It appeared that a web of mentoring connections was supporting Stevie and also John.

Toward the end of the semester I took my daughter to a school play at FSUS called "Bye, Bye, Birdie." Here I discovered another side to Clyde. "What a performer!" I thought to myself. "He could act and make people laugh. He was wonderful, especially when he sang, "Oh, What do you do with these kids today?" After the play I complimented him on his strong performance, and I later praised it in class. Gradually Clyde began to respond, but I had reached him too late.

Despite my feelings that I was unsuccessful in creating an atmosphere where peer-mentorship would flourish, student journal reflections provided another perspective. Student comments included statements like: "I learned how to treat people nice when they are trying real hard"; "You can work with people you don't want to work with"; and "Difficult people are not as hard to get along with as long as you try."

Issues of respect

When establishing relationships with anyone, there has to be respect. My "data" tells me that I worked to establish and promote respect over the entire semester that bridges this story. I define respect very broadly. For instance, if you respect someone you will not interrupt him or her. To my students I emphasized that there are many ways to "interrupt," such as asking someone who is busy a question without observing what is happening. Other examples include cracking gum, tapping pencils or feet, not being on task, or interrupting another's concentration. I explained that even raising your hand while making noise, like "Me, me, me" is a form of interruption. "Many times," I said, "just by continuing to listen, your question may be answered." I also said that at such times they should record their questions so they can remember them.

Despite such explanations, interrupting was a persistent problem in this second language class. Two students in particular would ask similar questions before class had started; I knew that others would have the same questions. I would ask them to "save" their questions until class began. Initially, both students were irritated by this request but learned that I will call on students to ask questions as soon as the class settles.

The number of interruptions that occurred during listening comprehension exercises was also a problem. The audiotapes I played as practice exercises were very difficult for the beginning students and they require patience. If students practice listening, the exercises become easier. However, if students constantly interrupt, they break their concentration. Listening is a skill many of these students do not have in English. Continued practice, occasional reminders, and consistent modeling on my part, helped to make this level of inattentiveness less of an issue. Students' reflections in journals enabled me to realize that they were learning how to handle these activities and how to benefit from them. Eleven students wrote, "I have to pay attention more." Three wrote, "You have to listen at all times." Two others said, "You have to be quiet."

Put-downs were another concern of mine. Most high school students find put-downs difficult to cope with. One day, Rebecca's friends were not reacting to her jokes so she laughed at them whenever they made a mistake. During an activity where I had students check their quiz answers against their own notes, Josephine asked, "What if you don't have notes?" Rebecca laughed. Rebecca continued to look at others' notes, making derogatory statements. I asked her to stop talking and she laughed at me. When I called on her for a review answer, she said, "I don't know," and shrugged. I laughed at her. The class became silent. After letting the silence sink in, I said: "It really hurts to be laughed at. When we laugh at others, we're sending the message that they are too dumb to learn and that we are superior. We are also cheating them out of a chance to learn." This was difficult for me to say.

I made an effort to be fair with all of my students. One observer wrote that I use various methods to ensure that all students participate as equally as possible. I have also developed techniques to avoid calling on one student more than another. These methods of fairness are an integral part of my mentoring. As I reflected upon the feedback, I remembered overhearing a conversation between a new student and a former student.

"Did she ever write you up?" the new student asked. I had just issued this student a detention.

"Oh, yeah. She writes up anyone who does something wrong," the former student said.

Being fair by treating students equally is difficult but rewarding. I play games in class to increase cooperative learning and healthy competitiveness. I am conscientious about being consistent about who wins and who loses. Over time, the students usually insist that I give weaker students an advantage. It is they who ask that the rules be modified to further ensure fairness. One day Stevie suggested, "If it's a tie and they have never won before, why don't you let them win?" Students agreed that this rule should be made. One student wrote: "Those who need to be challenged should be and those who don't understand should be helped." By having responded to the students' demands for change, I had modeled respect for them.

I model respect by respecting my students. One day, two former honor students came into my classroom. One student looked around and said loudly upon leaving, "How can you deal with them?" I quickly responded in an equally loud voice, "This is my fun class." As I said so, I realized that it really was. They had challenged me. I had made a sincere attempt to get to know everyone. And, the class had experienced positive synergy.

It was then that I realized that Eileen McDaniel had exercised foresight. The Partnership Support Group had helped me to become a better teacher by facilitating my awareness of my role as both a mentor and learner.

Final reflections

When I began this reflective action project with the comentoring group I had mixed feelings. First, I had wondered whether the research would detract from my teaching.

But, I do not think it did. Despite the emotionally draining nature of this class, the final student grade average was 77 per cent. Importantly, I was able to reach some students I might not have reached otherwise.

Second, I had wondered if I would have the time necessary to do the action research required. In retrospect, I feel I have just scratched the surface. But, as I look back over the semester, I feel invigorated. As a professional I had begun to plateau. In my 14 years of teaching I had learned shortcuts. My research with the comentoring group made me aware of this paradox, which has convinced me to approach my learning differently.

Professional reflection on daily teaching and mentoring is extremely important but it is a deeply neglected area. As educators we are always being taught new ways to teach, but, as I learned from the comentoring group, we are not being explicitly taught to mentor. This research certainly made me more aware of this role in my own life. However, guiding someone when you do not know you are or where you are going is very difficult. Without some knowledge of self and of other, coupled with insight into how you actually teach and learn, mentoring becomes highly problematic. As one of student wrote, "There are things we need to know that we are not even aware of." The mentoring process can be a highly reflective area of study that needs to be investigated with patience and jointly with others.

Acknowledgments

I am grateful to my daughter, Seneca, and author William A. Kealy for turning my concept of the culture wheel into a graphic.

13 Mentoring Preservice Teachers: The Positive Impact of Professional Development Schools

Diane Sopko and Susan Hilgemeier

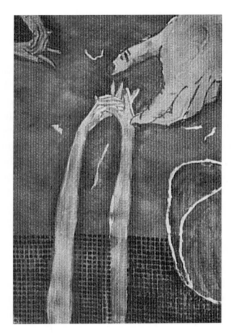

Figure 13.1: Hand that provides support to hands that aspire (Julie Johnson, 1998)

During many years of teaching in public schools, we saw new teachers come and go. Some novice teachers appeared to enter the classroom with the tools necessary for a successful first year, and others seemed less prepared for the task before them. As we observed these young people struggling to make meaning of the classroom, we remembered our own initiation into teaching and the personal isolation that we often felt in those early years. We remembered entering the classroom door and thinking, "Now what?" We thought we knew about theory but we did not know how we were going to use it on a day-to-day basis. Equally frustrating was not knowing whom to ask for help. Our new colleagues offered to help us in any way they could, but they really did not know what kind of assistance we needed. They could answer our questions when we figured what questions to ask, but they couldn't guide us in the right direction until we had a problem. Reflecting on our own teaching experiences, we realized that someone needed to "be there" for novice teachers, someone to mentor and nurture them through those difficult beginning years. As the opening artwork shows, hands were needed to provide support to hands that aspired (Figure 13.1).

Our search for mentorship was a personal and difficult one. Looking for a mentor or mentors to guide, nurture, and teach us was not easy. Sometimes finding the support we sought proved impossible. There were so many experienced teachers around us, yet the structure of the schools we taught in did not encourage symbiotic relationships in which novice and expert could collaborate to improve the practice of both. Even our student teaching practicums had limited mentorship possibilities – the luck of the draw. One cooperating teacher served as our model and adviser. That teacher had one semester to teach us how to run a classroom, to manage a room full of children, and to master the content we were required to teach.

Over time, our knowledge of teaching grew through trial and error, tips from the more seasoned of the faculty, inspiration from creative members, searches through teaching resource materials, workshops, and a desire to help students in our classrooms. Eventually we sought a more direct route for improving our own instructional strategies and knowledge of teaching by enrolling in master's degree programs. With these experiences behind us, we wondered how we could mentor and support the mentorship of preservice teachers as they navigated through the process of becoming teachers. Our desire to understand and improve the initiation of novices into the profession led us into teacher education.

A new kind of preservice teacher

Not long after entering graduate school, we both became involved in professional development schools (PDSs), where we had the opportunity to teach, observe, and mentor preservice teachers in action, on their way to becoming successful teachers. After working with many preservice teachers from both the traditional program and the PDSs, we intuitively sensed something was different about the young people "training" to become teachers in a professional development school program. We observed preservice teachers from PDSs who appeared to be confident, knowledgeable, and prepared. We talked with preservice teachers from PDSs who had a clear idea of what would happen in the classrooms they were preparing to enter as teachers for the first time. We observed preservice teachers who knew about children and learning and teaching. After brainstorming the possibilities, we arrived at one basic question: what is it about the professional development school experience that made these preservice teachers seem so well prepared?

To prepare preservice teachers for the classroom with more field experience than one semester during student teaching, the university in which we were studying and working had established several professional development schools (PDSs) based on the recommendations of reformers in teacher education (Goodlad, 1990; the Holmes Group, 1990; Sid Richardson Foundation Forum, 1990). Although the words "professional development school" have been attached to a wide range of concepts and practices, Goodlad (1995) concludes that "most commonly, they are used to convey the idea of a school that participates actively in the pre-service teacher education program of a college or university" (p. 7).

According to Darling-Hammond (1994), the PDS's aim is to provide new models of teacher education and development by serving as exemplars of practice, builders of knowledge, and vehicles for communicating professional understandings among teacher educators, novices, and veteran teachers. The professional development school concept holds promise for improving field experiences and for providing the preservice teacher with an opportunity for professional identity development. Such settings should enable the preservice teachers, like the students they will teach, to participate in multiple, complex, and concrete experiences essential for meaningful learning and teaching (Caine and Caine, 1994; Sylwester, 1995). Preservice teachers need to make connections between the theory they encounter in university classes and the way theory is interpreted in actual practice by classroom teachers (Abell and Roth, 1994; Book, 1994; Conant, 1951; Darling-Hammond, 1994; Goodlad, 1990; the Holmes Group, 1990, Sid Richardson Foundation, 1990).

We believe that the PDS setting may provide important experiences that help these novice teachers operate in an increasingly pluralistic society, understand how children learn, and discover ways to tap into that learning process (Caine and Caine, 1994; Gardner, 1993, 1995). Since preservice teachers need many opportunities to develop competent knowledge and practices essential for developing feelings of self-efficacy (Czerniak and Chiarelott, 1996; Darling-Hammond, 1994), we wondered what contributed to the self-efficacy of the PDS preservice teachers we observed. The structure of school-university collaboratives, we hypothesized, provided all the day-to-day diversity, complexity, and reality that beginners encounter in their first years of teaching and many opportunities for practicing teachers, university faculty, and peers in the PDS to mentor their professional growth.

Purpose of our PDS research

The three PDSs we discuss collaborate in partnerships with Texas A & M University. Each of the schools is located within a different school district in the surrounding area. While each school has a unique setting and structure, the schools prepare preservice teachers and also continue the education of experienced professionals to combine theory and practice. College students enter the PDS as interns the semester before student teaching to begin working in the real world of the school. The next semester they begin student teaching, assuming many of the responsibilities of the teacher. Some of the teachers in the PDS act as mentors for both interns and student teachers whereas others collaborate with university professors to teach college classes at the school campus. And, some of the teachers join action research teams to investigate concerns they have about their own teaching practices.

Looking at this complex real world, we began to wonder about how these schools affected preservice teachers who trained in them. We sought to understand the experiences that engage preservice teachers as they construct their personal understanding about teaching within the context of these PDS partnerships. In this chapter, we reflect on these questions:

- According to the stakeholders (preservice teachers, mentor teachers, and university faculty), which experiences enable preservice teachers to construct their personal understanding about teaching?
- Which experiences did stakeholders perceive as strengths for developing the preservice teachers' personal understandings about teaching? and
- Which experiences did stakeholders perceive as areas of concern in the preservice teachers' development?

Methods and tools of reflection

The data we used for this chapter comes from survey instruments developed by the National Education Association (NEA) for their Teacher Education Initiative (TEI) to analyze these specific PDS programs. In addition, we include interpretations of the PDS experience as perceived by focus groups and individuals interviewed in each of the three schools. Participation by preservice teachers, mentor teachers, and university faculty was voluntary. Survey codes identify the respondent (by number) and school (by letter) to provide an audit trail for researchers. Coding identifies individual respondents and their participation in focus groups. We examined data collected for the 1995–96 and 1996–97 school years. Two types of questions were used to gather data. One type consisted of direct questions with a Likert scale for responses; these questions were usually followed by an invitation for comments. Other questions were open-ended. During initial analysis, data from individual surveys were assembled and recorded on a master response sheet. Numerical data were analyzed using descriptive statistics. Written comments were analyzed for content using qualitative data analysis techniques.

Classroom teachers from each of the three PDSs, university researchers, and graduate students reviewed and organized the data. Work teams were formed from this group to read individual responses to each open-ended question and to organize the responses into viable categories (Erlandson, Harris, Skipper and Allen, 1993; Lincoln and Guba, 1985). The responses of multiple stakeholders provided triangulation and credibility to findings generated by the data (Lincoln and Guba, 1985). Our own reports generated on Texas A & M University's partnership with schools were reviewed by work teams for questions and categories concerning benefits, strengths, and concerns that participants held regarding the preservice teachers' experience.

While questions remained consistent each year, the wording chosen for many of the categories differed during analysis from year to year. This is, in part, due to the variations in work team personnel. Our analysis required a reexamination of data previously organized by other work teams. First, we reviewed tables from the studies and organized them to complete cross-group comparisons of findings for both years. All categories were reviewed for similarities and differences reported by all three groups of participants. Written responses were also reexamined for salient issues providing insights into the preservice teachers' experiences as constructed by those who have lived the experience, specifically, the preservice teachers, mentor teachers, and university faculty.

PDS participants

The participants in this study were all working within the context of the three PDS campuses as part of the university–school partnership program established with Texas A & M University and the three area school districts. The preservice teachers consisted of 50 interns and student teachers each for years 1 and 2. Survey responses did not indicate the status of the preservice teachers. Preservice teachers who were interns had not participated in the study previously. Student teachers may have participated as interns but we could not determine this information based on the surveys. The number of mentor teachers increased from 32 teachers in year 1 to 67 teachers in year 2. Mentor teachers mentored either interns or student teachers. Again, response forms did not indicate which type of preservice teachers was being mentored. Many of the same mentor teachers participated in both years of the study. The increase in numbers, however, implies that either mentor teachers were more willing to participate in the second year or the distribution and retrieval of surveys were more efficient. Although the number of university faculty was five for both years, faculty members may have been different in some cases.

Setting and on-site investigation

Each of the schools in this study identified the professional development of preservice and inservice teachers as part of their mission statements. Two of the schools in the NEA/TEI study were elementary schools within the College Station/Bryan area, and one was a junior high in a nearby rural school district. In one elementary school, 60 per cent of the faculty at that school served as mentor teachers. In the second school, all classroom teachers mentored a preservice teacher each semester. In the junior high, teachers worked collaboratively with the university to mentor preservice teachers as they developed and used interdisciplinary units. University course work was delivered on site by university faculty, graduate teaching assistants, classroom faculty, or a combination of these parties at each of the schools. The schedules, responsibilities, and experiences of preservice teachers were unique to each site.

Findings of teacher growth and development

The findings in the NEA/TEI study for the first two years suggest that the preservice teachers' experiences in these PDS sites provide an excellent opportunity for positive professional growth and development. Answers to survey questions concerning the quality of the clinical experience, the preparation of preservice teachers, and the comparison of PDS preservice teachers to their counterparts in traditional programs reveal a positive view of the PDS program. Since preservice teachers are taught by university faculty while they are observing the practices of inservice teachers, we closely examined responses in the study regarding the connection between theory and practice. The strengths of partnerships and concerns of participants were found in their responses to two questions. The first question is: "Overall, what do you feel are the strengths of the partnership (teacher education program)?" The second question is: "Overall, what do you feel are the weaknesses of the partnership (teacher education program)?" The responses to these questions were particularly enlightening because they provided an open forum for participants to present their point of view. Written comments were categorized inductively in the original analysis. We reexamined these comments and categories for further insights in the analysis of data. Categories found to be important to the research questions are discussed in the following sections. Each group of stakeholders is represented.

Quality of the clinical experience

The reader should keep in mind that the preservice teachers in the PDS schools are mentored by both practitioners and university faculty in the context of the school before they begin their student teaching semester. The preservice teachers also have the support and encouragement of their peers in the PDS. This situation encourages a community of learners comentoring one another as they share knowledge and experience. Many times, the preservice teachers expressed to us in personal conversations how valuable it was to have the support of not just one teacher, but many teachers; of not just one peer, but many peers. We therefore have concluded that the preservice teachers viewed this mentorship (and comentorship) as a valuable component of their teacher training program.

Mentor teachers and university faculty were asked to judge the quality of the clinical experience in terms of change when comparing the current partnership with the past traditional teacher education program. Sixty-two per cent of the mentor teachers in both years of the study believed that positive changes occurred for the preservice teachers. The primary reason they gave for positive change in the quality of the clinical experience can be attributed to the additional time that preservice teachers spend in the classroom. Positive change was viewed by some mentor teachers to be the result of the additional feedback given to preservice teachers by their mentor teachers concerning professional development.

Most of the preservice teachers in the first year of the survey thought that they received a quality clinical experience in PDSs that had a positive impact on their preparation to teach. In the second year of the study, the preservice teachers believed that there was an increase in the quality of their own experiences. The preservice teachers' comments reflect their perceptions of improvement in their preparation for work in the classroom. A small number stated that PDS clinical experiences were an improvement over those offered through a traditional program.

The preservice teachers' comments attributed the quality of the clinical experience to what they referred to as "great experiences" that they had in PDS programs without explaining further the meaning of "great experiences." We were unable to identify specific experiences that preservice teachers were referring to because they did not list them. The experiences to which they are referring, we believe, were those that they encountered on a day-to-day basis in the school and classroom where they were able to observe mentor teachers. "Witnessing teachers in action," was how one preservice teacher described this strength of the PDS. Some preservice teachers, however, were specific about what they believe contributed to the quality of their PDS program. One explained: "I gained hands-on experience, evaluated different discipline techniques, observed classroom management, [had] classes (TEED) taught by mentor teachers, taught lessons to students, [and] implemented my ideas in real situations, [in] classrooms." "The actual experience of planning, writing, and executing lesson plans," was important to another. One preservice teacher thought the great preparation was because they were able to "learn to write lesson plans and units, use all your classroom management skills learned, [and] get wonderful resources for the future."

Comentoring in the PDS

The comentorship that inservice teachers and university faculty can give to preservice teachers appears promising. The surprise and confusion that novices feel when they discover the the complexity of teaching can often be attributed to the simplistic representation of teaching in their university courses. Perhaps preservice teachers within a PDS appear less confused and more in touch with the "reality" of teaching because they encounter the real school with two support systems at the same time. They receive instruction in their education courses and methods courses from university faculty, as they observe and work with their mentor teachers in classrooms, where they "work with students first hand and observe [children's] interactions with teachers and peers" [preservice teacher].

This atmosphere enables the preservice teacher to form strong bonds with mentor teachers and maintain relationships with university faculty who are often seen by preservice teachers in traditional programs as out of touch with the reality of schools. Preservice teachers value their relationship with mentor teachers. One preservice teacher in our study commented that "Relationships with mentor teachers are priceless." Another preservice teacher agreed almost word for word: "The mentorship that comes from such a program is priceless." "Getting to work with so many quality teachers, watching them in action, and hearing their theories, strategies, and advice," were important strengths of the PDS according to one preservice teacher. One perceptive preservice teacher went much further in describing the relationship of the various stakeholders. She explained: "There is a unity between the college professor, the building principal, teachers, and cohort. There are a lot of personalities involved and this collaboration is still strong and desired. I enjoy the feeling of acceptance and appreciation the cohort is given."

All university faculty surveyed in both years believe the quality of the clinical experience had positive changes for preservice teachers because of the mentorship of inservice teachers. Preservice teachers, explained one university faculty member, "Saw many more connections between professors' claims and teacher actions and student outcomes. Preservice teachers are simply better prepared to be teachers. They have moved farther along the novice-expert continuum."

The contribution of inservice teachers to the development of the preservice teachers was also acknowledged by another professor who stated: "Preservice teachers have increased knowledge about how schools work. They have extended experience in the classroom. Inservice teachers are truly involved in the school experience." Preservice teachers were cognizant of how the classroom teacher provided them a model to observe and an opportunity to test what they learned from university faculty. "This program provided a lot of practical applications of the things we have learned in our theory [education] classes. I enjoyed the opportunity to teach the lessons I wrote," stated a preservice teacher. "The program also allows students to put all the theories that they have learned into practice," was another's comment. "We are able to be directly involved in a classroom," explained one preservice teacher, "to see how a class is run is definitely the strength of this program. Also, having our university classes so directly tied to our assigned classrooms."

Connections between theory and practice

Mentor teachers and university faculty were asked questions regarding increased connections that preservice teachers made between theory and practice in the PDS setting. Most of the mentor teachers who participated in both years of the study saw positive changes for the preservice teachers. Written responses indicate that the mentor teachers observed preservice teachers putting theory into practice. As one mentor teacher stated: "Explaining why and how you teach is self-revelatory." Another mentor teacher explained "theories become real when applied to actual situations."

University faculty, in both years, also saw evidence of positive changes in preservice teachers' ability to make connections between theory and practice. One of the university faculty members believes preservice teachers have opportunities for practical application of theory. This belief is supported by the comments of preservice teachers. One university faculty member, however, observed little or no change in the preservice teachers' understanding of putting theory into practice. Even though all groups believed there were some positive changes in this area, the university faculty did not believe that mentor teachers and university faculty were optimizing opportunities for preservice teachers to make better connections between theory and practice. Perhaps some of the mentor teachers in this study did not reflect on the role of theory in the decisions that they make in their planning and teaching. On the other hand, they may simply fail to articulate to their preservice teachers the role theory plays in their decision making or to use lay terms to describe the role of theory. After reviewing the data, we believe that open, synergistic discussion between university faculty and mentor teachers would promote a more reciprocal understanding of theory in practice and enable them to comentor preservice teachers more effectively.

Benefits of the PDS experience for preservice teachers

While many mentor teachers did not comment specifically about the benefits preservice teachers received in a PDS, others did reveal their thoughts regarding these benefits. When asked what the strengths of the programs were, mentor teachers in both years of the study responded that the practical, hands-on, real-life experiences in the classroom were valuable to the preservice teachers' professional development. A mentor teacher explained:

> The PDS allows the university student to experience the complex world of teaching over a reasonable and realistic span of time. Children become the focus for developing techniques for teaching concepts and results are vividly observed by the university student.

Some mentor teachers observed that opportunities to become familiar with school facilities and routines early gave the preservice teachers an advantage as student teachers. Preservice teachers could move into student teaching with practical knowledge behind them and could assume the responsibilities of a classroom teacher more quickly. Classroom management skills acquired during the PDS were also viewed as a strength. Imbedded in the PDS experience are many opportunities for preservice teachers to work with children and to observe and participate in instruction, either as a tutor, as an instructor with small groups of children, or as an instructor for whole class instruction. One mentor teacher gave this example of how personal experience prepares preservice teachers:

> Our student teachers experience a great deal of increased responsibility, because they are already familiar with [the school] layout, environment, and school policies. My student teacher's observation time was greatly decreased. She was actively teaching before student teachers in a traditional setting.

Another mentor teacher stated "They leave confident about student teaching! They have a repertoire of instructional and managerial tools for teaching based on experience." Another participant explained what she saw as an advantage for preservice teachers:

> I feel that more exposure to children is the biggest strength of the program. An advantage the PDS intern has over other students teachers who have not gone through a PDS school is, because they have been able to teach lessons, they are more prepared to student teach and do a better job at it.

Mentor teachers often perceive their roles as a positive influence. Much of the knowledge that a preservice teacher acquires during the PDS experience concerning routines, management, and instruction is attributed to exposure to the mentor teacher's model. The PDS experience was viewed by some as providing a more holistic view of the teaching profession. A shorter time in the school or a more traditional teacher preparation program may not have the same effect. One mentor teacher stated:

> College students are impacted in a very positive way through the partnership. They are a part of the daily school setting, and have much more time to work with teachers than in traditional settings where they come and go. They also see more instruction and have the opportunity to practice methods in this environment.

The mentor teacher's role was not limited to mentorships in the classroom. Some participants believe that classroom teachers who serve as course instructors were a positive influence. One mentor teacher explained: "They are being taught by professionals who are currently in the classroom rather than people [university professionals] who have been away from the classroom for years." Another participant stated: "The teachers who teach the courses are very knowledgeable and creative in their teaching." One mentor teacher was more democratic when discussing the contributions of different educators: "The program allows students [preservice teachers] to have input from both the college classroom and the classroom teacher to help them gain a broader perspective."

Stakeholders' concerns about the PDS experience

When asked to describe any weaknesses in the partnership (PDS), participants had fewer written comments than when discussing strengths. The greatest weakness perceived by all stakeholder groups was communication. Two mentor teachers thought the distance between the university and schools contributed to poor communication. "The weakness has been communication with the university. We feel removed, possibly due to the geographical distance between the sites." Another explained, "Communication – there is a need to meet more regularly to discuss concerns."

Some preservice teachers also saw communication as a weakness. "I felt there needed to be more communication between the university and the elementary schools," was voiced by a preservice teacher. "Communication between university liaison, school principal, mentor teachers, and preservice teachers is very weak," stated another. The number and per cent of comments citing communication as a concern dominate the responses of mentor teachers when they wrote about the weaknesses of the PDS programs. Half of the mentor teachers in the first year of the study and 40 per cent of the mentor teachers in the second year felt that communication among stakeholders was an issue. University faculty also listed communication as a concern. Slightly less than half of the preservice teachers in both years of the study felt that communication with parents was a weakness of the program. This perception may be because the preservice teachers interact with parents at the discretion of the mentor teacher.

Another area of concern of mentor teachers was the stress and demands of the PDS program on preservice teachers. A few preservice teachers had written comments categorized as feeling overwhelmed. What was most surprising was that the number of comments that fell into this category is so small. The demands of a full schedule of course work with all the reading, lesson plans, units, journals, and so on, were considerable. PDS students then spent the rest of the day immersed in the classroom activities. One preservice teacher captured the problem: "There is little time during the school day for the preservice teacher to work with other PDS [students] on projects, and so on, or their college classes." Another commented: "I know that we have a lot expected of us, but I wish we had more time or a longer semester to get work done." Our personal experiences working in PDS schools support this concern. We often heard appeals from stressed students who thought they had too much work to do for our teacher education classes and who did not get enough sleep. The availability of resources was a weakness expressed by each of the groups.

Increased feelings of teacher self-efficacy

We found evidence that preservice teachers in the PDS program gain increased feelings of self-efficacy. When preservice teachers in the first year of the study were asked how they would compare themselves to preservice teachers in traditional programs, their responses overwhelmingly reflect the value they give to the experience and the confidence they acquire as a result of the PDS experience. Forty-four of the 50 preservice teachers in that year thought they were significantly more able than traditionally prepared preservice teachers to enter teaching. The second year survey document did not ask this question of preservice teachers. Most often, preservice teachers' comments reflected feelings of self-efficacy. For example:

- "The feeling that everything I do is related to my class is awesome."
- "I feel like I am truly prepared to teach."
- "We gain confidence," and
- "You are more prepared and know what to expect when you begin student teaching."

Twenty-one per cent of the mentor teachers' written responses agreed with the preservice teachers'. Comments from them include:

- "I had a student teacher who had been through the program, her level of confidence and ability were much higher than traditionally trained preservice teachers."

- "These preservice teachers are more confident with their teaching strategies. They have already tried different strategies and they feel confident with small and large group teaching."

Mentor teachers in the second year of the study also expressed how confident PDS students are when compared to their peers in traditional programs.

One preservice teacher correlated time to improved teaching. "The more time you spend in the classroom the better teacher you will be," she said. Improved teaching strategies, we believe, may depend on more than time. Beyer (1984) points out that prolonged field experience seems to have the tendency "to produce and perpetuate strategies that are congruent with existing institutional and professional expectations" (p. 36). This would not be a problem if each PDS teacher or university instructor who serves as a mentor was using practices that were consistent with research in teaching/learning, reform efforts to introduce standards for content areas such as science, mathematics, and social studies, and recent research on the human brain. (See, for example, Caine and Caine, 1994; Sylwester, 1995). Even in less-than-ideal circumstances, the contribution of the PDS experience to the self-efficacy of the preservice teachers is important. Our own interactions with preservice teachers support this finding. Repeatedly, preservice teachers have shared their belief that the PDS experience served as a springboard for confidence. The experience they received in this context was critical in their development. The mentorship by many allowed them to emulate or reject the practices they observed in a reflective and supportive environment.

The PDS as today's reality

The purpose of our investigation was threefold: to identify experiences in PDSs that enable the preservice teachers to construct their personal understanding about teaching, to identify experiences in the PDSs that the stakeholders viewed as strengths, and to identify those experiences in the PDSs that concerned stakeholders. Since each preservice teacher's classroom, mentor teacher, and personal constructions of teaching are different, we must assume that each preservice teachers' experience and interpretation of that experience are unique.

Three findings

First, we can conclude that all stakeholders viewed the time the preservice teachers spent in the PDSs as valuable to their development as novice teachers. Less clear, however, is how that time was spent in each classroom and how the specific PDS experiences in the classroom that engaged them contributed to their development personally. As Goodman (1985) found in a case study of early field experience, what students learned depended upon a number of variables: "the individual student, the cooperating teacher, and the ecology of the classroom" (p. 44).

Based on their written responses we were able to place mentor teachers', university instructors', and preservice teachers' comments for both years of the study into several categories. Each group identified hands-on experience in the classroom as very important. In the classroom, they reported, preservice teachers encountered the reality of classroom management and developed personal relationships with children and other professionals. Participants also identified opportunities to observe instruction, plan lessons with their cooperating teacher and peers, participate in instruction, and reflect on their successes and failures as beneficial to the preservice teachers. Opportunity to observe a variety of teaching styles, to see master teachers in action, and to learn routines of the classroom and school were considered valuable. All of these experiences, we concluded, contributed to the construction of their personal understanding of teaching.

Second, some strengths in the programs were identified. All stakeholders viewed the extended length of time that preservice teachers spent in the classroom as one of the most important strengths of the PDS programs. Logically, one might infer: the more time they were able to experience teaching, reflect, and increase their understanding of what goes on in the classroom and the school, the more self-confident they grew. All of the experiences in the preceding paragraph were viewed as strengths by the participants. These experiences, we believe, contributed to the feelings of self-efficacy preservice teachers expressed. Participants thought the growth in self-efficacy of preservice teachers was a strength of the PDS program. There was also evidence that preservice teachers were able to make connections between the theory of teaching and practices of the classroom teacher. Another strength attributed to the PDS experience was the overall preparation of the preservice teachers for student teaching.

Third, those experiences identified as concerns were relatively few. Communication in several areas was cited by all groups as the major concern. The stress and demands made on the preservice teacher and the availability of resources and supplies were a concern for a small number of participants. Overall, few made comments concerning weaknesses in the PDSs. There were suggestions for program improvements at each site. The general consensus was that the PDS experience was one of quality that expanded the knowledge and understanding of preservice teachers positively.

The PDS experience for preservice teachers is promising, based on the data collected in the NEA/TEI study. We agree with Lortie (1975) who, in his sociological study of teachers, found that the opportunity to practice teaching "has the texture of reality. The [mentor] teacher is concentrating not on an ideal state of affairs but on the how of teaching, and . . . suggestions can be demonstrated" (p. 71). This idea appears to be the case for the preservice teachers in this study as well. In addition to their mentor teacher, preservice teachers were mentored by other practitioners and university faculty who were able to share their personal knowledge of teaching within the context of "real world" classrooms. The preservice teachers believed their PDS experience was in touch with the reality of today's schools and children.

The PDS as tomorrow's promise

We believe that the PDS program holds promise for creating well-trained, capable educators. Getting students into classrooms early in their educational careers; opening school doors for these preservice teachers so they can connect theories learned in the university to classroom events; and guiding students who believe in teaching-learning effectiveness are all critical components to the success of any professional development school. Mentoring, and in turn being mentored, by master teachers, peers, and colleagues in a PDS program may be one avenue for ensuring that preservice teachers know how best to engage our children because they have observed, tried, reflected, and learned. They have been *in* the classroom, not the least of which involves wiping noses and kissing banged-up knees, dealing with angry parents, and crying over lost puppies.

When these preservice teachers enter their own classrooms for the first time, they will bring with them all of the experiences and knowledge they have gathered along the way. They will also carry with them the legacy of their mentors to help prepare them for tomorrow. Goodlad (1990) states that "few matters are more important than the quality of the teachers in our nation's schools" (p. xi). The professional development school program holds promise in providing excellent teachers to teach the students of the twenty-first century.

During this writing reflection, we realized something that had arisen unexpectedly during our investigation of the PDSs. While the PDS's original intent was for experienced teachers to mentor preservice teachers, an added bonus emerged – comentoring. The mentors and preservice teachers began to mentor each other, contributing to the professional growth and development of one another. Experienced teachers undertook a dialogue among themselves about how to mentor more effectively, and also how to teach in a way that produced authentic learning. The preservice teachers discovered that their peers possessed valuable knowledge that they could use as well. The preservice teachers shared their stories, enabling peers to increase their personal understanding of the reality of schools. With expanded understanding came more effective teaching as well as better prepared teachers.

The comentoring that occurs among the different stakeholders in the PDS adds strength to strong and promising programs by enhancing the knowledge of all participating educators. Comentoring enables both inservice and preservice teachers to adopt a proactive stance to improve their own teaching and learning. University and school professionals have an opportunity to comentor and collaborate as they prepare better teachers for our nation's schools. Comentorship is symbiotic, a relationship in which novice, master, and higher education faculty are encouraged to share, and to learn from one another, in a trusting environment. Comentorship is a relationship that is open to the discovery of new knowledge that could improve the practice of all educators and, thus, benefit the children within our schools.

Our research related to professional development schools continues. We plan to investigate more fully the experiences of preservice teachers in a PDS to uncover how the experiences affect their teaching practices over time. We hope to follow many of these novice teachers into their careers to examine the impact of PDS training on the successes and failures they encounter in the world of the classroom. Through our research we hope to strengthen the voices of those who mentor and comentor. This way, we can help to create a fuller awareness of the important contribution that teacher mentors, preservice teachers, students, and others make to teacher education.

14   A Mentoring School Leader:
Successes and Trials of the Voyage

Edward M. Vertuno with Carol A. Mullen and
Fanchon F. Funk

Figure 14.1:   A sign of the times: A school's dual identity (William A. Kealy, 1998)

Being a leader of a K–12 school during the 1970s and 1980s was a challenging and awesome assignment. The educational, political, financial, and other battles were intense and difficult. Nonetheless, some leaders not only survived, but prospered in this environment. Why do some leaders succeed while others fail? Do mentoring and comentoring play important roles in the success of such leaders and their institutions? And, just how does a leader deal with the daily challenges and trials of operating a school and yet still find time, energy, and enthusiasm to serve effectively as the principal mentor for all sectors – including students, faculty and staff? This chapter relates the story of such a successful school leader who used his people-oriented mentoring style to help others build with him a synergistic, learning team approach to the affairs of a university school. Not only were he and his school effective during his lengthy tenure as lead mentor, but the comentoring environment of Florida State University School (FSUS) continues to thrive, even serving as a model for other schools.

My mentoring journey begins

After arriving at Florida State University School in the role of principal in 1971, I, Ed Vertuno, worked for one year with the director. During the second year the director became immersed in the Florida State University's presidential tasks. So, I performed in his capacity. During my third summer in 1973, the director became assistant vice president at FSU and I became the acting director. Soon I was appointed director of FSUS. For the next 17 years I was the school's leader.

In this chapter I look back with fondness on this highly influential time in my own professional development and particularly in the changing direction of FSUS. Like a ship that leaves port only to dock again, I continue to live with the excitement of the "trials of the journey" that this course through life has evoked for me. My research story was told to Carol Mullen and Fanchon Funk during their tape-recorded visit to my office in February 1998. That conversation has been recreated in order to narrate my memory of some of the critical events spanning my two decades spent at FSUS. I see myself as a storyteller, and so the effort in this chapter has been to capture the conversational tone, style, and language of my original telling.

Shaping influences

Historically, FSUS was "a demonstration school" like most other university schools in the United States. We were doing teacher education activities with hundreds of observers every day of the week, including those who taught methods courses. We had two kindergarten rooms with a space in-between that was wired for sound. We would put people in that room with two one-way mirrors, scheduling nine observers an hour from the area of elementary education. That's the kind of activity that we valued at FSUS; it's what we did that defined us. It was essentially a very routine school that also served as an "employment plum" for professors. When university faculty came to work at FSU, they would send their kids to us. The school had a largely white ethnic student population. More than 75 per cent of the kids had university-based parents.

In the 1960s the Board of Regents began to question the purpose of laboratory schools in general and whether they should continue to exist in Florida. The first thing that the Regents did was to debate, something like this:

"Well, we'll close the laboratory schools – they're not doing anything special anyway."

"But we're doing student teaching!"

"Yeah, but you can do that in the public schools, it's more realistic."

The FSU President and the dean of the College of Education at that time both had kids enrolled, which may (or may not) have had something to do with their decision to save the school.

When the mission of the school was redefined during the 1969–71 era, the Regents informed us that we would stay open if we could adapt to a research mission. Our progress would, additionally, be evaluated at each year. The Regents phased out most of the student teaching activities. They created a four-factor admissions policy – race, sex, IQ, and socioeconomic background – in an effort to match the distribution of students in the surrounding area. Some impact was immediately experienced. University faculty reacted emotionally when they learned that they would no longer receive an automatic invitation to send their kids to us.

That meant that the children of faculty were to be admitted like everyone else. There were parents to whom I had to say "no." They would respond, "I'll bet your kid is here," and I'd say, "No s/he's not." My oldest boy waited nine years before he was accepted at FSUS. This worked to my benefit because I didn't have to take any nonsense. I'm glad to say that the admissions' policy to FSUS has, from then onwards, been strictly administered.

The FSUS faculty experienced a great deal of turmoil. They had been hired for teacher education but were suddenly switched into a research mode for which they had little training, and even less interest and time.

When I came to FSUS in 1971, teachers with master's degrees were being hired. But while I was there, we hired those who also had five years teaching experience. We did make an exception for a Spanish teacher who had done student teaching with us and was "gang-busters."

As another change, an executive board was appointed which made final decisions on student admission and more. The board continued in that capacity for five years and then it became an advisory board. As a member, I would meet with the others once monthly, almost like a school board. This board had university representatives plus someone from the Commissioner's Office and the Leon County School Board. These people didn't have anything to do with us in the sense of control, but we wanted their advice and input; moreover, this connection gave us some respectability. We immediately ran into problems though. It proved very difficult for us to get relevant research from the university faculty, and they also began taking their research projects elsewhere. We also found it challenging to attract low-income and African-American students. As one response, we ran a school bus to bring children to FSUS.

More change

After I arrived at the school in the early 1970s, it underwent evaluations for the next few years. The Board of Regents decided whether or not we should receive appropriations. The other thing that happened was a significant change in the promotion policies affecting FSUS faculty. The criteria had been exactly the same for our teachers as for FSU faculty regarding publication and research activity. Under my direction, a change in policy was implemented, regarding tenure and promotion for school faculty, to reflect the kind of work that they actually do and contributions that they realistically can make.

About this time, we started to focus on promoting the school. I would go to the FSU departments and their faculty meetings to encourage colleagues to do research projects at the school. I said to my FSUS faculty that we needed to provide the appropriate conditions for research development. I encouraged them to see that the most uncomplicated role for them to play was to participate in facilitating others' studies. For a period of time our annual research report typically encompassed about 60 projects. Occasionally, a researcher would do something less than demanding, like watch a kid balance on a piece of gym equipment. At FSUS we were doing what was necessary to survive and gain respectability.

But our research development vision and course was not without severe tensions for me. For example, we had faculty members like our 55-year old kindergarten teacher who had given her life to FSUS. I knew that she, like most of the other teachers, was not going to suddenly write a book. She had kids from early in the morning to late afternoon. She didn't have the time or energy to be in the library every night because she needed time to recover from her day. To some extent, then, we also had to do what fit us, not just the university.

Then the Teacher Education Centers came into being, allocating money to purchase consulting services from university faculty. We took advantage of this opportunity, developing a core of teachers who did outside workshops. These teachers gained tremendous credibility while working extensively and even conducting workshops on weekends. So we "rode that horse" for a while, which seemed to satisfy people for a period of time.

We also had a brilliant teacher in mathematics who developed training materials to help teachers prepare kids for the state test in mathematics. This is one story of collaboration that I'm very proud of. I remember this particular teacher showing me the materials that he had developed. I was so overjoyed that I exclaimed that we were going to contact every curriculum person and department chair in the state to make the math curriculum available, and we did. He had put my name on his project and when I asked him to remove it he protested, but finally agreed. FSUS got recognition from that project. We promoted it all over Florida, and we were the first on that one! When I think about it, I was just running the place. It was the teachers who were doing the exciting work and making an impact.

Big payoff

In 1976, I went to the Panama Canal Zone with folks from various departments in the COE (College of Education), the University Graduate Dean, and the Dean of the Faculties. At the time, the COE ran a college program in Panama and a high school completion program. We returned from that trip with a contract to the effect that FSUS would provide all of the curriculum and guidance materials for that program. I was able to rotate my secondary faculty to Panama for this project.

On the way back from the initial trip to Panama, the dean of the faculties and I had an opportunity to talk. I let her know that the FSUS needed a special tenure and promotion track, judging faculty members on what they actually did as opposed to what the university was doing. She said, "Send me some ideas on it," and after then we implemented a process that is still in place. Despite changes, this process continues to reflect what the teachers are actually doing.

In the middle of all of these changes, I got a new director of research who worked with us, but then left. I again found myself also serving in the role of director of research. So, I responded by doing what I did best, which was to promote FSUS to the COE departments at FSU. You see, at the school we continued to focus on supporting others' research projects. We had several colleges and schools, such as the COE, psychology, and music conducting their research at our school. I sold my soul. If someone walked in with a project, we did it unless it was bizarre. There weren't many of those, but we did have one professor who wanted to do a project at the school on assembling grenade launchers for the army to determine how long this would take. We decided that this was something the school didn't want to sponsor.

But most proposals for research study were accommodated. Of course every time we facilitated a research project, the teachers' load would increase, even when they performed as a passive participant. But such acceptance was a real contribution on their part, and they got credit on their annual "brag sheet." This work also gave the FSUS teachers some stature, and, once in a while, they came up with a project on their own, like the math project.

In the late 1980s a school parent, who was a staff member in the House of Representatives, got some people to help us draft the Laboratory School Bill. The focus of this Bill was on laboratory schools, stipulating them as public schools in the state of Florida and confirming their affiliation with sponsoring universities. The idea behind the bill was that laboratory schools should have more substantive functions than just day-to-day school activities, while still being subject to annual appropriations and changing political winds. The Bill passed in 1989 but the governor vetoed it. We put it through again and it was passed in 1990. During the year of transition, I became really "disaffected," as they say in the army. Much of the intent that we had when we drafted that Bill was changed by the DOE (Department of Education) interpreters. There were two ongoing programs wherein we had shared hiring, assignments, and salary with the COE. We were able to get Ph.D. faculty members assigned one-half time to both units, securing a better link between the school and the college. This brought fresh ideas for curriculum development and research to the school. But the new doctoral faculty were not certified nor were they interested in becoming so. When it was determined that all faculty would be certified, the arrangement collapsed.

Decisions on few shoulders

While running FSUS, I got exposed to the kinds of things that happen when operating such a place, such as building problems and faculty and staff turnover. One time, the pipes burst during a cold spell and the kids were sent home in the morning.

Regarding faculty turnover, I thought that we did a good job of hiring minorities. In fact, I used to think that our numbers made the COE look good because the college would aggregate the COE and FSUS numbers in the yearly report. For example, I hired an African American principal who served for 13 years during directorship. We worked well together.

I invited professors from the COE to teach classes at FSUS, but almost invariably this didn't work out well. College professors generally don't like to fuss with parents, and the parents do like to get involved. Just the routine discipline of handling sophomores in high school is a challenge for most professors. These levels of encounter take a special knack.

Empowering the faculty

One of the more interesting projects we started occurred in 1986. One morning the dean of education called me over for a meeting. He announced that he wanted the British Infant School Program, a unique participatory approach to elementary education, which was then housed at Hartsville Elementary School, to be implemented at FSUS, and that he wanted me to facilitate this transition. "Who, me?" I was taken aback. I realized that I had one brief moment to drive a bargain. I said,

> Okay, but first I'll need five years with an ongoing evaluation process that will give us time to make the program work. One-year evaluations can prematurely show that a program isn't working, and I wouldn't want to be shortchanged in such a way. Also, this will prove to be a major effort because we are going to need to group kids, K–1, 2–3, 4–5, and so on, and we will be doing some other innovative things. Second, I have a faculty position available and want to hire somebody from England for two years to assist with the program. And third, I want to spend some money to send my faculty to England for three weeks to work with the program at another school.

I wanted to send some of the teachers to England to work with Carolyn Schluck for six weeks. I needed the dean's support to use part of my own budget for this training. He was silent for a moment, but agreed. All three of my conditions were accepted and also honored.

We sent a group of our faculty to England and they came back excited and inspired. While the faculty were in England *they* hired their new peer teacher and brought her back. We also got the five years of implementation and evaluation that I had negotiated.

We started the British Infant School Program with an orientation for parents. We explained that with this new program they would become part of the research. The dean assigned a senior faculty member to develop a research design for the program. We explored such topics as multiaged grouping of students; the whole language approach to reading and writing; and cooperative learning. One result was enthusiasm for learning among the students involved. Another was a publication by our English colleague, Margaret Hargreaves. We had a few families who elected not to have their children in the program.

We ran the British Infant School Program for approximately five years, and it was an empowering learning experience for those involved.

Students vital to research

One commitment that we made to university researchers was to insist that our students be made available for their projects. During our briefings to parents, I would conduct the meetings. I told them that we were not going to hurt their child in any way, or do anything without review, and that no unauthorized person was going to question the students. If we had a sensitive research project proposal – and we did send a couple to the Human Subjects Board for review – the parent was given the final say regarding their child's participation. We had one child who refused to work with the researcher, and so I had a conference with the mother who was upset. I pointed out that it was the second time that her daughter had refused to cooperate with a researcher. This time, she had torn up the research material. I said that we couldn't allow for such outbursts. The parent decided to withdraw her child after I explained the nature of our business as a university school. I emphasized that we were evaluated on our ability to work with the university. If we couldn't provide the necessary support, then we would jeopardize our future as well as the opportunity for students to be in a unique learning environment.

Appreciator role

People used to say to me, "I'll bet you took this job at FSUS to work your way into a position in the college." I would respond, "No, I love K through 12 work, and I do not have my aspirations set to work at FSU." I did agree to teach the university principalship course for several years, however, and the university students seemed to really enjoy it.

I was clearly a school person. As an officer in the National Association of Laboratory Schools, I ran the annual meetings. I would make presentations when asked. We did in-service at a community college where I talked about the school and its personnel policies.

I do not perceive myself as a scholar. I view my role in life as an *appreciator*. Without appreciators around, nobody's work would be viewed as important. My strength lies in my ability to talk and especially to listen to people. My brother-in-law who is a scientist would say ask me, "Just what is it that do you do all day long?" When I'd reply, "Talk to people," he'd say, "You get paid for that?" "You bet," I'd respond, "It's hard work, but it's worth something over the long haul when it's done well."

A personal treasure

If you were to ask me what I treasure as my most important accomplishment at FSUS, I would say keeping the school open. It's hard to grasp now, but in the early 1970s our ability to remain open was constantly "ify." I will always remember the week of Thanksgiving in 1981 when FSU was in a budget crisis, as was the state of

Florida. There were roll-back monies going to the governor's office. The dean of the COE called us into session saying, "FSUS will temporarily close at Christmas, and it will close permanently in June." Why he didn't say permanently at Christmas, I don't know. But we came *that* close. In a week's time we were able to marshal some help from people, including our alumni, which was small at that time because we only had about 100 graduates each year. We turned it around. I don't want to make this sound dramatic, it's just that it was our primary function, from 1971 to 1982, to remain open.

As things settled down and a new dean took over, we stopped doing student teacher and observer work by Board of Regent's fiat. We could accept a preservice teacher who had very special needs only. For example, we accepted one such student with muscular dystrophy and another who was visually impaired. Occasionally, a student teacher would need an alternative placement experience. It was thought that the FSUS experienced faculty could help in all such challenging situations. We gradually began to relax our student teacher placement code and to accommodate routine placements.

Respect for the faculty were always looming issues for me. For example, my faculty could always do their own photocopying and call long distance. It doesn't sound like much, but there are schools where teachers aren't permitted such freedoms. What's the hidden message? We can trust teachers with our kids but not with copying machines? The real treasure for me was that FSUS survived and functioned in unique ways for the betterment of our students and faculty.

Not all peaches and cream

We pushed on having school faculty governance and site-based decision making even before these innovations became a fad. Because of our genuine cooperation and mutual dependence, we functioned pretty well as a unit. Life at FSUS went well, even though it wasn't all peaches and cream. The faculty were angry with me a couple of times. One time I let the faculty know that they could meet me in the cafeteria the next afternoon. I invited the teachers to ask me questions they might have about any topic. I put out potential fires by using this strategy of communication on more than one occasion.

At a later time, the faculty were once again excited about an issue, so I asked them to send their questions and concerns to me via a designated teacher. At the meeting, this teacher pulled out questions from a box, and I responded to each one. Every principal I knew who experienced friction with their faculty did so either when something vital was hidden or when something important was not explained. I used to tell our graduates that if you can't explain something to your own grandmother that you plan on doing, then refrain. I applied this logic to my own leadership style.

This isn't to imply that at FSUS we were always in agreement about issues of concern. I believe that it's smart to listen to people. One incident comes to mind regarding a physical education teacher who had been with us since 1971. She was an outstanding teacher who was becoming somewhat stale in her work. This period of time corresponded with our chance to connect with IBM. We had talked IBM into giving us a classroom of computers. Our guidance counselor urged me, saying, "Why don't you ask the physical education teacher if she'd be interested in directing our new computer laboratory? She's already working with computers and the needs of the school on her own time." So I did. I listened. And to this day, that same teacher runs an outstanding computer program.

Mentoring teamwork

When I reflect on those whom I missed at the school with my move to a new job at FSU in 1991, it's the teachers who rush to mind. I remember a miracle that we "pulled off" in 1987. We were scheduled to do a spring musical, yet the school had scheduled football and the music practice at the same time. The music director approached me, saying, "Ed, these kids are coming in hoarse, they can't sing at night." So, I went to see the football coach. The coach and the music director got together and arrived at a solution. They agreed to alternate the schedules, with football practice early one day and late the next. With the emphasis on sports over the arts at most schools in the US, including our own, the football coach could have "dug his heels in." But he responded constructively. That's why working at FSUS was so rewarding. We kept focused on the kids *and* why we were there, which helped us to function as an effective team.

Another project we took on in the mid-1980s came about when a department chair of home economics in another school asked us to develop a full-service school program. In response, we developed a family friendly full-service school operation and even became a magnet in the state. We would send people out to schools to explain our program. We did the same thing with block scheduling. I had read about the Pythagorean Plan about block scheduling and those faculty who were interested in the possibilities became involved in mentoring efforts. The plan was fully implemented the year after I left. As I look around the county, it's clear that our work outside the school played a significant role in promoting interest in block scheduling.

Caring and sharing

Even though it has been a decade since I was the director of FSUS, I still feel attached because of all the years I worked there. I still care. It was a hard decision for me to take up the university administrative position. During the first few years in my new COE position, I still crossed the walkway over to FSUS everyday and taught a class in speech and debate. The course was offered early in the morning so that I would not have to miss a class session due to any scheduling conflicts. I enjoyed teaching that course and coaching the debate teams, and believe that it is a real advantage for people to have debate skills. I miss that K–12 contact with the kids.

Shifting cultures

Because I am presently responsible for the placement of student teachers throughout the state, I continue to spend time at FSUS. This gives me the opportunity to interact with the present director, both principals, and the faculty. When I'm there, I visit with faculty who are supervising our student teachers. I want to ensure, to the best of my ability, that everything is going okay. I also join faculty for coffee break to chat in a more relaxed way.

As another ritualistic practice at the school, I used to give the female cafeteria workers a corsage the first day of the year. I viewed the cafeteria as the school kitchen. Good things happen in kitchens – people talk and show warmth. In addition, I came to appreciate that janitors and cafeteria workers are critical to the operation of the school. I remember my first high school principalship when I was trying to write my dissertation while working full-time. Living a short distance from the school, I'd say goodnight to my wife and walk to the school to write. I must have been having a great time being principal because as soon as that maintenance fellow would come by I would immediately have cause to stop working on that dissertation. We would roam around the building inspecting things that needed to be done. Then the next night the same ritual would take place. It took me two years to write that dissertation.

When I came to FSUS to assume a new position, we had a maintenance crew working during the day and night. The night crew supervisor and I hit it off. It got so that if he noticed something that didn't seem right he would call me at home. One weekend morning I walked into the school. The supervisor was already there! He told me that he had been driving by the school when he noticed a door swinging open. He responded by deciding to check to make certain that the proper work order and repair papers had been filed. Once again, I learned from this experience how important it is for me to listen to different kinds of people who teach me about my own environment from their own perspective.

How the FSUS building actually came into being is another interesting story. It was shared with me by Dean Mode Stone (who is deceased). Dean Stone sat in my office one afternoon. I can still see him. We were almost touching knees because I had moved into a smaller office at FSUS to accommodate the needed space for new programs. At that time in 1952, the school was located on the old part of the FSU campus. Dean Stone reasoned with the spouses of the legislators, explaining that he wanted a new school building that their kids could use whenever their families came to Tallahassee for the legislative session. The problem of whether legislators could bring their family to such sessions had been unresolved up until then. But that's a glimpse into how the new building, conveniently located near the COE, came into being. However, with the passing of time, and with the implementation of the mandatory selection policy that cut off guaranteed admissions for students, some of these relationships wilted. The new Board of Regents' regulations changed the climate; we had to fight for survival.

Twice speechless

Speechlessness is not typically characteristic of me. However, I experienced this in 1991. I had just told my FSUS faculty at an after-school meeting that I had accepted an administrative position at FSU. Even now, I struggle to remember my words because there was so much emotion in the room. The faculty then hosted a university-wide retirement party and gave me a certificate for a cruise vacation. They felt that this would be something I would enjoy with Bev, my wife, and they were right. The cruise is one of my special memories that continues to link me across time to the faculty and our feeling of celebration.

School legends

Many school legends have survived. One is connected with the various buses we used. In 1971 FSU had gone out of the vehicle business, so we obtained one of its buses. We used that bus until we wore it out. Eventually, we bought our own bus that had the occasional habit of breaking down. One day, a teacher who had taken students to Disney World experienced the breakdown 200 miles away. It was early evening. He called asking whether he could have permission to get motel rooms. I said, "Fine, do that and come back tomorrow. We'll call the parents right away." The local county superintendent provided a bus the next day. I admit that I do rest a little easier at night without the possibility of such trials looming.

A capstone address

A capture experience in my professional life involves the graduation speech that I gave on June 6th in 1994 at the school. Here is the commencement speech that I delivered.

> Thank you for inviting me to participate in this happy occasion, the graduation of the class of '94. You know, for me, this is a first.
>
> When invited to speak at a graduation, it's a great temptation to write THE SPEECH, to strive for those words of wisdom/advice that will echo through the years, something you'll always remember. But a quick survey of even this audience, alert and attentive as you are, would reveal the sober truth. No one ever remembers what their graduation speaker said – most don't even remember the speaker's name unless they have saved the program. As you can see, happy as I am to be here, the challenge is quite real; the prospects for success, cloudy.

So, in the face of the evidence, I've decided to be more moderate in my expectations. I would like to concentrate on two of the next few days in your life. Tonight, Friday, and Monday next. Tonight, you deserve all the congratulations that will come your way. Indeed, I add mine to the chorus of well wishes. Enjoy the moment. You've earned it. And it will last, this special Friday, through the long, happy weekend ahead.

But the congratulations will eventually subside, even the best of Project Graduation parties will end, and we hope the weekend will close with the hoped for sunset. But it's over too soon and suddenly you're faced with the question that puzzles us all: Is that all? What's next? Well, what's next is Monday morning and all the Monday mornings of your life. Indeed, if there is a universal challenge that faces us all, it's the Monday mornings of life. It's what being an adult is all about. Some of us, a bit older, find them harder to handle. I hope that will not be your experience. I pray that you will approach Monday morning with a sense of anticipation, enthusiasm, and commitment.

With anticipation – for what lies ahead in the adult world, for life has much to offer you. Financial success, family love, friendship, art, beauty, and more, and you'll be free to work for your goals and those things that you think will make you happy.

With enthusiasm – for the challenge of life. Success won't come easy; but this life's tasks must be embraced willingly with courage and dedication, with a willingness to work hard and risk failure. To make the attempt and fall short is no disgrace. Indeed, it is often the human condition. But never to have tried is never to have truly lived.

With commitment – to make your life and this country work. Much will depend on you as you face the special challenge of your generation. What is that challenge?

It will be your task starting Monday, to prepare yourself to run the engine of society, government, and business well into the twenty-first century. Success or failure will depend upon your efforts. You cannot fail if this nation and its citizens are to prosper, if this nation's traditions and promise are to endure. We pray you will be equal to the task for the challenge is real. Michael Novak, the philosopher, puts it this way:

> All it takes for a free society to fail is for a single generation to abandon the ideals and habits that constitute free institutions. The history of the human race is mainly a history of tyranny; political and economic freedom comes with no guarantee. It is entirely possible that the free society such as we know it in the United States will burn out like a comet that swept through the darkness for a little more than two centuries and then disintegrated.

We don't want this happen. You must not let it happen.

We will all depend upon you as we depended upon another generation 50 years ago.

Monday next. June 6, 1994 marks the 50th Anniversary of the Allied Invasion of Normandy. D–Day. There are probably some in the audience this evening who were there; many of us participated vicariously. Surely all of us are aware of the commemorative events that are occurring this week to mark the occasion. I don't think that it stretches the point too much to suggest that you, the class of '94, share more with those young men and women of 50 years ago than you might think.

Picture them approaching the invasion beaches.

They were equally as young, many only 18; they were scared; they were facing a decidedly uncertain future; and they were about to forsake the fragile security of the landing craft to face the greatest challenge of their young lives, the opportunity, the necessity, indeed the mandate, to defeat the German Army in the Battle of France and Northern Europe. They did not flinch, and they succeeded in their crusade. Our presence here tonight is ample evidence of their historic accomplishment and the legacy for succeeding generations. How different it might have been if they had failed. We are the richer for their efforts and their sacrifices. Now, willingly or unwillingly, it's your turn, Monday next.

You're probably apprehensive of the future. You're about to leave the illusory security of the high school to face your generation's special challenge, the building and running of this country well into the twenty-first century. Within the next 10 years you will be raising families, running businesses, affecting policies – leaving your imprint on all levels of the American Enterprise. Yours will be the real burden of ensuring that the American Dream becomes improved for all citizens in the years ahead. It is a challenge well worth accepting. More importantly, no one else can do it.

Whatever this nation becomes in the next 50 years will be a direct result of the effort each of you makes to insure that our country prospers in the next century. You will be following in the footsteps of the young people of Normandy, the Great Depression, Gettysburg, Plymouth Plantation, and the Mayflower. The baton of responsibility and performance is being passed to you along with a special invitation to join with your forebears to grow and to help this country grow. We'll be eager to see what you do. You can surely do it!

The school name

Although the school name has changed over time, I prefer the informal, culturally ingrained name, "Florida High." When I arrived in the 1970s, it was called the University School. Years before that the name was Demonstration School; the name "Demons" comes from "demonstration." The Demons were a school football team and mascot that Alumni still refer to endearingly. When the dean of education reorganized the college in 1992, he called it the Developmental Research School; everybody thought this name was a mouthful. Florida DRS also came about as a name, but it was a long time before that happened. In the mid-1980s the university president reconstituted the advisory board for the school. One member argued that "Florida High" was an inaccurate name, creating the impression that the school had only a secondary function, not an elementary one too. This member then donated the sign that marks the school today, the one with two names on it! (See opening artwork, Figure 14.1)

During this conversation about the name of the school, I motioned that we call it The Florida State University School (FSUS). Although this may sound sensible given the school's affiliated campus function with FSU, the committee was without a consensus at the time. However, FSUS has become the school's official name.

The school journey continues

As the former director of FSUS, I felt lucky. When I look to the present and the future, it seems to me that Glenn Thomas, the recent director, is a visionary and an activist. Each time that I talk to this new leader I am impressed by his energizing vision and actions, ability to organize people and move them forward, and willingness to play on a global stage. The school is moving into a very different time and space with web-based learning sites, and this new director understands how to work with this momentum of change. He is already showing promise of effectively leading the school into the next century.

Cherished memories

Sharing these stories has brought to mind some fairly complex situations as well as a series of pleasant memories. I treasure my journey and the wonderful people along the way who have played a role in creating a stage for me to enact some of my professional dreams and now my most cherished memories.

And the voyage continues.

Leader and mentor success

Just as Ed holds cherished memories of his time at FSUS, those who knew and interacted with him during those times cherish their memories of him. Through his personable, proactive mentoring approach, he built synergistic relationships almost everywhere. People trusted him and knew that he was working everyday on their behalf. As a result, they wanted to help and support him in his leadership efforts for the school.

The FSUS has experienced amazing success over the years, during Ed's time and under subsequent leadership. The FSUS is regarded as one of the most effective schools in Florida. It is continually held up for its experimental successes as a model for other schools. Waiting lists are the norm for students wanting to attend this special school.

The high level of synergy evidenced in the school under Ed's leadership emanates from the mentoring and comentoring processes he put in place with others. As new threats and opportunities flowed through the FSUS, Ed functioned to assure a high level of school synergy by working with his faculty, staff, and students to set common goals; to relate interdependently; to empower them through their own efforts; and to allow all to participate in the affairs of the school. His openness and willingness for two-way communication across all sectors coupled with his flexible, active listening, and appreciative understanding style enhanced trust and credibility. His dependability, always being there when people needed him, inspired others to accept his leadership and efforts toward the accomplishment of agreed upon goals.

Ed's powerful and consistent mentoring approach during his FSUS tenure made him a effective and highly accepted director. His success as a lead mentor helped propel his school to be among the most notable in the state. This narrative of a mentoring school leader is about more than the shaping of the human journey of others – it also has a role to play in building tomorrow's schools and promising educational systems.

15   Lifelong Mentoring: The Creation of Learning Relationships

Carol A. Mullen and William A. Kealy

In the future, people must learn throughout their lives because of the rapidly changing circumstances and society around them. They must continue to learn, since they themselves will change. We view such lifelong learning as a process of "self-actualization of the individual" (Jansen and van der Veeen, 1997) that can be extended to groups, organizations, countries, and the global system. Lifelong learning can also be viewed as a "curriculum for human beings" (May and Furlong, 1997) that is inseparable from one's own life cycle and development.

With lifelong learning being an integral part of each person's life, what "learning model or models" might be especially effective to greatly enhance continuous learning? One such powerful approach is that of *lifelong mentoring*. Lifelong mentoring is a proactive engagement of learning and teaching that embodies unique possibilities for human development. This approach emphasizes intentional thinking with regard to how social relationship and context are created. We define the concept of *lifelong mentoring* as the process of continually seeking, finding, and reconstructing mentoring and comentoring relationships through which one can become enabled, empowered, and self-actualized. The Partnership Support Group (PSG), upon which this book is based, reflects this philosophy of lifelong mentoring. This school-university comentoring project represents a proactive approach to bringing together a school and university professionals within a framework of guided research practice.

The human life cycle can be described in lifelong mentoring terms. Just such a model has been developed by a former Texas-based university support group to which we belonged. At the completion of that project, the two of us created a human model of "multiple, intertwining circles" to capture processes of mentorship throughout life. Examples of the life cycle processes we identified include close and distant mentoring contact, highly structured learning activity, multiple mentoring figures/qualities, private and public stories, and various forms of communication. These communication patterns in mentoring relationships, programs, and organizations range from intense to halted to severed. Such elements also help to characterize lifelong patterns of mentoring. This organic model of lifelong mentoring is illustrated in Mullen et al. (1997), and, with greater detail, in Mullen, Whatley and Kealy (in press).

We, the authors of this chapter, are two teacher educator-researchers. Here we expand the notion of mentoring as something that is experienced contextually only to that having lifelong learning potential. We offer a new mentoring model and description to raise questions about, and to provide insight into, how mentoring networks generally work (see Figure 15.1, p. 193). With this model we highlight those needs, abilities, and resources that play a role in mentoring relationships and systems over time.

We both participated in the Texas network as a way of redefining mentorship in educators' lives and writings. Carol had been intimately connected from the study group's inception, initiating and managing a book project, and also preparing and editing the group's material for publication. Bill worked with Carol to develop and articulate a philosophical model based on the group's stories of mentoring. We draw upon this 1997 book to explore the concept of lifelong mentoring in a support group context. We also draw upon this new book on faculty comentoring within a Florida school-university environment.

Mentoring to lifelong mentoring

Some of us have, through mentoring practices, acquired specialized and advanced learning not available through textbooks and classroom instruction. In the case of the Partnership Support Group (PSG) in Florida, both novice and established faculty joined to conduct action research within a diverse study group; to develop new and empowering perspectives on mentoring issues; and to write collaboratively for a major book publication.

Lifelong mentoring gives "respectability" to the notion and expectation that many of us will require guided learning, from an outside source and stimulus, as we seek new skills or knowledge. People may find mentoring especially helpful during times of heightened adjustment, such as assuming a new position; moving from one career or profession to another; and advancing within a particular arena. With the new attitude toward aging that is gradually permeating society, and with the increased longevity of human life, perspectives on mentoring are changing. Mentoring has no age limit or any limits as such. Instead, mentoring is limited when constraints are placed on its proactive forms of guided learning and instruction.

In the past, mentoring generally occurred in conjunction with formal schooling or as part of a trade apprenticeship. Mentoring traditionally involves a one-on-one senior-subordinate relationship between the apprentice (or student) and a master craftsperson (or scholar) with expert knowledge in a profession. After one graduates from school or attains journeyman status, the mentorship period typically ends. Within this framework, mentoring is a unidirectional process wherein the more experienced person does the teaching and the neophyte, the learning. The traditional mentor sets or implies conditions for noncritical reflection and feedback whereby "authoritative knowledge" is mediated (Smits, 1997) and "satisfaction and recognition [are gained] from the accomplishments of his protégé" (Fleming, 1991, p. 28). On the other hand, the Texas and Florida support groups embodied a radically different understanding of mentoring appreciated through the practice of *being* a diverse support group studying itself.

Many traditional aspects of mentoring are changing, along with the view of what mentorship is, who benefits from mentoring, and what its purposes are in professional and academic life, and – we would add – life itself. A case in point is that many domains of society, such as business, government, and the military, are bringing the subject of mentoring into a public discussion that goes beyond the walls of colleges and trade schools. In fact, one could conclude from the current rise in book titles, magazine articles, newsletters, television programs, conference presentations, and focus groups dealing with mentoring, that mentorship is a topic much in vogue throughout society. It is faddish even. Leaders no longer see mentorship as an activity that occurs only in college or preprofessional training. Instead, it can be usefully incorporated in many other walks of life and at all levels of professional and self development.

The concept of mentorship should be expanded to include the notion that mentoring is not just a one-time occurrence. Rather, teaching and learning are ongoing activities throughout the course of one's life. The concept of lifelong mentoring takes its lead from the well-established idea of lifelong learning. Lifelong learning is, to us, a broader and deeper concept than those belonging to its family cluster, namely peer coaching, comentoring, peer tutoring, cooperative learning, and reciprocal teaching. To facilitate own our understanding, we define the concept of *lifelong mentoring* as the process of continually seeking, finding, and reconstructing mentoring and comentoring relationships through which one can become enabled, empowered, and self-actualized. We borrow from Dewey (1934) to illuminate the meaning of lifelong mentoring as the "activity setting" educators create as they shape experience, establishing conditions to promote "experiences that lead to growth" (pp. 39, 40).

Factors in lifelong mentoring

As a concept, lifelong mentoring represents an evolution of traditional mentoring arising from several societal trends. A primary factor in lifelong mentoring is the *changing population demographics* that indicate Americans are becoming increasingly older and more heterogeneous. As people live longer, healthier lives, the concept of retirement is giving way to "refirement" wherein the rekindling of second and third careers to enhance of one's later life are becoming commonplace. For these older learners, often more adept at the process of learning than younger novices, mentoring proactively continues into the later phases of life.

Mentoring programs for older learners have been implemented in a few universities and informally at many more. At Southern Illinois University, for example, retired faculty mentors lead a workshop that provides freshmen with a lifelong perspective on learning and the importance of developing support systems among peers. These students become exposed to a range of methods for viewing learning experiences as occurring throughout life. Retirees can also bring their special body of knowledge to arenas in which they perform as learners. However, the elderly are not normally considered candidates for mentoring. The problem? Mentoring is typically considered a sustained relationship between a youth and an adult.

Contrary to this out-of-date, limited notion of mentoring, there are rich and abundant examples of valuable mentoring relationships where the younger person serves as the mentor and the senior as the mentee. The international elderhostel program at colleges and universities provides meaningful, structured mentoring opportunities for those over 50. Another fascinating illustration of such "reversal" mentoring is seen in the growing trend to hire computer literate high school students in business, industry, and government to mentor workers on the use of computers and new information databases. Similar mentoring relationships occur on college campuses with students who mentor faculty and staff on how to use new technology innovations.

Mentorship can also be a beneficial adjunct to inservice training, particularly for those in nontraditional occupations with an increasingly heterogeneous workforce that includes women and minorities. Nonetheless, women and people of color require sponsorship to assume senior positions within university, school, and corporate hierarchies. Mentoring networks can provide synergistic advantages for women in particular. McElhiney (1990) describes such a network in empowering terms as a "mentoring model that resembles a web with the woman herself in the center controlling the strands, instead of a ladder in which the mentor above extends a hand to the woman below, works best for women" (p. 22). For women and minorities, mentoring can provide the specialized expertise and connections that facilitate their development as important contributors to organizational teams.

In American universities, minorities represented 12.3 per cent of full-time faculty from 1991–92 (National Education Association, 1993). This figure has not grown significantly, a sign that continues to point to the need for rigorous minority faculty recruitment. Faculty support groups can address this issue of unequal representation at interpersonal and institutional levels. Both the Texas and Florida networks found that the support group structure facilitates a nonthreatening space to ensure minority faculty representation in addition to diversity in viewpoints.

A second factor in the emergence of lifelong mentoring is the *impact of technology* and the resulting explosion both in the amount of information people have access to and the rate at which information changes. The rapid growth of new knowledge and the mushrooming outlets for its dissemination (e.g. internet and direct satellite broadcast television) challenge our ability to remain current in the know-how required to perform even our mundane daily activities. It is impossible in many cases to process the information available on a popular topic; to do so would over-task one's processing abilities. A larger body of task-relevant information inevitably yields a corresponding increase in the number of decision alternatives. This makes selecting the "right" information all the more critical and has, in part, fostered the appearance of information brokers, services, and software that perform what has traditionally been an important role of the academic mentor – that of directing novices to the most important works within a discipline. Technology has even progressed beyond this service to offer, through the internet homepages of many organizations, advice on how to create a successful mentoring program. Some sites on the World Wide Web even help to locate a mentor.

Third, and perhaps most important factor to the emergence of lifelong mentoring, is the redefinition of traditional roles and relationships. In particular, some teaching–learning relationships that were once hierarchically defined are now being recast in more egalitarian ways (Kealy, 1997). Feminist pedagogic analyses explore mutually supportive approaches to university teaching and research. Such studies offer ideas about, and examples of, how authoritarian structures can be made to shift where critically reflective, collaboratively-oriented communities are at work. Research into improved learning environments offers insight into practices that can benefit the establishment of empowering mentoring networks. Examples of feminist practice that can be transferred to the support group effort include interdisciplinary and transdisciplinary knowledge strategies for encouraging student and participant input. To clarify, lifelong mentoring is not equal to support groups; the former may be studied by learning teams that do not require lifelong engagement to be effective.

The collapse of some traditional mentoring relationship structures has had a pronounced impact in two ways. One, this has forced reexamination of the respective senior–subordinate stance of the mentor and the mentee to propose alternative roles, such as taking turns in research duties and rewards. Another change has been to approach the goal of a mentorship as a shared enterprise. This is exemplified in the concept of a "duography" whereby doctoral students and professors view themselves as partners in professional development; they may, for instance, produce a shared research agenda that has at its core issues of equality and power-sharing (Diamond and Mullen, 1999).

Two, the restructuring of relationships suggests potential and possibilities well beyond those of one-on-one mentoring dyads. Indeed, if mentoring is defined more as a process than an activity performed by an individual, then traditional roles of mentoring (e.g. nurturing, advising, befriending, parenting, instructing) may be performed by several people simultaneously. Basically this constitutes a decentralization of mentorship (and power-based relationships) into more of a "mentoring mosaic" (Kealy and Mullen, 1999). Within such a network, one person may serve as a subject specialist, another as counselor, still another as advocate, adviser, promoter. The development of an individual (or movement) may be the result of many influences, each fulfilling a different role: teacher, adviser, confidante, promoter, cheering section, parental figure, friend, career guide, and more. In the case of the Neo-Impressionist movement, Seurat was its "source" or originator; Dubois-Pillet was the movement's organizer; and Signac and Fénéon were promoters of the group's artistic ideas (Herbert, 1991).

Envisioning lifelong mentoring

At first it is difficult to imagine how the concept of lifelong mentoring translates into personal practical experience. What does lifelong mentoring look like? We, the authors, are struck by the impossibility of the mentor or mentee shadowing the other throughout an entire lifetime. Certainly this level of commitment was parodied in Voltaire's (1956) *Candide*. Candide was mentored by Pangloss, the philosopher-optimist, through a series of major disasters (e.g. earthquakes) and tragedies (e.g. flogging) only to conclude after years of momentous hardship that, regardless of the value of learning, the mentoring journey must be lifelong.

What does lifelong mentoring suggest, then? Mentoring for life does *not* imply or entail an extended one-on-one mentoring relationship against all odds (e.g. earthquakes and flogging). Rather, it suggests an ongoing commitment to seek opportunities for mentoring and being mentored as well as for learning and sharing the value of one's experiences. Today we live longer, are vastly more mobile, and are apt to transition in and out of all types of relationships on a more frequent basis than in the past. The point is that there are benefits in mentoring another – validation of one's learning, maturity, and professional knowledge not to mention the reward of aiding another's success – that make mentoring a relationship of special investment that differs from traditional teaching.

To characterize the practice of lifelong mentoring, we offer an orientation in higher education whereby the identity of mentor is made explicit and proactively constructed over time. Instructors, academic supervisors, or mentors can assist their students or dissertation candidates to develop a robust mentoring identity as professionals and researchers. Importantly, the mentor can display the potential for learning as a collaborator and for evoking in the other the potential to function as a guide. Those who promote quality relationships with their mentees can share not only research knowledge and skills but ideas and images of mentoring development. Students can greatly benefit from developing an image of themselves as mentors whose voices and stories matter. Among other things, they can learn to take responsibility for initiating agendas and projects, and for facilitating the new awareness of the mentor (Mullen, 1997c). Lifelong mentoring practices can thereby promote the distribution of power, teaching, and learning among individuals who work toward reconstructing their identities as comentors.

Questions that are relevant within the scope of lifelong mentoring include: What distinguishes lifelong mentorship of an individual from the long-term mentoring activity that occurs within a structured program of an organization? How does the idea of mentoring the elderly practically manifest itself, especially when the mentor is significantly younger than the mentee, the elder? By contrast, what innovative forms of mentoring can be proposed for or by adolescents? Do those who have the assurance of having succeeded in their careers (and having even guided others) perceive a need for mentoring? We only touch upon aspects of these questions throughout this discussion. Each one requires rigorous study.

A new mentoring model

From the perspective of lifelong mentoring, *resources, needs, and abilities* matter. These three components need to be integrated and together they characterize our new holistic model of mentoring. They play a role in determining mentoring relationships and contexts and, to a large extent, those aspects of mentoring that

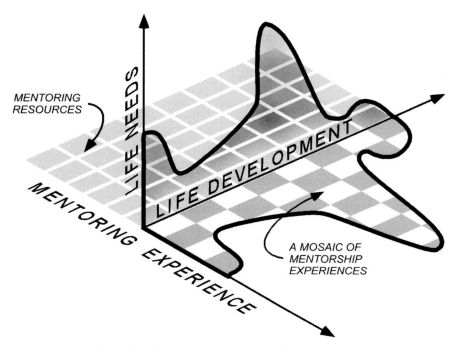

MENTORING
RESOURCES

LIFE NEEDS

MENTORING EXPERIENCE

LIFE DEVELOPMENT

A MOSAIC OF
MENTORSHIP
EXPERIENCES

Figure 15.1: A holistic mentoring model of abilities, needs, and resources
(William A. Kealy, 1998)

best nurture the mentee at a particular time. Based on mentor and mentee factors, we present a three-dimensional model in Figure 15.1. As this graphic shows, the horizontal axis extending to the right and its vertical axis represent, respectively, the changing needs and abilities of an individual over the course of a lifetime.

The other horizontal axis, and the horizontal plane it forms in the background, symbolize all of the resources that are available. Forward of this plane is another horizontal plane that denotes specific mentoring resources called upon given some-one's needs and abilities at a particular time in life. This checkered pattern depicts a mentoring mosaic, an ever-changing network of people who fulfill various mentoring roles. In such a context, protégés seek to fulfill their needs through different people performing various functions. Mentors who recognize protégés' needs may refer them to growth-enhancing contexts (e.g. conferences) or to people (e.g. other colleagues or students).

Head et al. (1992) suggest optimizing the functions of a network of secondary mentors to address shortcomings in the primary mentoring dyad. Watkins and Whalley (1995) assert that school-based mentoring can support the growth of beginning teachers through a process of team building. Herein multiple mentors offer resources and provide multiple ways of learning. This does not exclude the possibility for there to be a lead-mentor(s) through which wholeview organizational efforts are facilitated. Clearly mentoring can occur in forms other than a traditional, one-to-one mentoring dyad.

Figure 15.1 was not designed as a tool for identifying the mentoring components necessary when specific needs, abilities, and resources are already available. Rather, it depicts, in a three-dimensional display, the interplay of essential mentorship factors or components as a means of articulating the concept of lifelong mentoring.

Mentoring needs

A person's mentoring needs, the first component of the model, will vary in accordance with how his or her goals and needs change over life. We have greater needs, for example, as a student than we do as an established professional or even as a retiree. Additionally, throughout life our needs change. Self-concept theorists such as Maslow (1962) refer to an evolution of needs over one's lifetime, from survival and safety concerns to those of social acceptance and self-actualization (Joyce, Weil and Showers, 1992). The need for productive and satisfactory learning environments, for example, can be used to guide programs to build self-actualizing mentoring capacity. One purpose of support groups, then, is to bring together those with stronger and weaker mentoring self-concepts to create viable and fulfilling contexts (Mullen, 1997c).

Needs of protégés can be met by various functions fulfilled by mentors. In their mentoring model, Anderson and Shannon (1988) identified primary attributes of a good mentor as role model, nurturer, and caregiver who serves as a parental figure. Additionally, they specify functions of an ideal mentor: teacher, sponsor, one who encourages, counselor or problem-solver, and friend – one who accepts and relates to the protégé. The mentor as one who befriends is a theme emphasized by Gallimore, Tharp and John-Steiner (1992) who assert that attraction and attachment underlie all effective mentorships. Alternative models of intellectual friendship, emotional intimacy, and communication (Keyton and Kalbfleisch, 1993) offer perspectives on new forms of mentorship. These are all areas of potential needs.

From a sociocultural perspective, *joint productive activity* is a crucial ingredient in the formation and development of mentoring relationships (Gallimore et al., 1992). This example of comentoring is defined by forms of supportive mutuality; however, the concept of lifelong learning implies an even greater synergy. Although it is a concept whose time has come, it is also, in many ways, difficult to comprehend in its fuller scope and unfolding potential.

Mentoring abilities

In contrast to the needs components (shown in Figure 15.1) are one's abilities and the function they play in determining the appropriate mix of requisite mentoring roles. This is the "skill set" the mentee can bring forth in meeting his or her needs. Abilities of mentors vary with individual characteristics (and combinations) to include, for example, empathy, content specialization, networking capability and connection, goodwill, and social intelligence.

Regarding the abilities of mentors, questions to ask include: What character-istics make a good mentor, and can they be developed? And, how is "success" determined? Regarding the role of mentees, one question is, what is the capacity for self-mentoring or for monitoring one's progress? Might an example of self-mentoring be seen in Moon and Mayes' (1995) description of a "professional development portfolio" as a competency-based tool for preservice teachers? This kind of port-folio provides two functions: it serves as a vehicle for monitoring progress and for promoting reflection, and it also provides a documented source for providing evi-dence that learning has occurred. Both of these functions are akin to the mentee's cognitive ability and drive to direct self-development. To mentor oneself is other-wise a contradiction in terms – it depends on an outside source to stimulate, pro-mote, or guide some aspect of learning.

Finally, we ask, what about the potential for mutual mentoring, comentoring, or coauthoring in teacher development arenas? We have described this process in earlier sections and provided a number of examples, including the Texas and Florida support groups. These both illustrate new and beneficial forms of collaboratively-oriented research and pedagogy.

Mentoring resources

Resources for mentoring include time, space, and materials (Watkins and Whalley, 1995) as well as those in one's workplace, and personal and professional life. Resources in the protégé's environment include peers, mentors (e.g. teachers and advisers), administrators, and staff. Contexts that provide mentoring resources broadly include college, school, family, and church. Materials that are resources include books, computers, self-help guides, and films.

Mentoring embraces one's becoming, well-beingness, community, success, achievement, skills development, and other needs. These are largely determined by one's needs, abilities, and resources. For instance, consider a mature adult who suddenly acts on the urge to fulfill a lifelong dream of playing a musical instru-ment. In his autobiography *Piano Lessons*, radio talk show host Noah Adams (1996) chronicles his odyssey, at age 50, to learn to play the piano. He shares how he had resisted advice to take formal lessons from a piano teacher. In the end, ironically, the need for beginners to learn from teachers becomes one of the au-thor's deepest realizations and major recommendations.

There are other people whom Adams describes who had a powerful impact on his goal to play piano. There are role models in the form of famous piano players and figures like Glen Gould and Jellyroll Morton. There are people who know about the instrument itself in an historical sense who are holders of the tradition – people who represent the lore of piano playing and piano making. And, then there are people who are inspiring teachers. In Adams' case, there was an entire family of teachers to whom he became exposed who had a piano in every room of the home.

What he had created was a musical mentoring mosaic that wove together all of these resources combined with his own needs and abilities.

Mentoring needs, abilities, and resources can be combined in effective ways in various areas of our lives as capacity-building networks that ensure learning, wellness, and empowerment.

Lifelong mentoring: assumptions and postulates

What assumptions do people make about mentoring? What primary ideas about mentoring are advanced in the educational literature? What are examples of books and stories that unintentionally mentor through analogues yet have something important to say about the mentoring process? What assumptions do we, the authors, make about mentoring? One primary assumption we make is that everyone can benefit from mentoring in its myriad forms. We also make the assumption that mentoring not only occurs throughout life but that it is a fundamental source of life and growth. More specifically, we assume that individuals who value learning from others are more prepared to embrace reversals of the age/gender/racial mentoring norm (e.g. a dyad wherein the teacher is younger, female, or of color). We have considered our own assumptions about mentoring that resulted in the framing of certain postulates or beliefs (see Table 15.1).

Table 15.1: A manifesto of seven mentoring postulates

Postulate 1	Mentoring is for everybody.
Postulate 2	Mentoring is a lifelong pursuit.
Postulate 3	Mentoring is not just a teacher–learner relationship in the conventional sense, but it involves a broad array of different capabilities somehow suited to the mentor and mentee.
Postulate 4	Different people have different mentoring needs based on abilities brought to the relationship. Specific needs are shaped by particular life-situations (e.g. retirement, schooling, early phases of professional practice).
Postulate 5	Different people have different needs, abilities, and resources which determine the need for, and value of, a mentoring mosaic or collegial network. (One cannot "extract" all of the necessary resources from any one individual and can gain a great deal from exposure to a "collage" of many resources/qualities/abilities).
Postulate 6	Mentorship does not need to imply a hierarchical arrangement or status differential, nor does it need to imply that teaching and learning occur as a one-way street. Rather, the potential for synergistic comentoring exists between mentors and mentees. There are times when a more traditional arrangement is preferred or even required, as in an apprenticeship situation, and
Postulate 7	The potential for mentors to learn from mentees rises as mentors step back from endorsing traditional roles as knowledge-producers and seekers. Mentoring becomes paradoxically empowered as mentors' and mentees' roles become indistinguishable. Comentoring is a process wherein learning becomes greater than the capacity for individuals to produce on their own, without guidance or feedback. Attribution of who has done or created what part of a larger whole becomes "difficult" when comentors peak in their learning, shared understanding, and synergistic efforts.

Lifelong mentoring in the future

We are interested in the quality of life shared by those engaged in mentoring relationships and situations. We believe that an attitude towards mentoring as a lifelong process invites a deep and expansive approach to existence that can, in turn, help to fulfill one's personal and professional development mentoring needs and aspirations. Mentoring is, to us, a critical dimension of humanity and an embodiment of humanistic education. The philosopher Sartre (in Kaufman, 1975) named himself an "existential humanist" and valued the act of people who faithfully engage in the very search to liberate themselves. The idea is that through particular realizations individuals become more fully human. We believe that realizations can be promoted by the comentoring support group structure.

Although the concept of mentoring is commonplace, studies of lifelong mentoring are novel in teacher development, higher education, corporate life, and North America as a whole. The practice of mentoring through the "great questions of life," such as how human beings can meaningfully live their lives, was embedded in the interactions and writings of Socrates, Plato, and Aristotle (Noddings, 1995). Given the changing times and needs of human beings, what might lifelong mentoring mean in contemporary and future society? We encourage the framing of questions that can benefit the renewal of mentoring relationships and organizations.

What is the role of mentoring practices in helping to sustain relationships, academic lineage, organizations, and stories of genealogy? Conversely, why do so many mentoring relationships in education exhibit unhealthy elements, sometimes resulting in termination? Why is the responsibility for mentoring sometimes viewed competitively, and with suspicion or fear, that the mentored will outshine the mentor? What socializing experiences are needed for mentees who may experience negative mentoring and jealous mentors? Life-affirming perspectives on mentoring obviously go beyond technical considerations.

Mentorship may be similar to other "institutions" in life. As with a marriage, a mentoring experience can have a profound effect over the course of one's existence. By the same token, the prior knowledge and experiences of life can form a base that gives one a greater capacity for deriving the benefits of mentorship. It is useful to consider the validity and worth of mentorship as a lifetime enterprise. As such, mentorship is viewed not so much as an event but as an ongoing process that, like recreation, education, and worship for some, has the potential to become a fundamental component of living. These quality of life support systems are all defined by the resources they provide and by the needs and abilities of those who use them.

Lifelong mentoring requires us to ask larger questions of mentoring relationships – and particularly of ourselves. We can realize that mentoring takes many forms and, by doing so, take action by evoking desirable shifts in our mentoring processes and situations. For example, where one person may desire a shift from halted communication to intensity of contact, another may long for a change in the mentoring dyad to a mosaic of many (Mullen et al., in press).

Mentoring practices need to be studied in their particularities and broader implications, not just established and monitored out of need or in crisis. Even "practices of good management" have been theorized and applied to the corporate world. Many problems have resulted from "unstudied practices" and poor relations (Walton, 1986). Edward Deming's philosophy of participatory management has proven revolutionary. What would mentoring relationships, programs, and networks within universities and schools look life from the perspective of quality management? Given our commitment to the educational context (even though the corporate world is arguably just such a place and is relevant to a study of mentorship), we only wish to raise this question. We hesitate adopting quality control notions of performance in our lifelong approach to mentorship.

What we find attractive is that the Deming method of management supports engaging workers in honest dialogue about their own concerns. Senge (1990) goes further, making a critical distinction between "discussion" and "dialogue" in team learning processes within corporate settings. He views dialogue as the

> free and creative exploration of complex and subtle issues, a deep 'listening' to one another and suspending of one's own views. By contrast, in discussion different views are presented and defended and there is a search for the best view to support decisions. (p. 237)

Mentoring dyads and networks in schools and universities could gain from monitoring their patterns of dialogue and discussion. Discussion, as Senge strongly implies, can promote negative tensions through opposition, competition, and even sabotage.

Just as survival within the corporate world depends on knowing how to *Swim With the Sharks* (Mackay, 1988), the same could be said about higher education. Mentors (e.g. faculty) and the mentored (e.g. students) may be "trained" to function as powerfully opposing forces – what Senge calls the "the abstraction wars." Mentorship itself is steeped in university practices of abandonment, competition, and individuality. One acceptable mentoring practice involves the "process of the aftermath of having finished the dissertation [wherein] we [new graduates] must quickly learn how to fend for ourselves" (Mullen and Dalton, 1996, p. 61). The development of a robust mentor identity will help to ensure that the new graduate feels empowered to deal with abandonment and closure issues, which are very different.

The concept and practice of lifelong mentoring views graduate schools as reservoirs with the potential for ongoing, guided learning. University faculty can promote lifelong mentoring by developing more fully supportive networks for graduates to conduct research studies, find relevant work, and contribute to their fields. Graduate students can make formal requests that their mentoring issues and needs be addressed during the post-graduate phases of life. Given that the presence of women and minorities in higher education and positions of leadership is historically recent, there is a further need to equip mentors and the mentored with strategies for fostering lifelong mentoring.

The promise of lifelong mentoring

In this chapter lifelong mentoring is presented as a key concept and integral part of the human life cycle. It is also viewed as a powerful force in shaping mentoring dyads, groups, and organizational collaboratives. One implication of using lifelong mentoring as a concept and practice in education is that lifelong learning can be expanded to embrace mentoring processes. Mentorship can serve to promote a successful mentoring journey beyond one's immediate circumstances throughout one's career and life. Promising and effective mentoring begins with how we think about our past, current, and future lives in order to generate intentional thinking and feeling that steer how social relationship and context are created.

People and organizations need to self-actualize to enhance continuous learning and new possibilities for human development. This means that lifelong mentors will need to continually create robust relationships and systems through which they and others can more fully live.

Authors' notes

Newsletters covering mentoring topics include *Mentorship and Mentoring Practices*, produced by Mullen and Kealy, Cochairs of the mentoring SIG of the American Educational Research Association. *Mentor and Protégé* by Maureen Waters and *The Mentoring Connection* by the International Mentoring Association are two others.

For information on the retiree mentoring program at Southern Illinois University, consult the internet site, www.siu.edu/offices/iii.

The concept of *lifelong mentoring* is newly emerging in the educational literature. As of 1998, we found one instance of its use. This site, produced in the Netherlands in Dutch, is located at www.hva.nl/project/vhto/site/project2.htm. Importantly, it appears that the concept of lifelong mentoring had not reached North America. We hope that, with this chapter, we have signaled its arrival on our shores.

Part III

Mentoring Leadership

16 Multiple Level Comentoring: Moving Toward a Learning Organization

Dale W. Lick

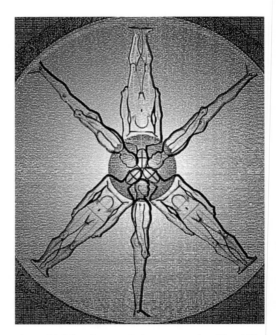

Figure 16.1: Multilevel synergistic comentoring (Rami Bitar, 1998)

How can we bring about positive and productive change in schools? This chapter narrates a powerful new approach to school change called the "whole-faculty study group process" that has the potential to increase school effectiveness, enhance student learning, and move schools toward becoming learning organizations. The core element in this transitional process is synergistic, multiple-level comentoring, teachers-to-teachers, administrators-to-teachers, and administrators-to-administrators. The discussion is based on my work in change management and experiences with the whole-faculty study group process in over 75 schools and 700 study groups in those schools. It provides both the practical knowledge required to implement and successfully use this new approach and a theoretical foundation to understand its key components. This chapter also draws many of the process fundamentals and practices from the comprehensive study group book by Carlene Murphy and myself (1998).

School change and comentoring teams

During the last 15 years, school reform and the improvement of schools have been the intense focus of almost every sector of our society. The general and educational rhetoric have been high but desired school results, in contrast, have been unimpressive. Even with the efforts of well-intentioned leaders and school personnel, logical and progressive solutions have either failed or had only limited success. Why? Simply put, substantive change, even positively perceived change, is difficult to bring about in long-standing, well-established organizations. Schools, like other organizations, are just not naturally open or amenable to major change.

Successful reform and school transformation will require different approaches and processes. In addition to determining what changes and reforms are required, we must also implement a significant transition process to help negotiate the societal, organizational, cultural, and interpersonal barriers relating to schools. We must find ways to transition individuals and groups from the old to the new paradigms, as well as transition the related processes and circumstances from the previous to the desired ones. Further, if genuine reform and change are to come to our schools, then teachers, administrators, and school personnel must be importantly and intimately involved in the process.

The professional whole-faculty study groups process represents one of the most successful and exciting new approaches to reform and change in education today. It gives, within reason, a school and its faculty the power to determine and transition to its own destiny. The process involves not just study groups, but the "whole faculty" being active in study groups and each group taking responsibility for an important part of the change or reform effort. The study group process, where properly implemented, has been unusually successful (Joyce, Murphy, Showers and Murphy, 1989). The study group approach is a holistic, practical process for facilitating major schoolwide change and for enhancing student learning in schools. The key strength of this approach comes from its self-directed, multilevel, synergistic, comentoring teams that form and creatively function as part of the study group process.

In this chapter I discuss comentoring groups, their function and dynamics, and the different layers of comentoring that can occur in the study group process.

Nature of study groups

It is common for small groups of teachers (i.e. study groups) to come together to promote collegial interchange and action, take courses, read and discuss professional literature, explore research findings, and introduce new instructional approaches. However, when properly utilized, professional study groups of teachers have the potential to facilitate major change and significant improvement in schools. I define a *study group* as a small group of school personnel joining together to increase their capacity (willingness and ability) through new learning opportunities for the benefit of students and the school. Ideally, professional study groups serve as a vehicle to integrate individual and institutional development through a set of personal and challenging relationships, creating conditions and circumstances where young people can learn to their fullest potential.

The whole-faculty study group process is a professional development approach that enables teachers to design their own learning and implement what they learn in their classrooms for the benefit of their students. In the process, all teachers in a school meet in study groups for serious inquiry and action research about student needs and classroom instruction. They also meet to explore applications that enhance student learning and improve school effectiveness.

Regardless of the size of school, grade level, or school demographics, study groups in general have two things in common – they are made up of adult learners and the faculty worry about logistical concerns such as meeting times, the group's organization, and the work of the group. Differences among schools' study group processes come mostly from how each faculty decides to initiate and implement the process. It should be noted that the study group process is *not* advised unless the whole faculty has an understanding of the process, acknowledging that a 75 per cent endorsement of one's colleagues obligates everyone to participate in analyzing (student data) and identifying (student needs).

Ends, means, and learning enhancement

In education we tend to have a problem in differentiating between "means" and "ends." The study group process is a means to an end, whereas the desired ends for this process are enhanced student learning and school improvement. In general, means are tools, methods, techniques, resources, or processes used to achieve the ends, and ends are results, outcomes, outputs, or products. Kaufman, Herman, and Watters (1996) remind us that one of the six critical success factors in education is "Differentiate between ends and means – focus on the *what* (the desired ends) before selecting the *how* (the means)" (p. 18). For example, desired ends for a school initiative might be an increase in student achievement and a decrease in negative student behavior, while the means to these ends might be whole-faculty training in several modes of teaching and organizing the entire faculty in study groups to support themselves in the implementation of new teaching repertoires.

The overarching academic goal of each school is student learning. Organizing study groups for the sake of having study groups is a disservice to the school and students. Desired professional ends of study groups are positive change in student learning and school improvement.

Transition through change

School reform, especially enhanced student learning, is difficult to accomplish and represents major change. It requires that schools and teachers deal with the natural resistance to change of people and organizations and the rigidities of an educational and social cultural system that has been in place for centuries. Why then is the whole-faculty study group process so effective? Study groups allow for the creation of individual, team, and schoolwide comentoring processes that provide new and appropriate learning opportunities, reduce resistance, and modify the culture enough to permit change. The study group process encompasses the key elements of change management required for transforming organizations and their processes, including

- strong change sponsorship;
- the building of individual, team, and school resilience (i.e. the ability to demonstrate both strength and flexibility in the face of disorder and change) so that people and schools can be more change-adaptable;
- effective comentoring (i.e. collaborative and synergistic study groups having common goals, interdependence, empowerment, and participative involvement;
- modification of the educational and school culture; and
- foundation building toward a learning organization.

The typical major components of the whole-faculty study group process are

1 supporting the implementation of curricular and instructional innovations,
2 integrating and giving coherence to a school's instructional practices and programs,
3 targeting an identified schoolwide need,
4 studying research on teaching and learning,
5 monitoring the impact of innovations on students and on changes in the workplace, and
6 acting as a vehicle to accomplish many vital purposes (Murphy and Lick, 1998).

In particular, the study group process, as a professional development model, is an integrated, cocreative learning experience for adults that is student and teacher centered, experimental and research oriented, reflective, holistic, supportive, inspiring, and empowering.

Commitment and change efforts

An important factor in dealing with major change is building of commitment for desired change projects and their ramifications. Commitment building is creating a foundation for personal, political and institutional acceptance, encouragement, and support for the study group process. Effective commitment building leads to meaningful and positive work and results. What helps make faculties committed and want to continue the study group process year after year are its contributions to both their increased effectiveness and positive, measurable results with their students.

As schools attempt to build commitment for study group efforts, an understanding of the four roles of change – change sponsorship, change agent, change target, and change advocate – is valuable. A *change sponsor* or *sponsor* is an individual or group who has the power to sanction or legitimize the change or efforts of the study group, such as the school board, the superintendent, the principal, a department chair, a combination of these individuals, or the faculty itself in certain circumstances. Strong sponsorship is critical to effective commitment building and successful change, and sponsors have the responsibility to decide what initiatives will be authorized, communicate their decisions and priorities, and provide the encouragement, pressure, and support necessary for study group efforts.

Change agent or *agent* is an individual or group who is responsible for implementing the desired change, and typically includes teachers and study groups in school alteration or innovation, as well as administrators and supervisors. A *change target* or *target* is an individual or group who must actually change, and most often includes students, teachers, and administrators who must transition for an initiative to be successful. A *change advocate* or *advocate* is an individual or group who desires a change but does not have the authority to sanction it, and often includes study groups, the principal, or nonschool people who recommend an initiative but have no power to approve it. For example, if a school considers an initiative involving computer-assisted instruction, the board, superintendent, and principal who authorized the initiative would be the sponsors, the principal and teachers who were responsible for implementing the initiative would be the change agents, and the students and teachers who actually had to change would be the targets. Others who support the initiative but without authority to approve it, such as parents and other groups, would be advocates.

Universal change principle

In general, the more people understand and the greater their competence, the more committed they become. They feel like they have a greater sense of control over a change or at least know what to anticipate, giving them an increased sense of comfort and security and potentially reducing their resistance to the change. These notions lead naturally to the accessible but powerful change principle that I call the *universal change principle*. As the name implies, it has applicability almost everywhere in change-related efforts and denotes that: *learning must precede change.*

Application of the universal change principle does not guarantee all resistance to change will be eliminated and that all desired changes can be accomplished. However, proper application of this principle does significantly enhance the likelihood of desired changes happening. Notice the principle implies "no surprises" and for large change efforts, such as major school initiatives, there must be a lot of learning, possibly several well-planned iterations of appropriate learning.

For instance, suppose a principal wants the mathematics faculty to implement a new teaching approach in algebra. If the principal just announces that teachers will use the new method next semester, teachers will often resist rather than facilitate the principal's decision. If, on the other hand, the principal employs the universal change principle, he or she would ask, "What learning must take place before this change can be successfully implemented?" In response, the principal might consider a series of learning opportunities and discussions about the new teaching approach. This series would need to include why the new method is important to improving student learning and to the faculty and school; what the implications are for students, faculty, and school; and when and how this new approach will be implemented. Providing these learning opportunities does not guarantee that everyone will be on board, but it will significantly increase the chances for its successful implementation.

Cultural change

What is school culture? *School culture* is the social and normative glue that holds together the educational aspects of a school (Birnbaum, 1988). In a sense, it is the personality of the school. School culture is not always visible to outsiders and even to many within, but it is a powerful force that is always "there." The culture of a school sets values and establishes ground rules for how people think and behave, and for what they assume to be important. Since my interest in culture focuses on the relationship of culture to change (e.g. student learning enhancement and school improvement), I will use a definition from a change perspective. School culture reflects the interrelationship of shared assumptions, beliefs, and behaviors that are acquired over time by members of a school (Conner, 1993). The key building blocks of culture are assumptions, beliefs, and behaviors. If a school changes one or more of these, it represents a change in the school culture. One of my goals is for schools to carefully alter some of these building blocks to allow for desired changes in student learning and school improvement.

Realigning a school culture, a *cultural transformation* or *cultural shift*, requires a modification, in some measure, of assumptions, beliefs, or behaviors to make them more consistent with the desired new directions of the school. One important strength of the whole-faculty study group process, and its multilevel comentoring components, is that it has the capability to bring about a cultural transformation and, through the shift, desirable changes in how the school functions.

Process guidelines

The study group process, in the context of the school's improvement or transformation plan, is the means for educators to acquire and develop the knowledge and skills necessary to help them enhance student performance and increase school effectiveness. Carlene Murphy, a study group process expert with schools, has found that these 15 guidelines help study groups to achieve their desired results.

1 Keep the size of the group to no more than six,
2 do not worry about the composition of the study group,

3 establish and keep a regular schedule,
4 establish group norms at the first meeting of the study group,
5 agree on an action plan for the study group,
6 complete a log after each study group meeting,
7 encourage members to keep individual logs for their personal reflection,
8 establish a pattern of study group leadership,
9 give all group members equal status,
10 have a curriculum and instructional focus,
11 plan ahead for transitions,
12 make a comprehensive list of learning resources, both material and human,
13 include learning opportunities and training in the study group's agenda,
14 evaluate the effectiveness of the study group, and
15 establish a variety of communication networks and systems.

Content of the process

The content educators must possess or acquire to achieve their intended results is critical to the study group process, including what teachers investigate and study and what they do to become more skillful in the classroom with students. If students are to become more knowledgeable and skillful, then teachers must change some of the academic content they teach and increase their repertoire of instructional strategies to deliver that content to students. A positive professional outlook embraces the notion that educators are always "a work in progress," in the process of developing or becoming more effective practitioners.

Study groups generally work with a combination of five staff development content areas: academic knowledge, instructional strategies, instructional skills, management, and belief systems. The promise in the study group process is that teachers will become more knowledgeable and effective, raising the students' rates of learning in personal, social, and academic domains. It has been shown that learning rates of students can be increased by having teachers focus on instructional strategies that make the educational environment more active, and that encourage higher order thinking and teach social skills.

A decision-making model

The first decision to be made in the whole-faculty study group process is whether or not the process is to be put in place at a school. This is a key decision, since a positive conclusion commits *every* faculty member to participate in a study group. Once a positive decision has been made to implement the study group process in a school, the following cyclical decision-making model for the balance of the process has worked successfully in various schools:

1   analyze a wide range of data and indicators describing the status of student learning and the condition of the learning environment,
2   from the data, generate a list of student needs,
3   categorize student needs and prioritize the categories or clusters,
4   organize study groups around the prioritized student needs,
5   create a study group action plan,
6   implement the study group action plan, and
7   evaluate the impact of the study group effort on student performance (Murphy and Lick, 1998).

The cycle is continued by repeating step one and the balance of the model.

Comentoring and team building

In Chapter 3, I discussed comentoring, team-building, and synergistic relationships and the power of these to build especially effective learning teams. That discussion is now directly applicable to study groups and the whole-faculty study group process, because synergistic comentoring study groups are the *soul* or essential part of the study group process.

In constructive comentoring groups, each person acts as a sponsor, advocate, guide – or teaches, advises, trusts, critiques, and supports others to express, pursue, and finalize goals. Also important is being competent, unexploitive, positive in attitude, and involved. Ideally, in a comentoring situation, each member of the group offers support and encouragement to everyone else, which expands individual and group understanding, improving the group's effectiveness and productivity. This is exactly what happens in a properly applied study group process, the study groups, in great measure, become synergistic comentoring teams. The Partnership Support Group (PSG), discussed earlier in this book and that worked to create it, as well as examples in many other chapters, are helpful illustrations of synergistic, comentoring teams in action.

Effective comentoring groups are capable teams. A comentoring group will not live up to its capacity if it does not have genuine teamwork. Teamwork is what typically differentiates an effective comentoring group from a less successful committee or group. *Teamwork* can be defined as the willingness and ability of members of a group to work together in a genuinely cooperative (i.e. interdependent) manner toward a common goal or vision. According to Conner (1993), "Teamwork requires insight and ideas, open discussion, and respect for the values and input of others" (p. 190). Teamwork is the vehicle that allows common comentoring groups to attain uncommon results.

The synergistic process is an extremely powerful approach for increasing the effectiveness, productivity, and quality of comentoring groups. However, creating strong, effective comentoring groups means taking the necessary steps to build synergistic teams. Developing synergistic teams requires groups to be proactive and intentional, and make a substantial commitment and effort.

Multilevel comentoring

The study group process described in this chapter is a powerful approach to school change and the enhancement of student performance. It not only provides a new set of procedures for learning and action research for the faculty, it also puts in place a schoolwide development program for multilevel, synergistic comentoring teams. I introduced procedures for learning and action research in early sections of this chapter. Using the foundation that I have established for team-building, I will now focus on issues related to development.

The people or groups involved in the study process are the *initial and sustaining sponsors* (i.e. those that provide the initial or sustaining legitimization of the effort – the school board, superintendent, principal(s), and the faculty/administrative leadership council); *change agents* (i.e. those who are responsible for implementing the changes – the principal, a leadership team, a coordinating council, and study groups); *targets* (i.e. those who must actually change – the principal, the teachers, and the students); and *advocates* (i.e. those who desire the changes but have no authority to sanction them – students, parents, and business and community leaders). One of the strengths of the process is that these groups become synergistically interwoven as comentoring teams, dramatically increasing the potential for productive change in the school.

The leadership of the school, typically the board, the superintendent, and principal(s) must decide whether to support the study group process before it can be taken to the faculty. These decisions constitute a serious "buy-in." It lays a *sponsorship base* for their becoming a comentoring group involving the study group process and its activities. This leadership support is a public expression for their faculty's full-fledged commitment to such efforts. Once the leadership forwards the initiative to the faculty, the faculty can either accept or reject the study group process for their school. If they accept the study group process (by a majority vote), they know that it binds every teacher to a faculty-led, change process in the school and within a study group structure. This decision is vital since it represents *whole-faculty change sponsorship*.

After its approval, the principal typically appoints a leadership group of teachers for the process, a *focus team*. The focus team, along with the principal, learns how to initiate and implement the study group process, develops a step-by-step plan, works with the faculty to implement the process, and then directs and monitors the overall functioning of the process. Under the title of *instructional council*, the focus team meets every four to six weeks together with representatives of each study group to discuss what study groups are doing and to address concerns and more.

These arrangements provide three additional opportunities for comentoring: the relationship between the focus team and the principal; the functioning of the focus team itself; and the interaction within the instructional council involving the teachers of the focus team and those representing the individual study groups. These provide occasions for the creation of synergistic comentoring to enhance communication, interdependence, and empowerment of all involved. They also generate circumstances for sustaining sponsorship of the overall study group process and for providing transitioning activities. Effective synergistic comentoring in these relationships helps develop unity of purpose and a supportive environment for the work of study groups and their coordination.

The most important comentoring opportunities, though, come in the study groups themselves. For them to reach their greatest effectiveness, they must clearly set common goals, work interdependently (mutually dependently and genuinely cooperatively), empower one another (appreciate and value the input of others), and, in a balanced fashion, openly share their ideas. It is here that the substance for meaningful change is formed and that the buy-in for real transformation in the classroom and school forms.

Among the other levels of involvement that are valuable to the study group process are the students, parents, and community. These "domains" have a great deal to do with what changes and will work in the schools. Students become fascinated with the action research and colearning that teachers are doing in their study group efforts. If made to feel part of the "reform team," they become more amenable to new approaches and materials that teachers introduce. Students, too, can participate in a form of synergistic comentoring with their teachers and classmates as the study group process permeates learning in their school and community.

Finally, a major benefit that seems to accompany the growing synergistic comentoring relationships is a vertical synergistic and comentoring enrichment, from bottom to top and vice versa. This enrichment further strengthens team-building, sponsorship, advocacy, support, and commitment to fundamental and substantive changes in school culture leading to enhanced student learning and school improvement.

The multilevel, synergistic comentoring discussed in this section is depicted in the artwork that opens this chapter. Each person in Figure 16.1 represents one layer in the multilevel comentoring relationship. The circle encompassing the heads and shoulders reflects the powerful and creative synergy in these relationships leading to the unusual effectiveness of these different participating groups and the organization as a whole.

Moving toward a learning organization

The whole-faculty study group process has been shown to be unusually successful in bringing about meaningful school change and enhancing student learning. A properly applied study group process represents the key elements for successfully managing major change. It not only critically determines the most important needs to be studied and effected, but it also generates a transformational process that effectively transitions people from where they were to where they must be for the desired results to be realized. This process involves massive change management that advances a focus on imperative changes, sponsorship, preparation of change agents, commitment of targets, reduced resistance, advocacy, knowledge of change and change principles, organized processes for transition, comentoring group synergy, learning team development, and school and educational culture modification.

The study group process, through the above key elements of leading and managing change, provide a structured movement for a school toward becoming a learning organization. The process generates collective vision, inspiration, energy, participation, and synergy. Learning, continuous improvement, and change become the norm of the workplace and organizational culture. All of these help the school to become more effective.

School transformation and multilevel comentoring

The effective transformation of schools to meet future needs has shown itself to be difficult to accomplish. A decade of rhetoric and serious efforts have left us wanting and frustrated; most efforts have failed or only been partially successful. Why? Because it is hard to bring about the necessary transformational change in long-standing, well-established organizations such as schools. Their cultures, the same ones that have been successful and stable in the past, are not naturally amenable to transformational change. To successfully implement desired major change, we must not only decide what change is essential, but must also put in place a significant transition process to negotiate school barriers.

17 From School to Family: A Voyage of the Soul

Frances K. Kochan

Figure 17.1: A school community called family (Julie Johnson, 1998)

How can you transition a school and its personnel from a relatively typical day-to-day environment to one that inspires, generates hope, and motivates actions of leaders, teachers, and staff to innovative new practices, relationships, and effectiveness? In particular, how can a school and its members create and sustain a sufficiently high level of synergistic comentoring to build an empowering "family" atmosphere, one with a sense of unity and community among administrators, faculty, and staff that supports and nurtures those within, enhancing student performance and school effectiveness?

During my 26 years in education, I have worked with wonderful people who have helped me to learn and grow. One experience in particular has had a profound effect on me. It involved working with my colleagues to change our relationships, thinking, actions, culture, and ourselves. What began as a project became a way of life. This experience taught me more about myself and how synergy between people can create a new reality than I could have believed possible. It became an adventure – part of my personal and professional voyage toward wholeness – and it had a similar effect on many who experienced it. This chapter is the story of this voyage. It describes a process we went through as we changed from an organization called "school" to a community called "family."

Creating a synergistic comentoring community

The traditional view of the organization as operating mechanically is giving way to new images (Kochan, 1996). The recent emphasis is on organizations as social systems comprised of individuals, symbols, relationships, and communication patterns (Fullan with Stiegelbauer, 1991; Senge, 1990). Public schools, which have long been organized around a mechanistic production model, are being challenged to change; the same is happening for institutions of higher education (Kochan, Anderson-Harper and Beck, 1998). This challenge brings with it a call for systemic restructuring which requires changing relationships, organizational cultures, and mindsets. Creating communities in which teachers work collaboratively, share successes and failures, accept responsibility for decision making, and feel secure and happy, are major goals in this restructuring process (Sergiovanni, 1994).

In 1989, the Florida State University School (FSUS) embarked upon creating such a collaborative environment. The effort was aimed at changing the character and relationships that existed among those within the school, their families, and the community. Although the process began as a means of addressing the need to work more closely with families, it became a major organizational reform effort.

The school received a grant from the Florida Department of Education to develop a program to strengthen relationships between the school, families of the children it served, and the community. There were three administrators at the school: the director, the secondary school principal, and myself, the elementary principal and coinvestigator of the grant. We joined with the Florida State University College of Education to facilitate the project. This partnership with several departments within the university proved extremely productive. We learned from one another, conducted research together, and published our findings. These relationships were instrumental in dealing with the various barriers that existed between the school and university.

The project director was responsible for the coordination of the project, and was assisted by two members of the faculty, who were assigned to the project on a full-time basis. Consultants from the state department served as project advisers that enhanced our ability to understand the perspective of stakeholders in the community.

Once we had the grant, the director of FSUS asked the faculty and staff if any of us were interested in taking a leadership role in the project endeavor. Thirteen individuals volunteered to assist and became the program steering committee. Permitting faculty and staff to volunteer to lead was a crucial yet unplanned factor in the success of the effort. During the evaluation phase of the project, numerous comments were made about the importance of this event.

The faculty decided to implement the program in three phases: the first year, we would seek to create a new internal culture; the second year, we would work with families and establish support systems for them; and the third year, we would focus on expanding our outreach efforts to join school, family, and community. This chapter deals with the first 18 months of our voyage and how this process created a *synergistic comentoring community*, impacting the school.

Building "family"

The initial phase of the restructuring process, described here, centered on changing the internal operation and governance structure of the school. The steering committee proposed creating a decentralized governance and management system through small working groups called "families." The rationale was that before the school could work effectively with families, it would have to become a family itself. The conceptual framework for this restructuring effort was "school as family." The metaphor of "family" was selected in the hope that it would evoke a sense of unity and community among faculty and staff. There is evidence to support the use of metaphor as a strong force in motivating people and in influencing their emotional responses to an idea (Lakoff and Johnson, 1980). This seems to have been the case in our situation because participants remarked: "Family is the heart of this. It is what people are responding to," and "Family is a philosophy. It is an internal thing. People are responding to that."

We created five family groups. Each involved a particular aspect of the school or its population. The families were school policy, family, faculty, students, and community. Each family had the responsibility for assessing the needs of their topic area and proposing actions to meet those needs. They were also responsible for providing individual support to their members and for assisting in school governance. We defined family as "a unit that supports and nurtures those within it." A pictorial representation of the family's essence as a series of overlapping, interconnected persons is shown in Figure 17.1.

We used Stinnett and DeFrain's (1986) and Curran's (1983) research on the characteristics of strong families as a framework for building our family relationships. These researchers found that strong families have six characteristics: commitment, communication, coping skills to manage resources and make decisions, appreciation, spending time together, and emotional and spiritual wellness. We disseminated this information about strong families, discussed it, and tried to focus our energies on incorporating these characteristics into our operations, our interpersonal relationships, and the manner in which our family groups functioned. From the mentoring perspective of this research and the community project upon which this chapter is based, "family" is a good example of a synergistic comentoring team.

All members of the faculty and staff, including administrators, selected the family group they wished to belong to. Five individuals volunteered to become family facilitators. They assumed the responsibility for assisting the family groups in their work. The families were to serve as support systems for their members and as policy making bodies for the school.

Impact of the faculty family

My role in the "School as Family" effort was unique. I chose to become a member of the Faculty Family. Members of this family were charged with dealing with the welfare and concerns of the faculty. There were 13 members with teacher representation from elementary, middle, and high school levels. I was the only administrator in the family. A cafeteria worker was also a family member. We agreed that we were equal in this family and that we must respect confidentiality. We also determined that the family facilitator, not I, would take concerns to the administration. Our facilitator was an experienced faculty member. About him, family members said, "He has been here a long time. They respect him." I was careful not to talk about family issues to my administrative colleagues. When we came together as a family, I did not think of myself as an administrator, but as a part of my family unit.

The Faculty Family's first action was to redesign the faculty lounge. Members redecorated it, enhanced communication by installing a bulletin board, converted the lounge to a "no smoking" area, and found alternative locations for smokers. These combined actions provided a catalyst for other "families" to take action. Evidence of change seemed to stimulate a belief in possibilities and encouraged other families to take action. As one member of the Student Family said, "The Faculty Family started it all by making the teachers' lounge nicer."

The Faculty Family worked to develop a community spirit among all. One avenue for doing this was by changing the agenda and organization of faculty meetings. The Faculty Family became involved in setting the agenda, adding a period when people shared "family" news, and arranging for refreshments to be served. They created a mentorship program for new faculty and instituted a "getting to know you" activity.

One of the most powerful outcomes of our Faculty Family activities was the establishment of a faculty ombudsperson whom we described as someone who "investigates and tries to resolve problems between people." The Faculty Family shared their idea and job description with the faculty and staff at a school-wide meeting at which the administration also spoke for the proposal. The faculty voted unanimously to select someone to serve in this capacity. Seventeen people consented to having their names placed in nomination. Although there would be no extra pay for this task, there were many who believed in it strongly enough to assume this role. Members of the Faculty Family met individually with school staff before selecting someone. This position changed the dynamics of relationships between teachers, administrators, and staff. During the first year, the ombudsperson dealt with many issues, only one of which had to be brought to administration for resolution. Faculty and staff began resolving their own problems. As an administrator, it was a relief not to have to deal with some of these issues. As a Faculty Family member, it brought a sense of satisfaction and success.

Our family worked out a system for meeting together in the morning before school started, usually twice a month. Since time was limited, we became adept at dealing with issues quickly or assigning members to work together to draw up a proposal or plan for action.

Humor was often a part of our family interactions. For example, when trying to organize a social, a note came out to us saying, "There will be a report on a potential trip to Pogoland. Please be sure to attend the meeting." The Faculty Family focused on the idea of modeling positive behavior and relationships to establish a tone of unity and community in the school. As the facilitator stated, "The best way to change others is to model the behavior yourself. I have tried to keep it positive." During the year, each family had a day away from the school where they could meet as a family. We met at one of our family member's home. Our day turned out to be a cold one that led our host to prepare a fire in his fireplace. There, warmed by the crackling flames, we planned for the year. We shared not only our ideas, but ourselves.

At the end of the year, our facilitator told us he planned to retire from teaching. He spoke with each of us about who we thought should be our next facilitator, and then one among us assumed the role. At our last meeting together our family facilitator said, "You all have been great. You don't know how much it has meant. I have felt like we were a family, not a committee." As we bid farewell, I felt strong emotion. The moist eyes of my colleagues told me that we had indeed become a family – with all that that signifies.

Understanding the process

As we engaged in the process of "becoming" together, I became more bonded to the members of my family and to the school organization. I could sense the closeness occurring within each family and in the school. Developing an interest in what others were experiencing, I began a formal case study of the process. As a participant–observer, and a member of the Faculty Family, I had access to the historical data, transcripts of interviews conducted by an outside evaluator, and survey and other assessment results gathered by an internal evaluator. One of the aspects I examined was the impact on the individuals involved.

During the past decade there has been a growing body of research on creating systemic change through developing collaborative and supportive environments (e.g. Fullan with Stiegelbauer, 1991). Although the literature supports the centrality of the teacher in the restructuring process, there is scant research examining the impact of participation on those involved in them (O'Donoghue, 1994). What has been explored tends to deal with elements of the effort rather than descriptions of the whole process (Lieberman and Miller, 1992). A review of research on the impact of participatory decision making, suggests that benefits may not have direct effects on decision outcomes, but might result in positive effects on morale and satisfaction (Estler, 1988). Chapman (1990) found increased trust, control, and commitment in those involved in implementing such efforts. When restructuring includes increased empowerment, researchers have found associations with job satisfaction, climate, and commitment.

In a study asking teachers what they thought the impact of increased site-based management might be, respondents listed potential positive effects as increased teacher collaboration and higher self-esteem. However, they thought that such reform efforts would increase tensions and pressure for teachers. They were also concerned that site-based decision making processes would require teachers to be away from their classroom. They believed this would have a negative effect upon student learning (Hallinger, Murphy and Hausman, 1993). Changing hierarchical governance structures to shared management models has not always resulted in increased empowerment. In studying a mandated restructuring effort in Australia, O'Donoghue (1994) discovered a lowering of teacher morale. The researcher believed this negative impact resulted because teachers did not have a voice in the restructuring model.

These conflicting findings have most often dealt with examining a particular aspect of restructuring, such as empowerment, to identify the effect upon the organization or individuals concerned. I sought to understand the restructuring experience holistically from the perspective of those involved by examining and describing a school engaged in restructuring. In what is shared here, I dealt with the question, "What are the positive aspects of involvement in the "school as family" restructuring effort on school personnel?"

The method of inquiry I used was a case study that employed ethnographic techniques. Data samples were collected over an 18-month period. I reviewed documents, conducted interviews, and made observations. I examined 206 documents generated by project staff, family groups, consultants, and evaluators. Forty interviews were conducted involving 78 individuals. I completed 22 of these interviews and shared transcripts with the interviewees for verification and revision. I made notations dealing with atmosphere, tone, and other pertinent ideas.

My observations allowed me to get a "feel" for the context in which activities occurred. I formally observed 24 meetings; informal observations occurred daily. Among aspects examined were the setting, participants, activities, interactions, frequency and duration, and subtleties (Taylor and Bogdan, 1984). I recorded substantive ideas and conversations in my field notebook.

Additionally, I gathered and analyzed data in phases: phase one covered 6 months; phase two, 9 months; and phase three, 3 months. Although planning, implementation, and evaluation occurred throughout, the major focus of phase one was planning, while phase two was concerned with implementation, and phase three dealt primarily with evaluation. Analysis occurred on a continuous basis. I grouped comments, outcomes, statements, and actions by what appeared to be positive and negative aspects of involvement.

Then I developed six case studies, one for each family group and one for the school as a whole. A cross-case analysis of case studies was conducted to determine how often and in which families positive and negative effects impacted individuals. A quantitative decision-rule was applied across the cases to determine if a category would be included or discarded.

Issues of research quality

I used standards of quality in conducting my research. When dealing with consistency, I applied Guba's (1985) logic that considers whether the data that has been collected makes sense, not whether the results hold true in all settings. I also dealt with questions of neutrality as does Patton (1990): "Qualitative objectivity has to do with the quality of the observations made" (p. 337). The use of triangulation, collection of data over time, verification of data by participants, data collection by multiple persons, all support the quality of the observations made.

Research findings

Outcomes

At the end of the first year, an outside consultant conducted a problem/benefit survey to determine the positive outcomes achieved and to identify concerns. Findings indicated that the restructuring effort was extremely successful in creating a sense of family, empowering faculty, and developing shared governance. There were 7 major student benefits, 10 teacher benefits, 4 benefits for parents, and 13 benefits for the school. Among the most prominent were:

- a sense of family has permeated the faculty and staff,
- improved relationships between teachers, students, and parents have developed,
- staff, parents, and students feel that their input makes a difference and that their knowledge and expertise are more respected now, and
- school personnel are working together better as a team. (Foster, 1990, pp. 40–5)

While there were problems identified, few were rated as serious or very serious by the majority of the faculty. The two problems most frequently noted as "seriously inhibiting progress" were the lack of written student discipline policies and inconsistent standards in disciplining students. Faculty indicated that a proposed set of policies being developed by the student family would help resolve these problems.

The major problem identified in implementing the "school as family" restructuring effort was the time required. Faculty and staff were conducting family activities in addition to their normal job load. Although they sometimes had release days or were paid to come in on a Saturday or during summer months, there was some increase in stress because of all that had to be done. However, faculty indicated that they were willing to continue the endeavor because they believed in what they were doing and were witnessing positive results from their efforts.

Participation in this successful restructuring effort appeared to have positively impacted feelings, attitudes, and relationships of those involved. Table 17.1 displays these effects.

Feelings

Participation in the "school as family" effort had an impact on how people felt about themselves, the organization, and their place. On the personal level, changes

Table 17.1:   *Impact of participation in "school as family" program*

Theme	Category	Sub-category
Feelings	Personal	Sense of identity
		Feeling valued
		Personal/professional growth
		Belonging
	Organizational	Feeling connected
		Increased commitment
		Empowered
Attitudes	Internal	Trust expanded
		Increased tolerance
	External	Increased acceptance
		Expanded connections
Relationships	Empathy	More interconnections
		Deeper concern
	Interaction	Communication
		More conversations
	Synergy	Increased levels of professionalism, interdependence, and empowerment

in the culture appeared to have made people feel more secure. Someone described it as a "sense of identity." Another called it "rootedness." A third remarked, "I know my job is important now. That makes me happier."

A typical remark was: "This has changed me. Every project I do now I think in terms of family. I have changed my orientation in and out of school." Individuals spoke of "being valued" and "appreciated." Statements such as, "My involvement in the 'school as family' effort has been a very positive influence on my life," and "These people can see that this is going to make their lives better," were prevalent. There were many comments about seeing people become "rejuvenated" and "recharged." People spoke of this endeavor as being an "avenue for personal and professional growth."

These feelings also extended to how individuals perceived themselves in relation to the organization. Numerous remarks were made about feeling "connected" and of "committing themselves" to the "school as family" effort. Stated one respondent, "I am amazed. I am committed to doing my part. It is teaching me something."

People demonstrated commitment in a myriad of ways: Meeting before or after school and on Saturdays without compensation; assuming additional responsibilities, and developing materials and willingly sharing them. As one person stated: "In the past I was sort of an island unto myself. Now I feel a part of something." Another said, "I think people feel like they are doing something – they are contributing something to the whole."

Individuals expressed the ways in which they felt differently about the organization through statements such as, "People were skeptical at first that this could work. Years and years of entrenched built-in operational barriers were there. I think we have started to break that down." As one person expressed it, "A lot of people knew there was something wrong. Now we understand the reasons better." Another said, "There is a change in spirit. We are happier, more productive. Something has been rekindled."

Feelings of being "empowered" and of "being able to do something" were common. One person explained it in this way: "I have been here since 1969 and I have never felt as comfortable. It is because we have gone at it from the bottom up rather than from the top down. After a while when it is top down, even if it is something that is right, the people who it is being done to feel helpless. We kept saying, 'they.' Now we say 'we.' We are it and we can make the change." Another stated, "It used to be that the administration told us what to do and we did it. We didn't have common goals. The families have given us a voice and people power. It is a means of getting things done." A third remarked, "It gives you hope. A few years ago we would not even have attempted to do what we have done. Now we will try again." Said another, "At first I thought 'this is too much. We can never create the kind of changes we need to make.' Then later I started thinking, we *can* change this place." Another said, "It has made me feel I have more control, not just at school but in all facets of my life."

Attitudes

This shared governance and community-building experience appeared to have altered attitudes toward those inside and outside the school. People talked about "appreciating each other more" and focusing upon "others" and their "struggles." There was talk about changing attitudes toward the administration from an "us-them" mentality to one of "we."

Attitudes towards one another also seemed to become more caring. There were numerous circumstances where people did special things to demonstrate appreciation. Sending notes, making announcements, and disseminating information in creative ways to highlight others' accomplishments became the norm.

Teachers' attitudes toward students were also affected. Teachers' talk about students changed from blame and even anger to a more compassionate stance. Teachers claimed that they "understood students better." Typical comments included, "I think there is more interaction between the faculty and students. Students say there is more concern for them," and "Our attitude toward students has changed from blame to wanting to help." Activities which resulted included a one-day conference for students based upon what they had identified as their interests and needs. Students were involved in the planning process. The conference was highly successful and students indicated they had gained much in terms of having their needs met. The entire faculty and staff took pride in this activity and decided to make it an annual event.

Attitudes about parents seemed to change substantially. Many activities were planned to bring parents into the school and to reach out to them in other ways. Faculty inconvenienced themselves to meet the time schedules of parents. Conversations about parents became more supportive. Among the comments made were:

"It seems as if the school is becoming more oriented toward families"; "I am more open to saying things to parents;" "I become less upset when parents say they can't leave their jobs to come to school. I am more tolerant of family problems;" and "We build around family here now. The concept builds bridges to new ideas and concepts. Your attitude changes. You think differently."

Relationships

The third area in which change appeared to occur was in internal and external relationships. An important element in this change was increased empathy. Relationships seemed to become imbued with a deeper sensitivity and understanding among participants. The greatest impact seemed to be between those internal to FSUS. Teachers noted that being part of the school restructuring effort had changed their relationships with their students and their own children. Among the typical statements were, "As a total, this change fed back into the school and into the classroom, and into the way we treated children and talked with them. We never had worked as completely as this with children who needed help." Teachers spoke about being more interconnected, and one teacher said, "This empathy also affected relationships with parents and families." A typical comment was, "I think the family connection brought around the ability for parents to share and talk about it when they were sad. It was learning about forming deeper relationships with them." Actions such as meeting parents at their workplace and holding parent workshops were indicative of this newly expanded understanding.

Having opportunities to talk together, to share, and to get to know one another more personally seemed to be a strong factor in changing relationships. Commented one individual, "At the beginning we had the chance to share something personal with each other. That was important. It created empathy and understanding. We have one member that is 'different.' People will say, 'That's OK' It's like having a *real* family. When someone is different you just accept them." Comments that captured the essence of this expanded empathy included:

- I think we have become a family.
- We have a greater sense of unity. There is a stronger connection between us and the students.
- We have a common bond. People are doing nice things for each other. Those who were skeptical and aggressively against it have mellowed. This has brought us closer together. It has made an impact on how the faculty relates to one another and to the students.
- I have gotten to know other members of the faculty more personally. People become more human. Often you get to know people by rumor. You develop an impression. When you have physical contact you get to KNOW them.

A particularly powerful statement came from a teacher who had been at the school for years:

I have felt left out in the past. When I told someone something before, they said things like "you're naive." People used to come to my room when they wanted something. Now they come to talk about family things. People come in now who never came before. This family thing enlightens, empowers, and enriches. It has opened people up. We have a common goal. We care about each others' lives. We have lost our apathy.

Another improvement in relationships dealt with the increased capacity to communicate with those internal and external to the school. The family governance structure enabled personnel to communicate more effectively. Thus they were able to more easily resolve school problems. This enhanced communication also made people more able to relate to one another resulting in a more positive school climate. One statement noting this change was: "The program has opened up lines of communication. Teacher/teacher defensiveness is lessening. I don't hear much gossip. I don't hear the kinds of jabs I used to hear." Expanded and improved communication permitted people to develop closer relations. "The family group has been good," said one participant. "It has done a lot for promoting interaction and it has given me an opportunity to work with others." Likewise a feeling that synergy was present was represented in remarks such as:

- There is increased professionalism among faculty, more consistency through organization of policies, and more faculty get-togethers which have promoted unity and good feelings.
- There is more cooperation. This is a better place to be. There seems to be more harmony between students, and faculty and parents.
- There is an expanded feeling of closeness and caring between and among faculty. There is a greater degree of openness and sharing. People seem more trusting. It has provided an opportunity for the faculty to become closer.

Reflecting on the experience

The restructuring process at FSUS involved shared and participatory decision making, organizing participants in small support and work groups, the use of a family metaphor, and an intentional focus upon the needs of faculty, staff, students and families. (Whole-faculty study groups is a parallel process.) Our effort resulted in restructuring the governance system of the school. Individuals and groups within the school became a comentoring support system for one another. Those involved in this endeavor appeared to have experienced personal and professional growth, improved feelings about their role within the organization, improved attitudes toward others and the organization, and enhanced internal and external relationships. Although there were some problems associated with involvement, particularly with the time required to create the organizational change, people consistently stated and demonstrated that positive results were worth the added time required.

The positive impact of participation in the "school as family" effort was pre-sented as separate outcomes. However, there appeared to be connections that ex-isted between and among outcomes. This interrelatedness is displayed in Figure 17.2. In some cases it appeared that the interrelatedness was causal. For example, feeling supported in the organization may have changed attitudes toward adminis-trators that resulted in increased empathy and improved relationships, or the effects could have operated in the reverse order. This interrelatedness supports Werner's (1980) contention that "implementation is an ongoing construction of a shared reality among group members through their interaction with one another" (pp. 62–63). The starting point, or whether there was any single exact cause for the positive changes that occurred may be unknown. What *is* known is that the activities, processes, and participants changed the structure, functioning, climate, culture, and people in the school. The impact of this experience proved to be positive for the organization and those who operated in it.

The family metaphor served as a focal point around which people formed commitments to organizational change at FSUS. The metaphor of family provided us with a framework to support and mentor one another and enabled us to grow in understanding. This use of the family metaphor was a strong force in motivating people to participate in the change effort and to experience new attitudes and behaviors. The findings support Turner's (1990) assertion that organizations should consider adopting an operational metaphor as a part of restructuring efforts.

Findings dealing with this school restructuring process at FSUS verify re-search cited earlier that teacher self-esteem, job satisfaction, and morale can be raised when faculty are empowered and involved in decision-making processes. The ability to make changes that benefit students, teachers, and parents helped teachers view their work as more rewarding and meaningful. Such perceptions generated excitement and a stronger belief in the potential for change. Since teach-ers' mental health and attitudes are vital to successful change in schools (Fullan with Stiegelbauer, 1991), this finding seems particularly significant.

The family groups proved to be an excellent mechanism with which to create shared governance, enhance communication, and enable individuals within a group to stimulate and create change. The experience had a powerful personal and profes-sional effect on those involved. It supports Nias' (1989) assertion that: "Teachers are happiest in a social environment characterized by mutual dependency in which sharing is the norm and individuals do not feel ashamed to admit to failure or a sense of inadequacy" (pp. 152–3). Similar results were found among middle-school teachers who felt more empowered when working in cross-disciplinary teams than in subject departments (Husband and Short, 1994). This finding lends support to the value of involving people in creating collaborative networks that are personal and endearing.

Through the "school as family" effort, we created a caring community in which all were valued. As we changed, we modified how we related to one another, our students, their parents, their families, and our community. The story continues beyond the boundaries of this study. Florida State University School personnel developed curricular experiences focused on enabling children and families to

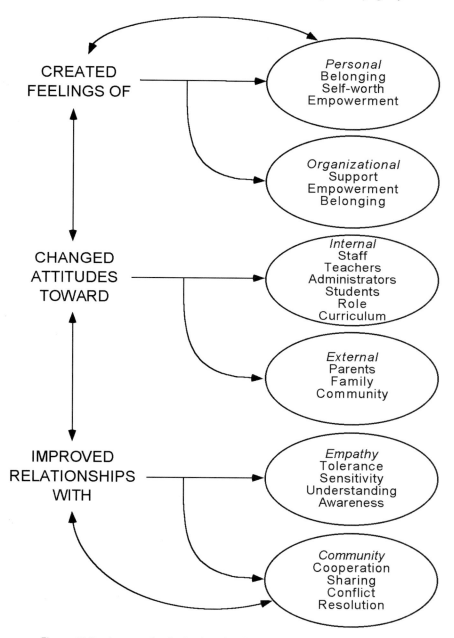

Figure 17.2: Impact of a "school as family" program on faculty involvement

incorporate strong family characteristics into their own families. School faculty and staff worked with community agencies to coordinate efforts to build and support strong families. Later, the FSUS community worked with schools and educational systems throughout the state, telling our story and helping others to create their own.

My own participation in the "school as family" experience has given me a new sense of hope. This writing has helped me to understand not only my own transformation, but what Lieberman and Miller (1992) call the "social realties of school improvement" (p. 95). Although I am no longer a school administrator, I will always be a part of the family there. Being a part of the comentoring publishing group is evidence of this. The story continues in my actions and in heart and soul. I am sure it also still resides in the hearts of many who experienced it. That in essence is what strong academic family is all about – establishing a legacy of love and hope, research and vision, and creating within the soul a capacity to pass it on (Kealy and Mullen, 1999). Fullan (1996) suggests that much of what stimulates positive change in schools is the emotion of hope, something often neglected in the development of organizational change. The telling of this story of my individual and shared school voyage "of family" is my way of passing on the hope.

Acknowledgments

Special thanks to Julie Johnson for the family artwork and William A. Kealy for professional design of my "School as Family" illustration. Sincere appreciation goes to Carol A. Mullen for encouraging me to join her mentoring faculty group and to write this research story.

18 A School Director's Vision: Lighthouse, Beacons, and Foggy Crossings

Glenn Thomas with Carol A. Mullen and Dale W. Lick

Figure 18.1: The lighthouse beacons/beckons
(Charly Andrews, 1998)

Why would a senior manager leave a comfortable post with the State Department of Education to enter the rough, real-world seas of school reform? This is what my colleagues queried me about when I became Director of The Florida State University School (FSUS) in 1997. My intuition told me that educational reform needed to be sown and nurtured at the school level to be successful. From this conviction, my vision compelled me to assume a new mantle of leadership, one where I hoped to lead major K–12 educational reform effectively, applying both comentoring and technology methods. This chapter relates my vision and initial reform forays into foggy crossings (see Figure 18.1).

The launching

I left a secure job to become a player in localized educational reform. As the relatively new director (superintendent) of FSUS, I am committed to fundamental school reform that uses "high tech" innovations to support an effective organizational culture (Naisbitt, 1984). My new place of work is a demographically representative school "district" of approximately 1 100 students (in 1997–98). This K–12 school serves much of the surrounding Florida area.

A three-masted mission

As a university school, FSUS supports a venue for current school contributors to conceptualize, prototype, evaluate, and disseminate research. It provides a "perfect port" with which to connect the routes of state department, university, college of education, and district systems. What distinguishes FSUS from other public schools is its three-masted mission to

1   provide an innovative demonstration site for excellence in K–12 education,
2   conduct quality action research and development to improve education systems, and
3   promote education and training for preservice and inservice teachers.

This unique, compound mission must be manifest at the university school in organizational risk-taking, innovation for results, and linkage expansion to communicate success. The Partnership Support Group (PSG) that created this book is one such dynamic example of how our three-masted mission can be realized by new awareness of how cross-campus faculty can further each other's research contributions for mutual learning and publication. From such a viewpoint, our organization is an ever-evolving unit demonstrating the capacity of becoming highly synergistic and effective. FSUS is fueled by core values, illustrated throughout these chapters, such as comentoring among and within student, teacher, and administrator cultures.

My contribution to our collective professional research story highlights, from a new director's perspective, how the university school culture is being continually rethought, if not reinvented, to achieve better results. In university school environments, as elsewhere, tension with innovative pursuits is a reality. Notably, school members can either provide reciprocal support to facilitate risk-taking or they can impede it. They can also promote results-driven innovation, or alternatively hide data. And, they can stimulate linkage or encourage isolation.

A boating expedition

Early on in my new post at FSUS, I was presented with an inspiring artwork by teacher Debi Barrett-Hayes. It is a print of "Breezing Up" by Winslow Homer. I look at this sailing drama on my office wall when I feel the need to be "anchored" or when seeking inspiration. The scene depicts three young boaters and an older one, each contributing something of value to their shared journey. They are all in an aligned vessel of sail, rudder, and weight.

I imagine that the route of the boaters' destination is uncharted. Consequently, an atmosphere of adventure and camaraderie pervades. The parties, knowing the destination of the port, are relaxed and confident. The hand on the tiller is young and new to the experience, while the one on the sail is familiar and assured. The weights of the sojourners are carefully distributed to balance the wind's thrust and the tide's unsteadiness. The immediate shared goal is to avoid capsizing the boat.

Over the course of the journey, the team's positions and roles will change as the effects of wind, tide, and evening are upon them. The boat will be challenged, responding unpredictably at times as elements conspire and human decisions are made, testing endurance. The lives of those on board will be put at risk. Over time, the boaters learn from each other and so become attuned to their rhythms in connection with those of the wind, sea, and night. They will become more proficient at forecasting movements at many levels in addition to the sheer handling of the boat. As individuals, and more importantly as a synergistic team, they will become somewhat adept during this journey in preparation for future sailing expeditions.

On the far shore stands the boating team's visual and spiritual guide: the lighthouse. Sometimes farther away to port, other times on starboard but always visible, the signals of the lighthouse guide the boat safely along the way. High above the shore's rocks and cliffs, the beams of the tower pierce the night's gloom. This welcoming beacon steadies the course not only for these boaters, but also for distant, larger ships – and for those who will come to traverse these unfamiliar waters. Beacons are used as signals within lighthouses to guide travelers to shore or to warn them of danger. Lighthouses are equipped with such revolving beacon lights to provide lifesaving guidance during foggy crossings.

Three beacons

The Florida State University School is the lighthouse in my story, and the university community its beacon. Their interrelationships and actions provide one of the dramas of this allegory. The other drama enacted herein arises from among the elements of the FSUS culture itself. Positioned in a visible spot on the university campus, our university school is expected to function as a reference point for innovative instruction, research and development, and service to aspiring and experienced educators. In effect, lighthouse beacons must cast three levels of light: one, a shorter, regional but broad beam; two, a larger, statewide, and more focused one; and three, a much larger, nationally and internationally accessible one that is laser-like and highly concentrated. These beams can together signal warnings of the "rocks" of resistance and reform. They can also signal the promise of a "safe harbor" to refresh and regroup before continuing the "journey" toward improved school effectiveness and enhanced student performance.

The regional beam requires a broad array of personalized and localized support from the school – and its associated networks of college faculty, state education department facilitators, and peer exemplary-like schools. The beam focused to the statewide horizon is targeted on issues of general concern to all schools. It is generated by the interpretation of legislation, administrative rule, and departmental initiatives for school policy. This beam must focus on planning implementation, products, "training," and evaluation to support statewide reform. It must also be able to signal where a potential risk, to a new law or regulation, has been identified, analyses conducted, and solutions piloted. This small-scale prototyping charts one means through an unknown strait. On the other hand, the potential for distance research, "training," and support becomes ever larger on national and international fronts.

Florida, as a bellwether or leading state, has a responsibility to share its experiences with curriculum standards, teacher performance appraisal, instructional delivery, and more. It is by aggregating these seemingly disconnected issues – that is, in linking, operationalizing, and systematizing them – that school–university leadership has a potent function.

The lighthouse keeper

As "keeper of the lighthouse," my role is that of lead-mentor, ensuring that "the lights" work as, and when, needed. There are many who contribute to this function and its beneficial outcomes, such as electricians, mechanics, carpenters, faculty, and school staff. These members work across many venues and for multiple purposes. But, through the keeper's leadership and their own, everyone has the potential to function within an effective team. The degree to which the team is effective is largely determined by the lead-mentor's willingness to develop vision, set far-reaching goals, successfully obtain resources, maintain a constructive climate, nurture planned change, and constantly check system processes. For many leaders, the convergence of professional and organizational knowledge, paired with desirable change, results in a foggy/elusive picture of the future school. Without the reassurance of a "lighthouse" positioned strategically along the route, the risk may be perceived as too daunting for the reward.

Building the lighthouse

Vision is the shared and inspiring framework for advancement among those who comprise the "inner organization." In its early phases, vision formation may be a one or more person's picture that is charted in a vague, but value-based, way coalesced from experience and trusted colleagues' ideas. The map that is drawn incorporates core organizational strengths and an orientation approach, sometimes of several years. The mentor-cartographer must develop a language to accompany this map, one that the entire crew will come to understand and feel ownership. It is necessary that this embryonic concept be clearly communicated; that it is flexible in design and process; and that it will anticipate growth, revision, and refinement, but also align with some fairly precise results.

A schematic blueprint of the future school, such as the one revisited on my wall during planning sessions, will permit vision to stretch, align, and calcify ideas and goals. This blueprint is an example of how I convey and foster a vision of tomorrow, one communicated to the "inner organization." The attempt is to create cascading change at the level of school, school–university partnership, and broader communities.

Language needs to be used to convey a vision of tomorrow's community-based public school. For example, I speak of a web-based campus for FSUS as though it were already a reality. This level of communication can help to facilitate the desired visualization in key stakeholders' minds, an emotional commitment, and an investment of energy and resources for the necessary transition to the future. This way of seeing tomorrow-in-today's world is especially critical for teachers and administrators of the school–university collegial culture. Vision has been an effective springboard in every organization in which I have participated. An exception to this was evident in the first school in which I taught. Administration functioned strictly top-down and human effectiveness consequently deteriorated.

Most faculties want to create improved teaching-learning settings but the urge toward innovation often proceeds without evolution of a "big picture." I agree with Senge (1990) that systems managers need to develop frameworks for seeing the whole, "for seeing interrelationships rather than things, for seeing patterns of change rather than static 'snapshots'" (p. 68). The belief that drives systems thinking is that organizations, such as schools, are "living systems" that are structured according to "rigid internal divisions that inhibit inquiry across divisional boundaries" and that must, for their survival *and* success, be viewed differently as complex ecosystems with underlying structures (p. 66).

In my experience, effective people within organizations will pull apart if they are not aligned with an integrated school vision. Committed team members become disillusioned and withdraw. Consistency of message, refinement of perspective, and encouragement of the university and community's input are also essential. This feedback loop clarifies issues and provides fuel for the emergence of vision at the grass-roots level. It helps with people's "implications of change" concerns, permitting simulations through "what ifs?" and "how does this affect me?" scenarios. This feedback loop also allows champions to be nurtured and to "take up the banner" for issues to which they feel committed.

Vision can be initiated and operationalized within either an administrative or teaching culture, but it is most powerful when interwoven through a supportive environment of comentors or peers. As school researcher Hargreaves (1992) suggests, "leadership is especially important here," paradoxically enough, as "dispersion of leadership and responsibility helps, playing down formal differences of status and investing visible administrative trust in the skills, expertise, and professional judgment of ordinary teachers" (p. 226). Practitioners of "quality" models realize that those who know the job the best must be empowered to have creative decision-making authority over important job functions.

The embryonic phase of vision is fragile. It needs the leader's direct, interpersonal, and daily sponsorship to legitimatize, influence, and gain public support. New visions stimulate organizations as well as camps of both supporters and detractors, and the largest group will be the onlookers. Leaders must recognize the difference between thoughtful, negative input and closed-minded resistance. Only the former can become a source of synergistic clarity and strength.

As goals and people become increasingly "aligned" under the emerging school–university–community vision, the organization draws in new thinking and renews its purpose. The members of the school who champion the vision feel energized, valued, empowered, and important in the decision-making process. Their contributions give substance to the picture, making the vision more accessible and meaningful. Most importantly, people's efforts make the picture creditable to themselves and to other team members. For those who wish to contribute, the leader must positively acknowledge all ideas and then evaluate the "fit" between them and the vision. This means that the ideas of others will be actively used, modified, or noted for other purposes, and hence acknowledged as valuable, a key part of empowerment.

As an analogy, people's organizational ideas are like "bricks" being donated from various sources to complete, repair, or refurbish a dwelling. Some bricks will fit on the exterior for all to appreciate; others are strictly structural; while still others are not useful for the intended project yet may have utility for another. Each brick has potential value and must be viewed as such. While it takes many bricks to build a lighthouse from nothing, it takes fewer to refurbish, reshape, or enlarge. The vision process needs careful balance between a top-down and a bottom-up approach – it must negotiate its way through a human-centered system, resourcing and researching worthy ideas, aligning existing strengths, and alleviating weaknesses. I agree with Grundy (1994) that "it is not sufficient for education systems to 'pass the buck' for educational improvement to teachers . . . It is important to understand the nature of the school as an organization which structures, enables and/or constrains educational work" (p. 24).

The responsibilities for, and effects of, institution-wide macro vision are synergistic and greater than the aggregation of each member's contribution at the local, daily level (Kealy and Mullen, 1999; Murphy and Lick, 1998). Each person within the organization will need to know that his or her vision matters to the evolution of the culture. I am reminded here of a quote that I see daily. Inside my daily planner it reads: "Anything that you vividly imagine, ardently desire and enthusiastically act upon . . . must inevitably come to pass" (source unknown).

Where progress is underway for developing and communicating the vision of a university school, the next phase is that of planning and alignment. As Joel Barker leadership theorist and writer asserts, "Vision without action is only a dream." The vision provides the map for advancement; our values become a compass upon which to measure the "rightness" of a course of action. The vision afforded by the lighthouse metaphor can provide an overall rationale and consistency across the many decision-making platforms of a mentor-leader. It creates a broad, shared conceptual framework for all members of the organization, despite variations in personal orientation and style.

Vision-based networks

Planning requires not only a global perception of the vision's promise, but also the reality of attention to both systematic and connecting details. Without this broad perspective, we lose major connections or may become sidetracked with "the more passive, disengaged colleagues in the profession" (Huberman, 1992, p. 138).

A genuinely compelling vision requires many fundamental changes to sub-systems and to linkages among them. It is not enough that we procure a brighter bulb for the lighthouse – electrical circuits may need updating; neighbors may need dialoguing; heating and cooling of the facility may need adjusting; and nautical charts may need revising. The more far-reaching and comprehensive a vision, and the deeper the meaningful attention on members' views, the greater the opportunity for massive system and subsystem changes. Such changes also have potential for increasing productivity, intensifying collegiality, decreasing disruptiveness, and reallocating resources. Suppose, for example, that the new brighter bulb served to actually decrease the total energy consumption of the lighthouse. Funds saved could be repurposed to improve radio communication, make overdue repairs, or even grant the lighthouse crew travel and release time for "training" in the opera-tion of new lighthouse systems.

Vision implementing plans often require the distinction and reconstitution of systems. Engineers have used the concept of a "black box" to describe a method for the development and improvement of complex nonorganic systems. The approach involves creating a common set of input, output, and exchange standards that fit into an architecture which can be modularized. For example, suppose we wanted to upgrade the electronic navigational system of the lighthouse. A traditional approach might be to trash everything related and start from "ground zero." The black box approach would be to define input/output standards, inventory existing components, study connections, and replace the necessary components. Whole system thinking, design, action, and evaluation lead to "modular" solutions that are more predict-able, flexible, and timely and less complex and costly than complete revamping. This is a necessary concept given the speed of technological change, the exponen-tial expansion of knowledge, and the reinvention of learning institutions.

Organizationally, the school is the hub of both statewide and local learning communities. At the statewide level, its networks with district, school leaders, and teams are in constant transition. Expanding, contracting, driving, and reforming all depend on the context. These learning alliances are formed around shared issues or visions. Issues tend to create temporal networks centered on explicit problem solving whereas vision-based networks display broader conceptual coherence across numerous specific issues. The narrowness and timeliness of an issue tends to drive short-term associations with an information base that is limited in scope.

Mentoring for success

Vision formulation provides a conceptual framework that gives direction; however, this process is far from neutral. Indeed, organizational members must monitor the value orientations implicit in a school vision. This process of examination and scrutiny can strengthen an organization and its vision by providing members with opportunities to communicate at a personal level of response, bringing forth their assumptions, beliefs, and values. Such peer team efforts can become occasions for mentoring networks in which each professional has experience or expertise to be shared. Other schools also gain after considerable effort has been made to reach consensus on language, goals, and outcomes within a school site. Mentoring network members must be open about their own assumptions, beliefs, and values, or at least be willing to explore them with others. Where these networks expose and affect professional assumptions and beliefs, comentoring or cross-learning becomes pervasive, and change can be realized.

Formerly, I participated in many statewide educational reforms initiated at the state department level. However, like other leaders, I did not understand the breadth of the local school organization commitment required for a paradigm shift to re-make schools. I had yet to understand that peer mentoring at all levels, and among multiple schools with similar assumptions and beliefs, was essential for positive change. The more radical the reform, the more effort network members must invest in joint communication and colearning. Learning through networking is especially important in the early years of school reform as the organizational culture and structure of the school are in transition. This process of institutionalization of reform can be described as one of "webbed mentoring," sometimes occurring at a distance, but increasingly close-up in work settings.

The best leaders of outstanding organizations mentor others to lead (Tichy, 1997). The local mentoring that drives innovation for results refurbishes existing relationships, or generates new ones focused on common goals. Mentor-leaders use the "power of position" to initiate organizational goals, operationalize them, over-come barriers, evaluate progress, and persistently repeat the cycle in ways to achieve "successive approximations of perfection." The real "work" of change must be made by committed organizational members who are mentored into leadership roles. They translate organizational goals and understand that macro goals are composed of specific team objectives often derived from the professional goals of members.

Some individuals at the team level must champion visions to become realities. These are potential leaders, and the more their capabilities and skills can be incul-cated into the daily lives of others, the more proactive and resilient the organization will be. The mentoring relationships established and sustained by the organization's chief officer are also critical to organizational success. Such relationships can be grouped broadly into either individual or "webbed" relationships. The rationale behind my "open door" policy is about proactive colearning with other profession-als, sometimes in group sessions. To be successful, these must be formalized into longer-term growth aimed at creating leadership.

If such group meetings do not produce more and better teacher and parent leaders, the chief officer-mentor will have difficulty affecting meaningful systemic organizational change. Planned change requires close mutual support. Peer comentoring allows for affirmation. It builds interdependence, empowerment, and participation, and targets those personal and collective areas needing improvement. Organizations undergoing fundamental belief examination and restructuring must have leaders who operate as a lighthouse with many beacons, serving multiple roles, such as vision communicator and systems builder.

Mentoring for leadership purposes uses a selection strategy that blends the logic of organizational positioning with the "karma" of personal understanding. It is a symbolic lighthouse in operation. While the chief officer-mentor needs approval and council as the keeper of the vision, the mentee-leader (or mentor-teacher) needs the same, only the latter functions as the developer and adapter and, more-over, the reflective guide and constructive critic. This synergistic process unfolds gradually over time, and it is generally fragile, intense, and time-consuming in initial phases of communication. But, as understanding and trust build, contact frequency and duration tend to decrease. A cautionary note is that mentoring relationships need "maintenance" to remain sound. Mentoring is an ongoing process, not a one-time encounter.

As a chief mentor like myself plans for change to remake the school environment, primary leaders who require mentoring can be identified using three organizational criteria:

1 *position*: How critical is this position to the success of the endeavor?
2 *representation*: How critical is this person to the success of the endeavor with respect to his or her perceived stature among peers?
3 *response*: How flexible is the person to new ideas and especially to the emerging vision?

Clearly the chief officer-mentor would look toward those representing all three criteria as the prime candidates of leadership. Others are considered to "shore-up" critical or weaker areas.

As a "mentoring map" for increasing the effectiveness and visibility of organizational leadership, I find the following principles useful:

1 pick the "easy" channels first. Mentor those having the greatest potential for success first. Success builds success,
2 plan to mentor representatives of all major constituents, but begin with those closest to the organization's core,
3 consistently paint the same pictures, using the same vocabulary, and be alert that "accurate language" is paramount in emerging relationships,
4 involve members of the organization in the information exchange to build organization confidence and trust. Confidence and trust are institutional change enablers,

5   remember that in the midst of change many are bewildered, others are averse, and a few champions can collectively mentor many others,

6   keep recentering everyone, and

7   remember that the more people can target desired outcomes, the more effective the organization. However, increased "targeting" also causes elimination of some functions.

I have come to believe that it is impossible to be all things to all people. Schools may no longer need to be visualized as large inflexible "monolithic" organizations. As we witness the direction of the global economies, we see networks of smaller, highly adaptable organizations that coalesce and disperse as economic or programmatic conditions dictate. The standard for the bottom line stays inflexible – "make a profit, stay in business." In the educational community, we often have not let parents', teachers', and students' choices drive our organizations because of the investment in sustaining "comprehensive" monolithic programs and organizations.

The "typical" large comprehensive North American high school is not the best setting for instructional purposes. In contrast, smaller "schools within a school," which are essentially self-contained career academies or other divisions, are beneficial. According to Lee and Smith's (1993) extensive school study, that included the public school system, restructured schools have the potential to become highly successful places of learning. They apparently promote less departmentalization, and more heterogeneous grouping and team teaming. Such restructured schools are communally organized places that have had a positive effect on student achievement and engagement. Additionally, large schools may not provide the best student security. Further, buildings of 300,000 square feet are expensive to build, and when neighborhoods transform into businesses, these schools are difficult to sell and recapitalize. Smaller may be a better option.

Creating a new climate

A critical distinction needs to be made between climate and culture. Climate is more concerned with common perceptions rather than with deeply held assumptions (Hellriegel and Slocum, 1974). Climate has the potential to play a key role in visioning and aligning values, expectations, means, results, and linkages both internally and externally. Such school climates are the counterpart of individual attitudes and are indicators of organizational health, adaptability, and change. Climates are also reflective of internal conditions that have powerful ramifications that, in turn, influence the organizational culture.

Major climate-related questions that lead-mentors must deal with include: How is the organizational climate determined by these different images of educational leadership? How do school inhabitants feel about their relative importance to the organization's image of leadership as well as to its goals and action-based methods for accomplishing them? Which members, in this scenario, play a team or lead role in facilitating and realizing results? Which members understand organizational alignment and so continually propose innovation? Which members have the ability and motivation to analyze relevant data to aid decision-making processes? Which school organizations function with climates that empower members and propel them toward excellence and effectiveness? Finally, which organizations demand the most administrative flexibility combined with professional accountability?

I am discovering that a highly effective approach for dealing with climate questions is for the lead-mentor to help create an environment where members accept the challenge to synergistically comentor. Very simply, this means that most members feel good about the organization; that they have a stake in what happens; and that they have something valuable to offer and gain. This level of involvement could produce powerful synergies, drawing extraordinary results from ordinary members. This kind of collaborative climate is especially important in a university school with its atypical three-masted mission.

Creating a new culture

As we refine our organizational climate, we must confront issues that are ambivalent, repressed, or overemphasized. Cultural manifestations – which are congruent through a system's climate, reward structure, and leadership – are mutually reinforcing and hence synergistic. Those that are incongruent reduce trust, effectiveness, and total positive result. Manifestations such as board policies, budget allocations, and performance evaluation reveal much about the values of those who lead and use the organization. Our visioning process at FSUS must identify cultural impediments and strategies to address them. Periodic systematic evaluation of everyone's progress on the journey promised by the lighthouse vision is imperative.

As a university school takes steps toward a vision, it is important that these be successive approximations of what members really want. Evaluation can function as a gauge of the length, duration, and direction of travel. How far have the parties involved traveled? What is the expected time of arrival for the sojourners? What route(s) did they choose for travel? These three questions undergird the vision-based network of the Partnership Support Group of school-university authors whose mentoring logs and journey gave rise to this book. New directions for mentoring can make use of these questions in order to shape the twenty-first century school environment. For me, and some invested others, this resembles a web-based, electronic campus impacting widely on the lives of teachers, students, parents, and administrators.

How can we fairly evaluate all school personnel across the common school? How do we account for their student performance and individual professional developmental constructs in a fair and collegial manner? Recently, at FSUS, we formed a "reconnaissance party" to study these issues. We proposed to faculty, staff, and administration key concepts to be incorporated into an appraisal system. Our rationale for advocating a new assessment system upholds that this necessary school reform will provide a fair, logical, and sustainable system which defines performance, has predictability, may become partially automated, and reinforces value.

The FSUS list of professional process outcomes for teachers covered reflection and analysis in the areas of assessment, critical thinking, diversity, role of teacher, technology, research, service, and more. These outcomes have yet to be documented. We have considered portfolios, surveys, action research, and professional articles. Staff would also have responsibility to support student learning as dictated by position, and they would have productivity measures unique to their duties. Everyone would serve an educative function.

We see a picture of "teachers as learners and students as workers" as long as we all continue to learn, devising student learning activities, and assessing student progress and our own. This is an effective methodology for learning the primary cognitive structures from which students will construct new understanding. The excitement students feel hypothesizing, researching, analyzing, testing, rethinking, producing, and evaluating is tangible because what they learn, they experience or make. And, they are "making" something for the first time that best suits *their* sense of relevance.

Shaping the new school

Humans are social creatures. Researchers have found ways to assess our predominant personality orientations. Holland (1996) has theorized six dimensions of personality (social, artistic, conventional, realistic, entrepreneurial, and investigative). Over a 20-year period, the Florida Department of Education administered a personality-type assessment (Holland's Self-Directed Search) to teachers around the state, and found approximately 80 per cent of teachers to be predominately "social." These findings are consistent with other national-level studies.

Since the majority of teachers are socially oriented, why do we isolate them in classrooms? Is this is the most productive environment for interpersonal growth? This model expects all teachers to have similar competency in all areas of the profession, which is not possible. Similarly, new teachers are too often "thrown to sharks" while next door there is a seasoned veteran at work. The challenge of becoming and remaining an effective professional is often not encouraged or compensated for within schools.

For students, we must question whether a school "world" educationally led primarily by "social" types provides an optimal learning environment and adequate real world mix. Entrepreneurial, conventional, and realistic types are seldom found in the classroom. Investigative and artistic types are also underrepresented. We must therefore strive to better represent these varied typographies to support our students' knowledge construction processes.

As we at the FSUS look to a new innovative facility to be designed and completed in a few years, our vision of teaching and learning must be concretely reshaped. To do this, we struggle to interpret existing educational research results and accumulated professional experiences while projecting to instructional needs of many years. From our visioning, planning, and reshaping efforts, four main principles have emerged.

1   Teachers need to collaborate in teams at all levels,
2   multifunctional learning spaces are needed so teachers can group students differentially,
3   technology can improve instruction and communication, and promote safety, and
4   facilitators must be as fully utilized by state, county, and city agencies as practical.

Redefining the teaching–learning place

It may be more productive for a team of teachers to manage instruction within a large, flexible, multipurposeful area. If we ask teachers to be accountable for their students' performance, we need to give them every advantage possible. The new space would have many computer work stations for student production. Here, students could be supported by the teachers as they collectively create, for example, multimedia products. Such functions might begin as isolated off-line activities. But, through the "artistry of teaching" the isolated activities would be connected in unique ways, analysis completed, and product created and disseminated.

Today with our 25–1 box model, we dare not ask a teacher to tightly concentrate on one child's "teachable moments" to the abandonment of the others. Suppose, instead, that a "team of teachers" worked with a "team of students" for multiple periods or even years in a facility that allowed differentiated activities, class sizes, and staffing. How much more productive can we be working synergistically together? How can we use mentoring and professional growth in this model to significantly enhance student and teacher performance?

Across Florida and the country, "schools within high schools" are being formed using some of these principles. These academies are demonstrating the potential for improved student performance as teachers and students work synergistically on relevant issues. A grounding concept for these emerging models is that they must maintain high standards of student academic, career, and personal achievement. However, without attention to the demonstrable relationship of these activities to core academic skills, neither teachers nor parents will be confident that students are prepared for postsecondary education or the workplace.

Students must be positioned as workers, and teachers as learners, in these new models. The "deeper learnings" can occur more effectively in an environment unfettered by traditional organizational constraints, including centrally-controlled, "one size fits all" time, space, and grouping arrangements. Emerging technologies allow us to leverage, in new ways, our surroundings and ourselves as well as time and spaces, and new synergies.

New currents in the tide

The new FSUS school will harness emerging technologies. Our goals are to reduce administrative overhead, improve fiscal control, promote student safety, and improve customer service. For example, we are currently researching "palm reader" technologies that allow electronic recognition of a hand. Such technologies could "take attendance electronically"; deduct school lunch costs from student accounts; allow computer access to student's webtop sites from any location in the school; and "check out" media center materials. Students can also access their webtops from remote locations, including intern workplaces and residence. This kind of access would allow us to extend and track both learning scope and time for learners. Webtops serve as "virtual bookbags" holding homework, assignments, notes, electronic versions of textbooks, multimedia presentations, student projects and portfolios, and more.

We are currently exploring internet cameras (mini-cams) as utility "video tools" for the new school. Such tools would allow other schools to view classrooms and download any materials. Likewise, educators from The Florida State University could "watch" student interaction. Parents could "visit" their children's classes. Teachers and administrators could use "real" examples of student misconduct with families. And, teachers could create electronic portfolios for promotion purposes. The key will be to provide as much teacher-centered, synergistic management of these systems while supporting improved student performance.

Remember, though, as we contemplate and apply such technologies that we *must* continue to focus all we do on the improvement of student performance, research and development, and dissemination of what works along with service to the educational community.

Reflections from the lighthouse

The currents continue to move sand, exposing rocks and covering them, but always in transition with the wind and tide. Channels migrate as sediments shift by unceasing battles of river and sea. Across that most turbulent battlefield, transit the boaters, each with a purpose and port in mind. Some mariners understand the relativity of charts, science of location, and significance of the lighthouse. Others are fearful; lacking skills, they remain close to shore and shun darkness. The experienced seafarers pursue richer voyages; they are confident and assured by the lighthouse that their course is worthwhile, even essential. They understand that the lighthouse can only mark positions, warning of impending destruction or promise of safe harbor. But they must also be responsible for checking depth, finding other markers, and using the water's movements to reach their moorings.

Lighthouses are not needed when there are no adventures. If the way is clean, safe, and known, channel markers or buoys will suffice. But the way of educational reform is sometimes foggy, partially charted, often tidal, and never safe. Visions are not clear even to leaders. As we mentor each other, we become more aligned and vision begins to take meaningful, pervasive shape, forms which promise success. Educational research provides charts for much of what we know, but mostly in the form of clues and generalizations based on a few circumstances.

Paradoxically, "good" research is frequently ignored, often because it demands a massive and collective shift at the organizational-cultural level. The manifestation of such change may impose new organization processes, perspectives, and ultimately values. However, the survivability of an organization is connected to its ability to persistently tack against the wind, while smoothly "coming about" as conditions change. The effort must promise the outcome of improved student performance and it must engage collective communication and synergistic relationship around an emerging vision.

The beacons of the lighthouse establish positions for voyages that will extend beyond their reach. The lighthouse encourages, assures, warns, and welcomes adventures. It redefines itself with more powerful signals to reach lost vessels. Its repairs are teamed, and its promise charted, in different lives and languages. Most of all, the lighthouse assures that those who journey are not alone. During foggy crossings, it is comforting to know that voyagers can use the rays to guide them through newly charted waters.

Epilogue: A New Mentoring Pathway has been Navigated: The Search Continues

Carol A. Mullen

What have we learned from this collaborative action research project? The Partnership Support Group discovered a basic principle of mentorship – that it is most empowering when combined in a comentoring, proactively supportive and synergistic framework. To assist others in navigating their own unknown pathways, I offer this post-reflection on our group process and book project. I discuss major areas of facilitation and hindrance that significantly shaped this, the work of our professional faculty network. I also offer recommendations for guiding action research in collaborative contexts that will hopefully be of interest to our readers.

Reflective conversation and assessment

At our last PSG meeting in May 1998, we met like travelers who had returned home to our gathering place – the resource library of The Florida State University School – to take a group photo for this book. After this celebratory moment, we had a reflective conversation about those salient group processes that had facilitated our work and that also hindered it. We listened carefully as each member offered a personal assessment of the experience. This turned out to be yet another constructive event in sharing viewpoints among our group of teachers, teacher educators, and administrators. While we shared and even debated perspectives, we worked at developing two network displays to exhibit our responses (see Figures 19.1 and 19.2).

As facilitator of the faculty support group, I thought it was important to bring formal closure to this particular project and to develop a collective assessment of the experience. Although I could have evaluated the group process alone, this singular effort would have weakened and even contradicted our synergistic comentoring practice. It would have also assigned too much importance to the evaluative role of the university researcher. Further, I wanted to learn from the others and to bring our joint assessment to the wider academic community as a framework for input and critique.

Educators are searching for effective and creative ways to foster the work of learning teams. We, in the teacher education profession, are learning how to bring together stakeholders across different but related cultures. Pounder (1998), as one example, explores in her cross-cultural study with schools how constructing knowledge, work-related tasks, and assessments or performance strategies all help to develop study group effectiveness.

The premise of *New Directions for Mentoring* is that reform in teacher education needs to find ways to include school professionals in designing, evaluating, and authoring research projects. Equality and power-sharing mean that teachers function not just as "organizational interfaces" but also as integrated team players and researcher-authors. For those educators who are committed to rethinking the profession, we hope to challenge some existing forms and inspire new ones.

Areas of Group Facilitation

A post-assessment, conducted collaboratively by PSG members, clarified areas that had facilitated our group process. We sketched two network displays which I later drew in PowerPoint. As the display "Factors facilitating group process" suggests, we experienced a high degree of positive synergy. Our talk about assessment was focused, energetic, and affirming, and not without productive tension. We developed consensus around nine areas of facilitation: *comentoring, openness, storytelling, leadership, active listening, field notes, synergy, appreciative understanding,* and *structured inquiry.* These elements overlap in meaning, but I shall briefly discuss each one in order to clarify the thinking of the group.

By *comentoring*, members described how they had all felt supported in their work through a process of guided and structured learning. They commented on how they had felt encouraged through my regular electronic communications, invitations for them to author their own chapters, and detailed responses to their questions and writing. These aspects of our project kept members informed and motivated about the project itself while being guided within the context of their own needs and interests.

Another primary dimension of our group process was *openness.* Members described this element/quality as meaning that the group was receptive to new ideas and influences as well as acceptance of each member. They felt that we were able to share vulnerabilities which, in turn, enabled risk-taking, the sharing of hunches and preliminary ideas, and a deeper level of trust.

Storytelling, another dimension, was equated with intuitive levels of learning that arose by and through the members' anecdotes about their mentoring stories and research. It was also described as a kind of "bonding glue" that animated our discussions, motivating participants to come to sessions to learn about one another's work, share and provide feedback, and produce.

Leadership was associated by members with my continual input and facilitative style which members believe orchestrated the entire group process. They talked about the comentoring environment that I had created and sustained through my vision, confidence, nurturance, commitment, organization, knowledge, energy, and synergy-building.

Field notes were made available to members based on my transcription of our taped sessions. This action research strategy was viewed as having promoted

Figure 19.1A: Factors facilitating group process (Partnership Support Group, 1998)

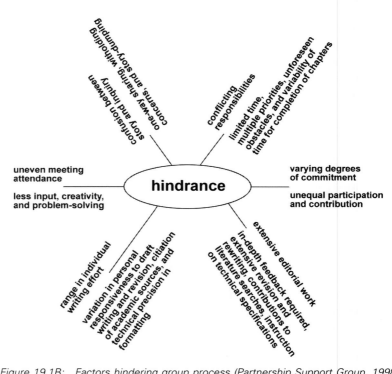

Figure 19.1B: Factors hindering group process (Partnership Support Group, 1998)

confidence in the practitioners who found it helpful to have access to a record of our dialogue for their own work.

Synergy was described as the inspiration and energy behind our three common goals: one, to function as an effective collegial network; two, to do action research in the area of mentoring; and three, to write meaningfully for self and successfully for publication. Members experienced interdependence and empowerment as well as involvement and convergence, all aspects of the synergistic process. Additionally, *appreciative understanding* was experienced through nonjudgment, empathy, community-building, connectedness, and active listening.

As another overarching point, members agreed that *structured inquiry* had been fundamental to our success. This area of facilitation had been framed by the reading packet of mentoring studies that I had generated, something that members added to. Another example of structured inquiry was the attention on focus during storytelling. Biweekly meetings were essential to the development of these patterns.

Areas of group hindrance

As Figure 19.1B shows four problematic areas compare with the nine facilitative dimensions that emerged from our group assessment. Members felt challenged when asked to identify areas of the group process that had interfered with the synergistic comentoring work of the group. They struggled while brainstorming to characterize obstacles or areas of hindrance that had adversely affected our effectiveness as a group. Nothing seemed glaring enough to commit to paper. Significantly, members found it easier to generate areas of benefit. Consensus was gradually arrived at, but members were tentative, qualifying their responses. It was as though members were responding somewhat protectively, a possible byproduct of close relations. In the spirit of the group, I attribute lesser status to Figure 19.1B.

Four areas were identified, with some hesitancy, as having hindered aspects of the group synergy and project: *uneven meeting attendance*; *conflicting responsibilities*; *varying degrees of commitment*; and *confusion between story and inquiry*. Later faced with extra months of extensive editorial work alone and with Dale Lick, I added, to Figure 19.1B, these dimensions: *range in individual writing effort* and *extensive editorial work*. Regarding "range in individual writing effort," the authors varied in their efforts to revise draft writing; to respond to detailed editorial feedback; to produce according to the timelines; and to work effectively with technology and electronic attachments.

Most chapters required "extensive editorial work" on draft versions. Areas of editorial work for this project included effective writing with and for impact; narrative voice development; contextual and general analysis; key exemplars and questions; metaphoric sensibility in textual language; thematic use of artwork; summary points and overview statements; inclusion of relevant literature; and correct use of the American Psychological Association formatting style, revised by Falmer Press. Despite the demanding editorial responsibilities, I felt pleased knowing that the authors appreciated and benefited from the feedback. This team project involved new learning for everyone, not just the novice writers and researchers.

Uneven meeting attendance was recognized as a problem but not all members were convinced that the group had, in some tangible way, suffered. Despite absences by some members, it was felt that our shared work, commitment, and vision had remained strong. However, for those few of us who had attended all meetings, we recognized that some loss was incurred in input, creativity, problem solving, and productivity without full membership. This loss became evident toward the end of the busy academic semester and school year. *Conflicting responsibilities* was identified as another problem and also the primary reason for the uneven meeting attendance. This dimension was further characterized as limited time, multiple priorities, and unforeseen obstacles in people's lives.

Members viewed themselves as having had different personal and group needs. These differences helped to account for the *varying degrees of commitment* and unequal participation within the group. *Differences between storytelling and inquiry* meant that one-way sharing sometimes occurred as people either told their story at length or explained a particular concept in the mentoring field. Someone jokingly described those people who joined us to tell their story only to not be seen again as "story dumping." We learned that stories were sometimes told without the intent to produce an inquiry, despite the common purpose of the group. However, even our story dumping occasions proved useful as these exposed us to a wide range of mentoring processes and programs available in educational contexts.

Creating a new mentoring pathway

This book could help university researchers, administrators, and teachers to create a new mentoring pathway in their own contexts. Our synergistic comentoring model of relationship and organization can assist others to create mentoring teams within guided learning spaces. Conversations about shared areas of interest require the willingness to openly engage in what may be of value to stakeholders who may be culturally different from oneself.

Recommendations: conducting collaborative action research

School-university organizations vary as their own unique cultures, and so I offer the following 12 recommendations with the understanding that context plays a critical role in shaping reform initiatives. As we all risk new forms of collegiality in our own educational domains, the availability of "best practices" in research will proliferate. With my own (shared) experience in mind, I view these aspects of the PSG faculty project as particularly noteworthy:

1   research, writing, and publishing experience on the part of the teacher educator-facilitator,
2   advanced publishing plans or contractual agreement for a book or theme issue with a journal,

3   invitations to practitioners to become part of a professionally diverse support group,

4   systematic framework involving planning, group process and productivity, and assessment,

5   strategies for developing and sustaining research-based publishing teams (see Table 4.2),

6   documentation of group process and case study analysis using a variety of methods,

7   selection of research topic to be initiated, negotiated, or refined by the group,

8   ritual of journal writing and sharing to produce helpful feedback from members,

9   attention on the quality of research and writing at all levels,

10 close editorial feedback and guidance on material prepared by participants for publication,

11 use of interrelated themes to connect individual studies as a whole research story, and

12 assessment of the project from participants' points of view, and disseminating results.

Reflective postscript

Educational cultures have yet to become places of productive and synergistic comentoring that benefit school participants as equal partners in research and publication. Support group structures can provide the guidance, reciprocity, and flexibility needed to give weight to the role of university faculty in fostering a new research culture. Psychological barriers become evident to cultural go-betweens like myself. We can discern a covert language of impossibility in utterances that highlight the impracticability of collaboration. "The other" is viewed as somehow unworthy or perhaps impenetrable. Such mindsets occupy those precious walkways that could otherwise link colleges of education with schools in more substantive ways. The widespread cultural practice that supports the service mentality of research laboratory schools challenged our support group and book production. We offer a view of productive resistance, or of what types of walkways one comentoring group can pave. The new stories that other groups and sites can tell are countless. Let us together pave walkways that matter.

Notes on Contributors

About the editors

Carol A. Mullen is Assistant Professor in Educational Foundations, Leadership and Technology, College of Education, at Auburn University, AL 36849–5221. At the time Dr. Mullen was Principal Investigator of this comentoring book project, she was affiliated with The Florida State University. She specializes in organizational and educator development from the perspective of mentoring research and practice.

Dr. Mullen has conducted research in schools, universities, and prisons resulting in numerous articles in educational journals. Dr. Mullen's other books are *Imprisoned Selves: An Inquiry into Prisons and Academe* (1997b, University Press of America); *Breaking the Circle of One: Redefining Mentorship in the Lives and Writings of Educators* (1997c, Peter Lang); and *The Postmodern Educator: Arts-based Inquiries and Teacher Development* (Diamond and Mullen, 1999, Peter Lang). *Breaking the Circle of One* won the 1998 Division K Research Award, "Exemplary Research in Teaching and Teacher Education," from the American Educational Research Association and the Athena Award for Excellence in Mentoring. Carol has guest editorial issues with *Latino Studies Journal*; *Theory Into Practice*; and *The Professional Educator*.

From this book, Dr. Mullen has learned that comentoring across diverse professional cultures is worthwhile and invigorating. School and university faculty can learn and benefit from being collaborating partners in research. Carol appreciated being let into the very special life-worlds of the author-participants. Email: mulleca@mail.auburn.edu.

Dale W. Lick is a past president of Georgia Southern University, University of Maine, and The Florida State University, and presently University Professor and Associate Director of the Learning Systems Institute at Florida State University, teaches in the Department of Educational Leadership. Dr. Lick is committed to new learning approaches to transformational leadership, managing organizational change, and learning organizations – all areas in which he has credentials. Included in 33 national and international biographical listings, he is the author of over 50 professional books, articles, proceedings, and 285 original newspaper columns. Dr. Lick is coauthor of the book, *Whole-Faculty Study Groups: A Powerful Way to Change Schools and Enhance Learning* (Murphy and Lick, 1998, Corwin).

It was fascinating for Dr. Lick to experience how quickly the comentoring group became a functioning learning team. The rapid movement toward synergistic relationships enabled members to assist each other with new understanding and writing. Email: dlick@lsi.fsu.edu.

About the contributors

Debi P. Barrett-Hayes is a National Board Certified Teacher at The Florida State University School. Debi is head of the Visual Arts Department and board member of the National Art Education Association and the Florida Art Education Association. Debi is a strong advocate for arts education in the general education. Currently FSUS is piloting a five-year project sponsored by the Getty/Annenberg Foundations called "Transforming Education through the Arts" challenge. Debi is an exhibiting mixed media painter. She is married to Martin and they have a creative child, Cosby. Email: dbarrett@mailer.fsu.edu.

Lori L. Franklin is a library media specialist at The Florida State University School with a bachelor's degree is in Mass Communications and a master's degree in library science. Lori enjoys interacting with teachers and children. She is proud of her family – husband Edward and children Casey, Will, and Matt. As a member of the comentoring group, Lori's eyes were opened to the many different personalities doing mentoring work in the school-university site.

Fanchon F. Funk is Associate Director for the Center for Performance Technology where she is involved in researching customer satisfaction for Florida school districts. She is also Associate Professor of Educational Leadership at The Florida State University. Dr. Funk, recipient of both the *President's Excellence in Teaching Award* and *the President's Continuing Education Award* at FSU, has been recognized by the National Association of Teacher Educators as "one of 70 distinguished leaders in teacher education." She has coauthored four books and produced articles. Her coauthored book, *Appleseeds* (1987), is considered essential reading by the National Endowment of the Arts. As one of the support group sojourners, Dr. Funk experienced the excitement of learning from the mentoring stories of the others.

David S. Greenberg spent the 1997–98 academic year as a French I/II instructor at The Florida State University School. A teacher of 40 years, Dr. Greenberg received a doctorate from The Florida State University in 1997 in French Literature, after having retired from teaching in New York State. He holds degrees and certificates in French, English, social studies, guidance, educational administration, and the language teaching profession. The support group process helped Dr. Greenberg to understand the mentoring research as well as writing for publication.

Freddie L. Groomes is Executive Assistant to the President and Director of Equal Opportunity and Pluralism at The Florida State University. Dr. Groomes is also an Associate Professor of Counseling and Human Systems. Freddie is a researcher and consultant who coordinates areas of diversity, executive recruitment, and general management. As a member of the support group, Dr. Groomes experienced a gratifying, unique professional opportunity.

Susan Hilgemeier is a doctoral student at Texas A&M University studying curriculum and instruction, and reading. She has served as the research assistant with the NEA/TEI grant. Susan taught reading in Texas public schools for 12 years. She has worked with disabled readers in middle school. Susan's dissertation is a study of teachers who were trained in professional development schools.

William A. Kealy is an associate professor in the Department of Educational Research at Florida State Unviersity in Tallahassee, Florida. His specialty areas of teaching and research include effective mentoring practices, instructional media design, and learning from graphic displays. Dr. Kealy has published numerous articles in addition to chapters in *Breaking the Circle of One*, *New Directions for Mentoring*, and *The Postmodern Educator*. From 1997–2000 he was co-chair (with Carol Mullen) of the Mentorship and Mentoring Practices Special Interest Group of the American Educational Research Association.

Frances K. Kochan is Director of the Truman Pierce Institute and Associate Professor of Educational Leadership at Auburn University, Alabama. She previously served as a Principal and Director of The Florida State University School in Florida. Dr. Kochan has extensive experience in K–12 education having served as a teacher, school principal, district office coordinator, and director of innovative projects. Her research interests include creating collaborative communities and organizational change. Dr. Kochan has published in numerous journals. In her role as a group member, she had the opportunity to rekindle relationships.

Sandy R. Lee is the Counselor for Families/Case Manager and Parent Involvement Coordinator at The Florida State University School. Dr. Lee holds a bachelor's degree in psychology, a master's degree in social work, and a Ph.D. in Marriage and Family Therapy. Her responsibilities include provision of family and individual therapy, and crisis intervention therapy for families and individuals.

Eileen McDaniel is the elementary principal at The Florida State University School. As a University School Associate Professor, she oversees many programs. Her experiences include over 10 years as an elementary teacher, a reading specialist and resource teacher for the elementary program, elementary guidance counselor, and the administrative assistant for K–12 programs before having become principal. Eileen is a doctoral candidate in Educational Leadership at Florida State University. Her dissertation focuses on alternative assessment. The book provided her with an opportunity to reflect and write on her professional life.

Margaret L. Ronald is Associate Professor of Spanish and Latin American studies at The Florida State University School where she has been teaching for the past six years. She is also working on her doctoral degree in international/intercultural education development at The Florida State University. Margaret is interested in women's knowledge, intellectual property rights, and environmental education. She obtained her BA from the Universidad de las Americas in Mexico where she studied anthropology and Spanish. The group provided her with a guided opportunity for reflective analysis of her teaching.

Diane Sopko (formerly Adoue) is Assistant Professor in instruction and curriculum leadership at the University of Memphis. Diane taught in Texas schools for seven years. Her research focuses on the impact of professional development schools on the mentoring experiences of preservice teachers.

Glenn Thomas is Director (superintendent) of The Florida State University School. Glenn has been a senior manager in the Florida Department of Education, secondary science teacher, and more. He has also served as a teacher union president. Glenn has designed a variety of "high tech" systems to support an effective, "high touch" organizational climate. Glenn's current focus is on meaningful statewide reform aimed at the improvement of student performance. The book project provided Glenn with a venue for articulating his vision of leadership.

Edward M. Vertuno is Director of Student Services at The Florida State University. From 1974 to 1991 Dr. Vertuno was the Director of The Florida State University School where he encouraged research opportunities. Dr. Vertuno has taught supervision of student teaching and the principalship. For this book, Ed recollected with fondness his life at the lab school.

About the artists

In memory of **Amelia Allen**, an honor role senior at The Florida State University who passed away, was multitalented and loved. She had hoped to become an accomplished artist and teacher.

Charly Andrews's art revolves around marine biology and mythical sea life. Charly plans to be a marine biologist and also an artist; she also hopes to develop her broadcasting interests.

Rami Bitar is a motivated artist and athlete who draws the human figure using digital graphics. He was selected as Florida Art Education Association's outstanding student-artist for 1998–99.

Cara Delissio is a senior who does not plan to pursue a career in the arts but still wants to develop her artistic skills. Cara enjoys realism; her subjects include landscape and relationships.

J. J. Fenno is a freshman whose works have been exhibited, receiving recognition by Scholastic Publishing and Beckett's Baseball Magazine. He created J.J. Enterprises to share his art.

Jeremiah Foxwell is a highly individualistic, ambitious youth. He makes music, but is not a musician. He makes art, but is not an artist. He is a collection of contradictions.

Julie Johnson has always created and she has won numerous awards for her artworks. Julie plans to get her Bachelor's degree in art education. She takes pride in being a peer mentor.

Nathan Kennedy enjoys computer graphic design, video games, and scuba diving. Nathan enjoys drawing from the imagination and his inspiration comes from digital technologies.

Katrina Kittendorf's artwork portrays feelings and involves color and energy. Her art is a vent for imagination. Katrina plans on pursuing a career in veterinary medicine.

References

ABELL, A. K. and ROTH, M. (1994) 'Constructing science teaching in the elementary school: the socialization of a science enthusiastic student teacher,' *Journal of Research in Science Teaching*, **31**, pp. 77–90.

ABERNATHY, K. (1997) 'The dedicated life,' *Interactive Teacher*, **2**, 3, pp. 14–18.

ADAMS, N. (1996) *Piano Lessons: Music, Love and True Adventure*, New York: Dell.

ADOUE, D. S. (1997) 'Mentoring preservice science teachers: The professional development school,' in MULLEN, C. A., COX, M. D., BOETTCHER, C. K. and ADOUE, D. S. (eds), *Breaking the Circle of One: Redefining Mentorship in the Lives and Writings of Educators*, pp. 87–100, New York: Peter Lang.

ALCOTT, A. B. (1968) 'Orphic sayings (1840),' in J. BARTLETT (ed.), *The Teacher Familiar Quotations* (14th edn., p. 590), Boston, MA: Little, Brown and Company.

AMERICAN ASSOCIATION OF TEACHERS COLLEGES (1926) *Standards for Accrediting Teachers Colleges*, Oneonta, NY: The Association.

ANDERSON, E. M. and SHANNON, A. L. (1988) 'Toward a conceptualization of mentoring,' *Journal of Teacher Education*, **39**, 1, pp. 38–42.

ANGELINI, D. (1995) 'Mentoring in the career development of hospital staff nurses: Models and strategies,' *Journal of Professional Nursing*, **11**, 2, pp. 89–97.

ARIN-KRUPP, J. (1992) 'Planned career mentoring,' *Mentoring International*, **6**, 1/2, pp. 3–12.

ASHTON-WARNER, S. (1963) *Teacher*, New York: Simon and Schuster.

BARNETT, B. (1990) 'Mentoring programs for administrator preparation of mentors and interns; perceptions of program success,' paper presented at the Annual Meeting of the American Educational Research Association, Boston, MA.

BARONE, T. (1992) 'A narrative of enhanced professionalism: educational researchers and popular storybooks about schoolpeople,' *Educational Researcher*, **21**, 9, pp. 15–24.

BEASLEY, K., CORBIN, D., FEIMAN-NEMSER, S. and SHANK, C. (1996) ' "Making it happen": Teachers mentoring one another,' *Theory Into Practice*, **35**, 3, pp. 158–64.

BEREITER, C. and SCARDAMALIA, M. (1993) *Surpassing ourselves: An inquiry into the nature and implications of expertise*, Chicago: Open Court.

BETZ, M. and FITZGERALD, L. (1987) *The career psychology of women*, Orlando, FL: Academic Press.

BEYER, L. E. (1984) 'Field experience, ideology, and the development of critical reflectivity,' *Journal of Teacher Education*, **35**, 3, pp. 36–41.

BIRNBAUM, R. (1988) *How colleges work: The cybernetics of academic organization and leadership*, San Francisco, CA: Jossey-Bass.

BLACKWELL, J. E. (1983) *Networking and mentoring: A study of cross-generational experiences of blacks in graduate and professional schools*, (Microfiche No. ED 235745 HE 016 725).

BONA, M. J., RINEHART, J. and VOLBRECHT, R. M. (1995) 'Show me how to do like you: Comentoring as feminist pedagogy,' *Feminist Teacher*, **9**, 3, pp. 116–24.

BONAR, B. (1992) 'The role of laboratory schools in American Education,' *National Association of Laboratory Schools Journal*, **17**, 1, pp. 42–53.

BOOK, C. L. (1994) *Professional development schools*, New York: Macmillan.

BOYLE, P. and BOICE, B. (1998) 'Systematic mentoring for new faculty teachers and graduate teaching assistants,' *Innovative Higher Education*, **22**, 3, pp. 157–78.

BROUCH, V. M. and FUNK, F. F. (1987) 'Prologue.' *Appleseeds: For beginning art teachers*, National Art Education Association, Reston, VA.

BYRNE, J. A. (8 June 1998) JACK: A close-up look at how America's #1 manager runs GE, *Business Week*, 98.

CAINE, R. N. and CAINE, G. (1994) *Making connections: Teaching and the human brain*, New York: Addison-Wesley.

CANFIELD, J. and HANSEN, M. V. (1996) *A 3rd Serving of Chicken Soup for the Soul*, Deerfield Beach, FL: Health Communications.

CAREW, J. (1998) *The Mentor*, Cincinnati, OH: Donald I. Fine.

CARTER, K. (1993) 'The place of story in the study of teaching and teacher education,' *Educational Researcher*, **22**, 1, pp. 5–12.

CHAPMAN, J. E. (1990) 'School-based decision-making and management: Implications for school personnel,' in CHAPMAN, J. E. (ed.) *School-based Decision-making and Management*, New York: Falmer, pp. 221–42.

CLANDININ, D. J. (1986) *Classroom Practice: Teacher Images in Action*, London: Falmer Press.

CLANDININ, D. J. and CONNELLY, F. M. (1992) 'Teacher as curriculum maker,' in JACKSON, P. W. (ed.) *Handbook of Research on Curriculum*, New York: Macmillan, pp. 363–40.

CLARK, R. W. (1988) 'School-university relationships: An interpretive review,' in SIROTNIK, K. A. and GOODLAD, J. I. (eds) *School-university partnerships in action: Concepts, cases, and concerns*, New York: Teachers College Press, pp. 32–65.

CLINTON, H. R. (1996) *It takes a Village*, New York: Simon and Schuster.

CLUTTERBUCK, D. (1991) *Everyone Needs a Mentor: How to Foster Talent within the Organization* (2nd ed.), London: Institute of Personnel Management.

COLBURN, A. (1993) *Creating Professional Development Schools*, Phi Delta Kappa Educational Foundation Fastback, #352. Bloomington, IN: Phi Delta Kappa Educational Foundation.

COLLINS, M. L. (1997) 'Imperatives for teacher education faculty in higher education,' *Action in Teacher Education*, **19**, 1, pp. 47–54.

CONANT, J. B. (1951) *On Understanding Science: A Historical Approach*, New York: The New American Library.

CONNELLY, F. M. and CLANDININ, D. J. (1988) *Teachers as curriculum planners: Narratives of experience*, New York: Teachers College Press.

CONNER, D. R. (1993) *Managing at the Speed of Change*, New York: Villard.

CORCORAN, T. B. (1995) *Transforming Professional Development for Teachers: A Guide for State Policymakers*, Washington DC: National Governors' Association.

COVEY, S. (1990) *The Seven Habits of Highly Successful People*, New York: Fireside.

CRONAN-HILLIX, T., GENSHEIMER, L., CRONAN-HILLIX, W. A., WILLIAM, S. and DAVIDSON, W. S. (1986) 'Students' views of mentors in psychology graduate training,' *Teaching of Psychology*, **13**, 3, pp. 123–7.

CROW, G. and MATTHEWS, L. J. (1998) *Finding One's Way: How Mentoring can Lead to Dynamic Leadership*, Thousand Oaks, CA: Corwin Press.

CURRAN, D. (1983) *Traits of a Healthy Family*, New York: Ballentine Books.

CZERNIAK, C. and CHIARELOTT, L. (1996) 'Teacher education for effective science instruction: a social cognitive perspective,' *Journal of Teacher Education*, **41**, 1, pp. 49–58.

DARLING-HAMMOND, L. (ed.) (1994) *Professional Development Schools: Schools for Developing a Profession*, NY: Teachers College Press.

DARLING-HAMMOND, L. (1996) 'The quiet revolution: Rethinking teacher development,' *Educational Leadership*, **53**, 6, pp. 4–10.

DARWIN, C. (1989) *Voyage of the Beagle*, New York: Penguin Books. (Original work published in 1839 by Henry Colburn)

DAY, M. (1997) *Preparing Teachers of Art*, The J. Paul Getty Trust.

DEWEY, J. (1990) *The School and the Society*, Chicago, IL: University of Chicago, Press. (Original work published 1900; revised, 1943)

DEWEY, J. (1929) *The Sources of a Science of Education*, New York: Liveright.

DEWEY, J. (1934) *Art as Experience*, New York: Balch.

DEWEY, J. (1965) *The Child and the Curriculum: Schools and Society*, Chicago: University of Chicago Press. (Reissued work published 1990)

DIAMOND, C. T. P. and MULLEN, C. A. (1997) 'Alternative perspectives on mentoring in higher education: Duography as collaborative relationship and inquiry,' *Journal of Applied Social Behaviour*, **3**, 2, pp. 49–64.

DIAMOND, C. T. P. and MULLEN, C. A. (eds) (1999) *The Postmodern Educator: Arts-based Inquiries and Teacher Development*, New York: Peter Lang.

DIAMOND, C. T. P. and MULLEN, C. A. (1999) '"Roped together": Artistic forms of comentoring in higher education,' in DIAMOND, C. T. P. and MULLEN, C. A. (eds) *The Postmodern Educator: Arts-based Inquiries and Teacher Development*, New York: Peter Lang, pp. 315–40.

DONOHUE, K. (ed.) ALEXANDER, J. (Intro.) (1997) *Imagine! Introducing Your Child to the Arts*, Washington, DC: National Endowment for the Arts.

DOWNER, P. (1998, May/June) 'The power of one,' *Moody*, **98**, 5, pp. 33–4.

EDUCATION DEVELOPMENT CENTER (1996) 'Telementoring: using telecommunications to develop mentoring relationships,' *Notes From the Center for Children and Technology*, **4**, 1, pp. 1–2.

ELBAZ, F. L. (1983) *Teacher Thinking: A Study of Practical Knowledge*, London: Croom Helm.

ELLIOTT, J. (1994) 'Research on teachers' knowledge and action research,' *Educational Action Research*, **2**, 1, pp. 133–7.

EMIHOVICH, C. (1992a) 'Teacher research: school/university collaboration from a new perspective,' *Florida Journal of Educational Research*, **32**, 1.

EMIHOVICH, C. (1992b) 'The teacher-researcher [special issue],' *Florida Journal of Educational Research*, **32**, 1.

ERIKSON, E. H. (1950) *Childhood and Society*, NY: Norton.

ERLANDSON, D. A., HARRIS, E. L., SKIPPER, B. L. and ALLEN, S. D. (1993) *Doing Naturalistic Inquiry: A Guide to Methods*, Newbury Park: Sage.

ESTLER, S. (1988) 'Decision making,' in BOYAN, N. (ed.) *Handbook of Research on Educational Administration*, New York: Longman, pp. 305–19.

FACULTY HANDBOOK (1991) Florida: Office of the Dean of the Faculties, The Florida State University. (Steve Edwards, Dean of the Faculties, Foreword)

FEUERVERGER, G. and MULLEN, C. A. (1995) 'Portraits of marginalized lives: stories of literacy and collaboration in school and prison,' *Interchange*, **26**, 3, pp. 221–40.

FLEMING, K. A. (1991) 'Mentoring: Is it the key to opening doors for women in educational administration?' *Education Canada*, pp. 27–33.

FLORIDA STATE COLLEGE FOR WOMEN (1920–31) *Florida State College for Women Catalogue*, Tallahassee, FL.

FLORIDA STATE COLLEGE FOR WOMEN (1951) *Florida State College for Women Catalogue*, Tallahassee, FL.

FLORIDA STATE UNIVERSITY SCHOOL (1997) 'Research and Development Guidelines, 1997–98,' Tallahassee, Florida.

FLORIDA STATE UNIVERSITY SCHOOL – FLORIDA HIGH (1998) 'Florida State University School – "Florida High" research and grant activity report, 1997–98,' Tallahassee, Florida.

FOSTER, G. (1990) *School as Family: Restructuring the Florida State University School*, Tallahassee, FL: The Florida State University School.

FROST, R. (1916/1971) *Robert Frost's poems*, New York: Simon and Schuster.

FULLAN, M. (1996) 'Emotion and hope: Constructive concepts for complex times,' in HARGREAVES, A. (ed.) *Rethinking Educational Change with Heart and Mind*, Alexandria, VA: Association for Supervision and Curriculum Development, pp. 216–33.

FULLAN, M. with STIEGELBAUER, S. (1991) *The New Meaning of Educational Change*, New York: Teachers College Press.

FREIRE, P. (1994) *Pedagogy of Hope: Reliving Pedagogy of the Oppressed*, (R. Barr, trans.) New York: Continuum.

FURLONG, J. and MAYNARD, T. (1995) *Mentoring Student Teachers: The Growth of Professional Knowledge*, New York: Routledge.

GALLIMORE, R., THARP, R. G. and JOHN-STEINER, V. (1992) *The Developmental and Sociocultural Foundations of Mentoring*, Columbia University, New York:

Institute for Urban Minority Education. (ERIC Document Reproduction Service No. ED 354292)

GALVEZ-HJORNEVIK, C. (1986) 'Mentoring among teachers: a review of the literature,' *Journal of Teacher Education*, **37**, 1, pp. 6–11.

GARDNER, H. (1993) *Multiple Intelligences: The Theory in Practice*, New York: Basic Books.

GARDNER, H. (1995) 'Reflections on multiple intelligences: Myths and messages,' *Phi Delta Kappan*, **77**, 3, pp. 200–9.

GEHRKE, N. (1988) 'Toward a definition of mentoring,' *Theory Into Practice*, **27**, 3, 190–4.

GIROUX, H. A. (1991) 'Democracy and the discourse of cultural difference: Towards a politics of border pedogogy,' *British Journal of Sociology of Education*, **12**, 4, pp. 501–19.

GLASER, R., LIEBERMAN, A. and ANDERSON, R. (1997) ' "The vision thing": Educational research and AERA in the 21st century, part 3: Perspectives on the research-practice relationship,' *Educational Researcher*, **26**, 7, pp. 24–5.

GOODLAD, J. I. (1988) 'School-university partnerships for educational renewal: Rationale and concepts,' in SIROTNIK, K. A. and GOODLAD, J. I. (eds) *School-university Partnerships in Action: Concepts, Cases, and Concerns*, New York: Teachers College Press, pp. 3–31.

GOODLAD, J. I. (1990) *Teachers for Our Nation's Schools*, San Francisco, CA: Jossey-Bass.

GOODLAD, J. I. (1995) 'Genesis and maturation of an initiative in educational renewal: A Janus look,' *Record in Educational Leadership*, **15**, pp. 3–11.

GOODMAN, J. (1985) 'What students learn from early field experiences: A case study and critical analysis,' *Journal of Teacher Education*, **36**, 6, pp. 42–8.

GREENBERG, D. S. (1997) *Catalysts for Closure*, Unpublished doctoral dissertation, Florida State University, Tallahassee, Florida.

GROOMES, F. L. (1982) *League of Mentors Handbook, Florida State University*, Office of University Human Resources. Tallahassee, FL: The Florida State University.

GRUNDY, S. (1994) 'Action research at the school level: Possibilities and problems,' *Educational Action Research*, **2**, 1, pp. 23–37.

GUBA, E. G. (1985) 'The context of emergent paradigm research,' in LINCOLN, Y. S. (ed.) *Organizational Theory and Inquiry*, Newbury Park, CA: Sage, pp. 79–105.

GURALNIK, D. B. (ed.) (1986) *Webster's New World Dictionary* (2nd edn.) New York: Prentice Hall.

GUZZO, R. A., SALAS, E. and ASSOCIATES (1995) *Team Effectiveness and Decision Making in Organizations*, San Francisco, CA: Jossey-Bass.

HAFERNIK, J. J., MESSERSCHMITT, D. S. and VANDRICK, S. (1997) 'Collaborative research: why and how?', *Educational Researcher*, **26**, 9, pp. 31–5.

HALLINGER, P., MURPHY, J. and HAUSMAN, C. (1993) 'Conceptualizing school restructuring: principals' and teachers' perceptions,' in DIMMOCK, C. (ed.) *School-based Management and School Effectiveness*, New York: Routledge, pp. 22–40.

HARGREAVES, A. (1992) 'Cultures of teaching: A focus for change,' *Understanding Teacher Development*, New York: Teachers College Press, pp. 216–40.

HARGREAVES, A. and FULLAN, M. G. (1992) 'Introduction,' in HARGREAVES, A. and FULLAN, M. G. (eds), *Understanding Teacher Development*, New York: Teachers College Press, pp. 1–19.

HARING-HIDORE, (HARING), M., FREEMAN, S. C., PHELPS, S., SPANN, N. G. and WOOTEN, H. R. (1990) 'Women administrators' ways of knowing,' *Education and Urban Society*, **22**, 2, pp. 170–81.

HEAD, F. A., REIMAN, A. J. and THIES-SPRINTHALL, L. (1992) 'The reality of mentoring: Complexity in its process and function,' in BEY, T. M. and HOLMES, C. T. (eds), *Mentoring: Contemporary Principles and Issues*, Reston, VA: Association of Teacher Educators, pp. 5–34.

HELLRIEGEL, D. and SLOCUM, J. W. (1974) 'Organizational climate: Measures research, and contingencies,' *Academy of Management Journal*, **17**, pp. 255–79.

HERBERT, R. L. (1991) *Seurat*, New York: The Metropolitan Museum of Art.

HOLLAND, J. L. (1996) 'Exploring careers with a typology: What we have learned and some new directions,' *The American Psychologist*, **51**, 4, pp. 397–407.

HOLMES GROUP (1986) *Tomorrow's Teachers: A Report of The Holmes Group*, East Lansing, MI: The Holmes Group, Inc.

HOLMES GROUP (1990) *Tomorrow's Schools: Principles for the Design of Professional Development Schools*, East Lansing, MI: The Holmes Group, Inc.

HOLMES GROUP (1995) *A Report of The Holmes Group: Tomorrow's Schools of Education*, East Lansing, MI: The Holmes Group, Inc.

HOLY BIBLE, NEW INTERNATIONAL VERSION, THE (1973) Grand Rapids: Zondervan Bible Publishing.

HUBERMAN, M. (1992) 'Teacher development and instructional mastery,' *Understanding Teacher Development*, New York: Teachers College Press, pp. 122–42.

HUSBAND, R. and SHORT, P. (1994) 'Teacher autonomy through shared governance: effects on policy making and student outcomes,' *Middle School Journal*, **26**, 2, pp. 58–61.

INTERNATIONAL MENTORING ASSOCIATION (1998) *The Mentoring Connection*, Quarterly newsletter of The International Mentoring Association, fall.

JANSEN, T. and VAN DER VEEN, R. (1997) 'Individualization, the new political spectrum and the functions of adult education,' *International Journal of Lifelong Education*, **16**, 4, pp. 264–76.

JEANTY, E. A. and BROWN, O. C. (1976) *Parol Granmoun 999 Haitian Proverbs in Creole and English*, Port-au-Prince, Haiti: Editions Learning Center.

JOYCE, B., BENNETT, R. and ROLHEISER-BENNETT, C. (1990) 'The self-educating teacher: Empowering teachers through research,' *Changing School Culture through Staff Development*. Alexandria, VA: ASCD, pp. 33–4.

JOYCE, B., MURPHY, C., SHOWERS, B. and MURPHY, J. (1989) 'School renewal as culture change,' *Educational Leadership*, pp. 70–7.

JOYCE, B., WEIL, M. and SHOWERS, B. (1992) *Models of Teaching* (4th ed.), London: Allyn and Bacon.

KAUFMAN, W. (1975) *Existentialism from Dostoevsky to Sartre*, New York: New American Library.

KAUFMAN, R., HERMAN, J. and WATTERS, K. (1996) *Educational Planning: Strategic, Tactical, and Operational*, Lancaster, PA: Technomic.

KEALY, W. A. (1997) 'Full circle: insights on mentoring from my mentor's heroes,' in MULLEN, C. A., COX, M. D., BOETTCHER, C. K. and ADOUE, D. S. (eds) *Breaking the Circle of One: Redefining Mentorship in the Lives and Writings of Educators*, New York: Peter Lang, pp. 175–88.

KEALY, W. A. and MULLEN, C. A. (1999) '"From the next scale up": Using graphic arts as an opening to mentoring,' in DIAMOND, C. T. P. and MULLEN, C. A. (eds), *The Postmodern Educator: Arts-based Inquiries and Teacher Development*, New York: Peter Lang, pp. 375–96.

KEYTON, J. and KALBFLEISCH, P. J. (1993) 'Building a normative model of women's mentoring relationships', paper presented to the joint Central/Southern States Communication Association, Lexington, KY.

KOCHAN, F. K. (1992) 'Research and practice: an administrator's view,' *Florida Journal of Educational Research*, **32**, 1, pp. 27–33.

KOCHAN, F. K. (1996) 'Factors influencing participation in school restructuring in Florida,' *International Studies in Educational Administration*, **24**, 1, pp. 39–45.

KOCHAN, F. K., ANDERSON-HARPER, H. and BECK, D. (1998) 'Collaboration: an essential element in curricular reform,' *Journal of Pharmacy Teaching*, **6**, 3, pp. 39–51.

KRAMER, R. (ed.) (1991) *School Follies*, New York: Macmilliam Free Press.

KRUPP, J. (1992) 'Planned career mentoring,' *Mentoring International*, **6**, 1/2, pp. 3–12.

LAKOFF, G. and JOHNSON, M. (1980) *Metaphors We Live By*, Chicago, IL: University of Chicago.

LEE, V. E. and SMITH, J. B. (1993) 'Effects of school restructuring on the achievement and engagement of middle-grade students,' *Sociology of Education*, **66**, 3, pp. 164–88.

LEVINSON, D. (1978) *The Seasons of a Man's Life*, New York: Knopf.

LIEBERMAN, A. (1988) 'The Metropolitan School Study Council: A Living History,' in SIROTNIK, K. A. and GOODLAD, J. I. (eds) *School-university Partnerships in Action: Concepts, Cases, and Concerns*, New York: Teachers College Press, pp. 69–86.

LIEBERMAN, A. (1992) 'The meaning of scholarly activity and the building of community,' *Educational Researcher*, **21**, 6, pp. 5–12.

LIEBERMAN, A. and MILLER, L. (1992) *Teachers: Their World and Their Work – Implications for School Improvement*, New York: Teachers College Press.

LINCOLN, Y. S. and GUBA, E. G. (1985) *Naturalistic Inquiry*, Newbury Park, CA: Sage.

LITTLE, J. W. (1990) 'The mentor phenomenon and the social organization of teaching,' *Review of Research in Education*, **16**, pp. 297–351.

LORTIE, D. C. (1975) *School Teacher: A Sociological Study*, Chicago, IL: University of Chicago Press.

MACKAY, H. (1988) *Swim with the Sharks: Without Being Eaten Alive*, New York: William Morrow.

MASLOW, A. (1962) *Toward a Psychology of Being*, New York: Van Nostrand.

MASSEY, W., WILEY, A. and COLBECK, C. (1994) 'Overcoming hollowed collegiality,' *Change*, **24**, 4, pp. 11–20.

MAY, S. and FURLONG, D. (1997) 'Teaching that fosters professional and social development (addressing the needs of adult learners in community-based and NGO settings),' *International Journal of Lifelong Education*, **16**, 4, pp. 308–19.

MAYNARD, T. and FURLONG, J. (1995) 'Learning to teach and models of mentoring,' in KERRY, T. and MAYES, A. S. (eds), *Issues in Mentoring*, London: Routledge, pp. 10–24.

MCCALEB, S. P. (1994) *Building Communities of Learners: A Collaboration among Teachers, Students, Families, and Community*, New York: St. Martin's Press.

MCDANIEL, E. (1988–89) 'Collaboration for what? Sharpening the focus,' *Action in Teacher Education*, **10**, 4, pp. 1–8.

MCELHINEY, A. B. (1990, Summer) 'Genesis of a planned mentoring program for re-entry women,' *Mentoring International/Career Planning and Adult Development Journal*, pp. 21–6.

MCPHERSON, M., with RICE, W. (1995) *One Kid at a Time: How Mentoring Can Transform Your Youth Ministry*, Colorado Springs, CO: Youth specialties and David C. Cook.

MERRIAM, S. (1983) 'Mentors and protégés: A critical review of the literature,' *Adult Education Quarterly*, **33**, pp. 161–73.

MILLER, J. (1997) *Draft Evaluation Processes: Personnel Manual no. 2*, Tallahassee, FL: College of Education/Florida State University.

MOON, B. and MAYES, A. S. (1995) 'Integrating values into the assessment of teachers in initial education and training,' in KERRY, T. and MAYES, A. S. (eds) *Issues in mentoring*, London: Routledge/The Open University, pp. 233–42.

MULLEN, C. A. (1994) 'A narrative exploration of the self I dream,' *Journal of Curriculum Studies*, **26**, 3, pp. 253–63.

MULLEN, C. A. (1997a) 'Hispanic preservice teachers and professional development: Stories of mentorship,' *Latino Studies Journal*, **8**, pp. 3–35.

MULLEN, C. A. (1997b) *Imprisoned Selves: An Inquiry into Prisons and Academe*, New York: University Press of America.

MULLEN, C. A. (1997c) 'Post-sharkdom: An alternative form of mentoring for teacher educator-researchers,' in MULLEN, C. A., COX, M. D., BOETTCHER, C. K. and ADOUE, D. S. (eds) *Breaking the Circle of One: Redefining Mentorship in the Lives and Writings of Educators*, New York: Peter Lang, pp. 145–74.

MULLEN, C. A. (1999) 'Whiteness, cracks, and ink-stains: Making cultural identity with Euroamerican preservice teachers,' in DIAMOND, C. T. P. and MULLEN, C. A. (eds) *The Postmodern Educator: Arts-based Inquiries and Teacher Development*, New York: Peter Lang, pp. 147–90.

MULLEN, C. A. (in press a) 'Constructing comentoring partnerships: Walkways we must travel,' *Theory Into Practice*.

MULLEN, C. A. (in press b) 'Innovations in mentoring: Creating partnership links in a Florida school-university collaborative,' *Florida Journal of Educational Research*.

MULLEN, C. A. and DALTON, J. E. (1996) 'Dancing with sharks: Becoming socialized teacher educator-researchers,' *Taboo: The Journal of Culture and Education*, **I**, pp. 55–71.

MULLEN, C. A. and KEALY, W. A. (eds) (1999) *Mentorship and Mentoring Practices Special Interest Group*, Newsletter of the American Educational Research Association, **1**, summer.

MULLEN, C. A. and KEALY, W. A. (eds) (1999) *Mentorship and Mentoring Practices Special Interest Group*, Newsletter of the American Educational Research Association, **2**, spring.

MULLEN, C. A., WHATLEY, A. and KEALY, W. A. (in press) *Widening the Circle: Faculty-Student Support Groups as Innovative Practice in Higher Education*, Interchange.

MULLEN, C. A., COX, M. D., BOETTCHER, C. K. and ADOUE, D. S. (eds) (1997) *Breaking the Circle of One: Redefining Mentorship in the Lives and Writings of Educators*, New York: Peter Lang.

MURPHY, C. U. and LICK, D. W. (1998) *Whole-faculty Study Groups: A Powerful Way to Change Schools and Enhance Learning*, Thousand Oaks, CA: Corwin.

NAISBITT, J. (1984) *Megatrends*, New York: Warner Books.

NATIONAL EDUCATION ASSOCIATION (1993) *Mentoring Minorities in Higher Education: Passing the Torch*, Washington, DC: National Education Association Office of Higher Education.

NIAS, J. (1989) *Primary Teachers Talking: A Study of Teaching as Work*, New York: Routledge.

NODDINGS, N. (1995) *Philosophy of Education*, Boulder, CO: Westview Press.

OAKES, J., HARE, S. and SIROTNIK, K. (1986) 'Collaborative inquiry: A congenial paradigm in a cantankerous world,' *Teachers College Record*, **87**, pp. 545–61.

O'DONOGHUE, T. (1994) 'The impact of restructuring on teachers' understandings of their curriculum work: A case study,' *Journal of Curriculum and Supervision*, **10**, 1, pp. 21–42.

PAGE, F. M. and PAGE, J. A. (1981) 'Laboratory schools: updated or outdated?' (ED 213672), Statesboro, Georgia Southern College.

PANNOZZO, L. (1998) 'What defines a profession?' *Accomplished Teacher*, **1**, 3. Southfield, MI: National Board for Professional Teaching Standards.

PATTON, M. Q. (1990) *Qualitative Evaluation and Research Methods* (3rd ed.), Beverly Hills, CA: Sage.

PEEL, B. B., WHEATLEY, E. A. and BRENT, R. (1997) 'The story of a successful higher education/public school partnership,' *SRATE Journal*, **6**, 1, pp. 3–6.

PETERS, T. J. and WATERMAN, R. H. (1982) *In Search of Excellence: Lessons from America's Best-run Companies*, New York: Warner Books.

POLLARD, A. and TRIGGS, P. (1997) *Reflective Teaching in Secondary Education: A Handbook for Schools and Colleges*, London: Cassell.

POUNDER, D. G. (ed.) (1998a) *Restructuring Schools for Collaboration: Promises and pitfalls*, Albany, NY: State University of New York Press.

POUNDER, D. G. (ed.) (1998b) 'Teacher teams: redesigning teachers' work for collaboration,' in *Restructuring Schools for Collaboration: Promises and Pitfalls*, Albany, NY: State University of New York Press, pp. 65–88.

PRESIDENT'S COMMITTEE ON THE ARTS AND THE HUMANITIES (1997) *Creative America: A Report to the President*, Washington, DC: US Government.

PRITCHETT, P. and MUIRHEAD, B. (1998) *The Mars Pathfinder Approach to "Faster-Better-Cheaper,"* Dallas, TX: Pritchett and Associates.

RAND, P. (1974) 'Florida High transforms theory into practice,' *Florida Flambeau*, pp. 3–5, February 12.

REITZUG, U. C. (1994) 'A case study of empowering principal behavior,' *American Educational Research Journal*, **31**, 2, pp. 283–307.

RESTINE, N. (1996) 'Partnerships between schools and institutions of higher education,' in ACKERMAN, R. and CORDEIRO, R. (eds) *New Directions in School Leadership: Boundary Crossings, 2*, San Francisco, CA: Jossey-Bass, pp. 31–9.

SAAVEDRA, E. (1996) 'Teachers' study groups: Contexts for transformative learning and action,' *Theory Into Practice*, **35**, 4, 271–77.

SANDS, R. G., PARSON, L. A. and DUANE, J. (1991) 'Faculty mentoring faculty in a public university,' *Journal of Higher Education*, **62**, 2, pp. 174–93.

SARASON, S. B. (1993) *The Case for Change: Rethinking the Preparation of Educators*, San Francisco, CA: Jossey-Bass.

SCHWAB, J. J. (1978) 'The practical: A language for curriculum,' in WESTBURY, I. and WILKOF, N. J. (eds) *Science, Curriculum, and Liberal Education*, Chicago, IL: University of Chicago Press, pp. 287–321.

SCOTT, M. E. (1992) 'Designing effective mentoring programs: Historical perspectives and current issues,' *Journal of Humanistic Education and Development*, **30**, pp. 167–77.

SENGE, P. (1990) *The Fifth Discipline: The Art and Practice of the Learning Organization*, New York: Currency.

SERGIOVANNI, T. (1994) *Building Community in Schools*, San Francisco, CA: Jossey-Bass.

SHOWERS, B. and JOYCE, B. (1996) 'The evolution of peer coaching', *Educational Leadership*, **53**, 6, 12–16.

SID W. RICHARDSON FOUNDATION FORUM (1990) *The Professional Development School: A Commonsense Approach to Improving Education*, Fort Worth, TX: Author.

SLEETER, C. (1998) 'Activist or ethnographer? Researchers, teachers, and voice in ethnographies that critique,' in DEMARRAIS, K. B. (ed.) *Inside Stories: Qualitative Research Reflections*, Mahwah, NJ: Lawrence Erlbaum, pp. 49–57.

SLAVIN, R. E. (1995) *Cooperative Learning: Theory, Research and Practice* (2nd edn.), Boston, MA: Allyn and Bacon.

SMITH, C. (1 April 1998) 'Businesses are learning the benefits of mentoring programs,' *Tallahassee Democrat*, D12–13.

SMITS, H. (1997) 'Reflection and its (dis)content(s): Re-thinking the nature of reflective practice in teacher education,' *Journal of Professional Studies*, **4**, 2, pp. 15–28.

STEVENS, W. (1972) *The Palm at the End of the Mind*, New York: Vintage Books.

STINNETT, N. and DEFRAIN, J. (1986) *Secrets of Strong Families*, New York: Berkeley Books.

SYLWESTER, R. (1995) *A Celebration of Neurons: An Educator's Guide to the Human Brain*, Alexandria, VA: Association for Supervision and Curriculum Development.

TANNER, L. N. (1997) *Dewey's Laboratory School: Lessons for Today*, New York: Teachers College Press.

TAYLOR, S. J. and BOGDAN, R. (1984) *Introduction to Qualitative Research Methods* (2nd ed.) New York: Wiley and Sons.

THIESSEN, D. (1992) 'Classroom-based teacher development,' in HARGREAVES, A. and FULLAN, M. G. (eds) *Understanding Teacher Development*, New York: Teachers College Press, pp. 85–109.

THODY, A. (1993) 'Mentoring for school principals,' in CALDWELL, B. J. and CARTER, E. M. A. (eds) *The Return of the Mentor: Strategies for Workplace Learning*, Bristol, PA: Falmer Press, pp. 59–76.

TICHY, N. M. (1997) *The Leadership Engine: How Winning Companies Build Leaders at Every Level*, New York: HarperBusiness.

TURNER, B. (1990) *Organizational Symbolism*, New York: Wa de Gruyter.

VANZANT, L. (1980) 'Achievement motivation, sex-role acceptance, and mentor relationships of professional females', unpublished doctoral dissertation, East Texas State University, Texas.

VERTUNO, E. M. (Speaker) (12 February 1998) interview with Mullen, C. A. and FUNK, F. F. (Cassette Recording), Tallahasse, FL: The Florida State University.

VOLTAIRE (1956) 'Candide, or optimism', in BLOCK, H. M. (ed.) *Candide and Other Writings*, New York: Random House, pp. 110–89.

VONDRACEK, F., LERNER, R. and SCHULENBERGER, J. (1986) *Career Development: A Life-span Development Approach*, Hillsdale, NJ: Lawrence Erlbaum.

WALKER, A. and STOTT, K. (1993) 'Preparing for leadership in schools: The mentoring contribution,' in CALDWELL, B. J. and CARER, E. M. A. (eds) *The Return of the Mentor: Strategies for Workplace Learning*, Bristol, PA: Falmer, pp. 77–90.

WALTON, M. (1986) *The Deming Management Method*, New York: Perigee Books.

WATERS, M. (ed.) (1998) *Mentor and Protégé: Accelerating Professional and Personal Development through the Art and Practice of Mentoring and Coaching*, **10**, 2.

WATKINS, C. and WHALLEY, C. (1995) 'Mentoring beginner teachers – issues for schools to anticipate and manage,' in KERRY, T. and MAYES, A. S. (eds) *Issues in Mentoring*, London: Routledge, pp. 121–8.

WEBER, A. (1996) 'Professional development schools and university laboratory schools: is there a difference?' *The Professional Educator*, **18**, 2, pp. 59–65.

References

WERNER, W. (1980) 'Implementation: The role of belief', unpublished manuscript.
WILLIE, C. V. (1988) *Effective Education: A Mentoring Policy Perspective*, New York: Greenwood Press.
WUNSCH, M. A. (1993) 'Mentoring probationary women academics: A pilot programme for career development,' *Studies in Higher Education*, **18**, 3, pp. 349–62.
ZEY, M. (1984) *The Mentor Connection*, Homewood, IL: Dow Jones-Irwin.
ZIMPHER, N. L. and RIEGER, S. R. (1988) 'Mentoring teachers: What are the issues?' *Theory Into Practice*, **28**, pp. 175–82.

Index

academe
  academic canons 50
  academic community 24
  academic environment 93
  academic lineage 129, 197
  academic mentor 190
  academy 49
action research 238
  collaborative action research 7, 63,
    242
active listening 243–4
Adams, N. 54, 195
administration (school and university)
    87–103, 122, 129, 147, 180, 231, 237,
    246
administrators
  female 89, 91
  male 90, 91–2
  K–12 administrators 91, 215
advising/counseling 83–4
advocate(s) 210
affirmative action 21, 79, 85
Affirmative Action Program 80
African American 21, 79, 93, 174, 176
Alcott, A. B. xiv
Allen, Amelia ii, 18, 133–41
alternative frameworks 123
American Association of Teachers Colleges
    23
American Educational Research Association
    53
Andrews, Charly 227
anonymity x, 58
appreciative understanding 243–4
appreciator 178
Arin-Krupp, J. 88
art
  art department 134
  art teacher 5
  artwork(s) x, 14, 59, 245
Ashton–Warner, S. 59–60

assessment/evaluation 3, 5, 150, 214,
    237–8, 242–7
  collective 242
  facilitation of group 7, 243–5
  facilitator 4, 216, 239, 242
  hindrance of group 242, 244–6
  post-assessment 243–6
author(s) 2, 10, 245
author phenomenon 57
authorship
  authorship negotiations 54
  authoring practice(s) 54
  authorship patronage systems 58
  authorship training 53–4
  coauthorship 4–5, 195

Barone, Thomas 50
Barrett-Hayes, Debi P. ix, 6, 15, 48, 228
barrier(s) 212, 214, 247
Beasley, K., Corbin, D., Feiman–Nemser,
    S., and Shank, C. 62
Bereiter, C., and Scardamalia, M. 31
Bitar, Rami ix
blueprint (schematic) 231–3
Bona, M. J., Rinehart, J., and Volbrecht,
    R. M. 30, 35, 52
book
  birth of a book 48, 54
  book expedition 20
  book-making 54
  book's "soul" 48
  grow(ing) wings 48–9, 69–70
  hardware images 48
  nuts 'n bolts 48–9
Boyle, P., and Boice, B. 3, 61
British Infant School Program 177

caring 180–1
  attitudes 221
  forms of practice 124
Carter, K. 1

Index

case study 54–70, 217–26, 247
change
   change agent defined 206, 210
   management 34, 202–12
   organizational change 223, 226
child development 118, 240
child(ren) 130, 135, 174, 224
circle
   academic circle 128
   spiritual circle 126–8
   therapeutic circle 128–31
Clandinin, D. Jean 19
Clark, R. W. 23
classroom 24, 72–7, 135–41, 148–56,
   157–71
Clinton
   President Clinton 140
   Hillary Clinton 139
collaboration xi, 22, 217–18
   barriers 24
   messy 59
collaborative
   inquiry 21, 33
   learning relationship 134
   model 33
   networks 224
   research communities xiii, 29
collaborator(s) 57, 59–60, 163
comentor(ing)/comentor(ship) xi, xiii–xv,
   10–12, 22, 30
   comentoring defined 11, 35, 52, 55–6,
      62–3, 127, 243
   comentoring model xi
   comentoring partnership 106
   comentoring strategies 65–8
   comentoring support group 54, 197, 223
   multiple-level comentoring 202–12
   rebirthed as comentors 10, 17
   (see "mentorship")
community 27, 49
   activist 134
   mentoring 15
   of learners 50
Connelly, F. M., and Clandinin, D. J. 19,
   30
Conner, D. R. 36–40
counseling therapy 21
cross-cultural study 242–3
Crow, G., and Matthews, L. J. 88

culture wheel mentoring tool 142, 150–1
curriculum development 175

Darling–Hammond, L. 31, 159
Darwin, Charles 4
data
   collection 57, 218
   field notes 243–5
   Likert scale 160
   methods and analysis 160–1, 164, 218–19
   numerical 160
   surveys 160–1, 219, 238
Delissio, Cara 87
Deming's philosophy 198
demographics 189, 204, 228
Dewey, John 23–4, 189
dialogue (versus discussion) 198
Diamond, C. T. Patrick 30, 191
discipling defined 127
dissemination 247
divergence 116–17
diverse 1, 21
   faculty/membership 66
   educators/professionals 60
   support group 20, 247
   heterogeneous group 236
diversity 22, 30, 41, 45, 84, 190
dual keyboards 111–12
   dual keyboarding partners 104
duography 191

electronic
   conversation(s) 115
   network/structure 21
equal/equality xiii, 21, 25, 191
   equal colleagues 100
   equal opportunity 82
egalitarian practice 24
   mentoring xi
Erikson, E. H. 144
Elbaz, Freema L. 1, 19
Emihovich, Catherine 27, 29
empathy/empathetic 54, 78, 222
   empathy defined 41
empowering/empowerment 97, 102, 125,
      177, 187, 210, 213, 221, 242, 245
   teacher empowerment 196
encaustic painting 133–4
engagement 110–11

expedition (boating) 228–9
Euroamerican 92

Falmer Press ix
family/families 181
  family relationships 149
  family as metaphor 224
  faculty family 215–17
  school therapist 129
  "school as family" 213–26
family-school-community partnership 28
Fenno, J. J. 125
Florida 27, 29, 60, 66, 122, 175, 188,
  230
  Board of Regents Policy 27, 173, 179
  certification 121
  Florida Department of Education 84,
    214, 238
  Sunshine State Standards 145
Florida State University, The (FSU) ix–xi,
  2, 10, 17–18, 20, 25–7, 49, 73,
  79–86, 173–82
Florida State University School, The (FSUS)
  ii, ix–xi, 2, 6–7, 10, 18, 20–1, 24,
  26–8, 49, 57, 62, 72, 90, 117, 119–21,
  126, 143, 146–56, 172–86, 213–26,
  227–41
  FSUS Knowledge Center (library) 22,
    26, 104–15, 146, 242
  FSUS's PLUNGE 141
  FSUS admissions' policy 173–4
  FSUS policy (other) 119, 215, 230
  web–based campus 231
Foxwell, Jeremiah 104
Franklin, Lori 6, 68–9, 143
"free–rider effect" xiv
Furlong, John 20, 187
Fullan, Michael 24, 217, 226
Funk, Fanchon F. 5–7, 173

Gallimore, R., Tharp, R. G. and
  John–Steiner V. 194
Gehrke, N. 76, 127, 131
Giroux, Henry A. 52
Goodlad, John 2, 12, 31, 33, 59, 61, 158–9
good-will 195
grades (student) 150, 154, 156
graduation speech 182–4
graphics 17

Greenberg, David S. 6, 78
Groomes, Freddie L. 6
guidance 126, 247
  guide(s) 74, 241
  guided learning 188, 246
Guba, Egon G. 160, 218

Hafernik, J. J., Messerschmitt, D. S. and
  Vandrick, S. 24
Hargreaves, Andy 24, 231
Haring, Marilyn J. xi, 2
Head, F. A., Reiman, A. J. and Thies-
  Sprinthall, L. 4, 193
hierarchy/hierarchical xi, 32, 191
Hilgemeier, Susan 6
Holland, J. L. 238
Holmes Group 12, 158–9
Homer, Winslow 228–9
hope 226

innovation(s) 148, 228
  innovative applications 17
  innovative instruction 229
  innovative mentoring xi
inservice teachers 228
institutional 11
  rank/status 55
  reform 21
interdependence 96–7, 186, 210, 245
interinstitutional
  partnership xi, 7
  research 26
isolation 228

Johnson, Julie 34, 71, 157, 213
journal (documentation)
  mentoring logs 7, 247
  student journal 153
  teacher journal 145–7, 151
journey 7, 186, 227–41
  doctoral 117
  mentoring 87, 172, 192, 199
  sojourner(s) 4, 18, 20, 88
  spiritual/analytical 54
  traveling 18
  traveling companions 20
  traveler(s) 86, 102, 242
Joyce, B., Murphy, C., Showers, B., and
  Murphy, J. 202

Kaufman, R., Herman, J., and Watters, K. 202
Kealy, William A. ix, 3, 7, 52, 129, 156, 172, 191, 193, 226, 232
Kennedy, Nathan 10
Kittendorf, Katrina 116
Kochan, Frances K. 5–7, 31, 214, 220, 225
knowledge xiii
    authoritative knowledge 188
    new 170, 188
    professional xiv

laboratory school(s) 4, 6, 18, 22–4, 28, 53, 56, 116, 149, 173, 247
Laboratory School Bill 176
Langston, Bill 79
language development 148–9
leadership 16, 88, 185–6, 198, 227–41, 243
    educational leadership 21, 84, 90, 116, 236–7
    leadership development 24
League of Mentors, The 6, 79–86
League of Mentors Handbook 80
Lee, Sandy R. 6, 117
Levinson, D. 79, 144
Lick, Dale W. 5, 7, 21, 31, 35–7, 73, 129, 232, 245
Lieberman, Ann 4, 217, 226
Life-affirming perspectives 197
lifelong mentoring 187–99
    lifelong mentoring defined 187, 189
    as organic/philosophical model 187–8
lighthouse(s) 7, 227, 230–3, 240–1
    lighthouse keeper 230
    beacon(s) 7, 229–30, 241
Lincoln, Yvonna S. 160
Little, Judith W. 31, 51
"lone wolf " 58

map(s) 4–5, 230
    concept map 7, 244 (example of)
    mentoring map 235
    road map xv, 141
marriage (mentoring as) xiii, 104–15, 149, 197
Maslow, A. 194
McCaleb, S. P. 60
McDaniel, Eileen L. ix, 6, 22, 62, 106, 130, 143, 155

mentor(s) xiii, 4
    lead-mentor 230
    Mentor 35, 137
    Mentor-cartographer 230–1
mentor defined 88
mentoring defined 13, 66, 188
mentor identity 198
mentor(ing) phenomenon 51, 79
mentor teacher(s) 162, 166–71
mentor training 198
mentoring/mentorship xi, 3, 6, 14, 21 (see comentorship)
    mentorship defined 51, 242
    career mentoring 138
    holistic mentoring model 192–6
    mentor-mentee relationship 71–2, 74, 80–6, 96–7, 110
    mentor-teacher 133
        mentor-teacher defined 139
    mentoring benefits 138–9, 165–6, 210, 245
    mentoring creative thought 137, 139–40
    mentoring leadership 193, 230
    mentoring literature 31, 196
    mentoring model 190
    mentoring (support group) mosaic 2, 4, 29, 61, 145, 191, 196–7
    mentoring norm 196
    mentoring opportunity 123, 137
    mentoring pathway(s) 1, 10, 31–3, 242–7
    mentoring phases 89
    mentoring postulates 196
    mentoring processes 186
    mentoring profiles 90–103
    mentoring programs 13, 80–6, 89, 138, 170, 187, 194
    mentoring relationships 99, 137–8
    mentoring synergy 73
    spiritual mentoring 6, 125–32, 133–41
    therapeutic mentoring 126
Merriam, S. 20, 127, 129, 144
metaphor 4
Miller, Jack W. xiii, 2, 28, 37, 62
minority/minorities 73, 79–86, 190
    ethnic(ity) 30, 84, 151
    faculty recruitment/hiring 176
mirror(s) 134, 173
Moon, B., and Mayes, A. S. 195

mother 152
  working 108–9, 144
Mullen, Carol A. ix–x, 3, 6–7, 12, 18, 21,
    24, 29–30, 32, 35, 43, 45, 52, 72,
    117, 120, 127, 129, 132, 143, 151,
    173, 191–2, 198, 226
Mullen, C. A., Cox, M. D., Boettcher,
    C. K., and Adoue, D. S. 3, 13, 16, 29,
    63, 89, 103, 132, 187
Murphy, Carlene 202, 207–8

narrative (study of) 12
  narrative research accounts 20
National Education Association 160, 190
network
  primary mentoring 193
  secondary mentoring 193
Neo–Impressionist movement 191
new directions xi, 1, 3, 6, 10–11, 14, 27,
    33, 49, 61, 237, 243
Noddings, N. 31, 197
novice-expert continuum 164

openness 243–4
organizational change 21

Page, F. M., and Page, J. A. 23
parent(s) 176, 178, 221–2, 240
  parent-mentor 152
  parenting education 118
participatory action research/framework 19,
    56
partner(s) xiv–xv
Partnership Support Group (PSG) ix, 1–4,
    10–11, 16, 19–21, 24, 35, 43–4, 49,
    63–70, 105–6, 117–18, 129, 132, 143,
    187, 209, 228, 237, 242–7
  partnership support groups xiii, 190
partnership(s)
  faculty 30
  partnership creation 7
pathway(s) 20, 242
pedagogy xiii, 195
Peel, B. B., Wheatley, E. A. and Brent, R.
    30–1
  support system 144–5
people of color 190
personnel
  school 1
  university 1

"Please Let Me I N" (poem) 64
Pounder, Diane 3, 242–3
power 32–3, 90
  power-laden xi
  power-sharing 140, 191
practitioner 1
preservice teachers 73, 157–71, 228
preservice teacher education 157–71
principal (school) 88, 107, 116–24,
    130
principal
  as encourager 118, 122, 124, 194
  as mentor 116–24, 172
  as research director 119–20
  principalship 121, 181
Pritchett, P., and Muirhead, B. xiv
productivity 3, 10, 209, 246
  joint productive activity defined 194
  productive resistance 247
portfolio
  professional development portfolio 195,
    238
  student (electronic) portfolio 240
Professional Development Schools 7, 132,
    157–71
professors/university faculty xiii, 3, 21, 23,
    26, 28, 50, 53, 57–8, 164, 166, 173,
    198
  retired faculty mentors 189
protégé(s) 4, 188, 194
publication 1–2, 10, 20, 23, 53, 247
  major book 188
  publishing experience 21
  publishing plans/contract 246

qualitative inquiry/research 59
questionnaire 63

recommendations 242, 246–7
reciprocal/reciprocity 22, 31, 144, 247
  reciprocal mentoring 19, 40
reflection 155, 240–1, 242–3
reform initiatives 3, 206, 246
  school reform 7, 202–6, 227–41, 237
research
  beginning/novice researchers xi
  community 33
  development 175, 229
respect 154–5

risk-taking 228–9
"Road Not Taken, The" (poem) 141
Ronald Margaret L. 6, 151

Sands, R. G., Parson, L. A., and Duane, J. 31, 61, 85
Sarason, Seymour, B. 23
school
  building(s) 236
  school climate defined 236
  school culture defined 207, 236
  demonstration school 173, 184
  Developmental Research School 184
  faculty governance 179
  Florida High 184–5
  K–12 curricula 134
  K–12 school 87–103, 116–24, 146–56, 172
  leader 172–86
  legends 182
  restructuring 213–26
  school's dual identity 172
scholarship xii
school-university xi, 2, 5, 12, 14, 32–3, 50–1
  community 20, 232
  culture 3, 12, 29, 119–20
  organization 246
  partnership 23, 231
Schwab, J. J. 33
self-actualization 187, 194, 199
self-efficacy 167–8
Senge, Peter, M. 198
shark(dom) metaphor 29, 32
Shrum, Donna 105–15
Slavin, R. xiv
Sleeter, C. 1
Sopko, Diane 6
sponsor(ship) 43, 74, 144, 194, 210
whole–faculty change sponsorship defined 210
stakeholders 160, 166–7, 169, 231, 246
star (shining) 135–7
  "What one star can carve" (poem) 33
status quo 54
stories of genealogy 197
story 106, 126, 245–6, 247
  mentoring story 188
  research story 85, 173, 226, 228, 247

research story defined 12
  success story 102
storyteller(s) 173
  storytelling 57, 106
stranger 60–1
structured inquiry 243–4
student performance 229, 239–41
synergy (see "mentorship") xiv, 5, 12, 34–45, 54, 223, 243
  synergy defined 36–7, 52, 55, 68
  audit 34, 42–4
  created 71
  culture(s) of synergy 1, 10, 31
  "oneness" 120
  synergistic "baby" 111
synergistic comentoring (practice) 3, 11, 17, 101, 125, 210–11, 213–14, 242, 246
  relationship(s) 26, 117, 134
synergistic mentoring 85, 87

teacher xiii
  as author 53, 56–7
  as researcher 56, 147
teacher education 171, 173, 175
  teacher education literature 49, 56, 63
teacher networks 32
teacher thinking 1
teamwork defined 209
  focus team defined 210
technology xiii, 21, 85, 107, 139, 141, 147–8, 190, 239–40
tenure and promotion 6, 28, 79–86, 175
Texas A&M University 159, 161
theory and practice 23, 164
Thomas, Glenn 7, 26, 185
Thiessen, D. 29
traditional mentoring 13
  grooming mentoring xi
  redefinition(s) 189, 191, 194
transcript(ion) 3, 55, 69

U.S. Commissioner of Education 140

Vertuno, Edward, M. 7, 25, 28, 117, 172, 185
vision 230–3
  vision–based networks 233
Voltaire's *Candide* 192

vulnerability 105
walkways 70
  adjoining walkways 22, 247
  energizing walkways 51–3
  paving walkways 1
Weber, A. 23

whole–faculty study group 7, 202–12, 223
  study group defined 202–4
wings ("grounded with wings") 49, 135
writing 245

Zimpher, N. L., and Rieger, S. R. 88, 127